Destination Resilience

The challenge of destination management is to track and understand trends on different levels, to consider socio-economic developments and to respond proactively by addressing the paradigms of sustainability and resilience.

By examining tourism and travel trends in a wide range of regions, this book offers new insight into the impacts of economic, social and environmental changes on destination management, governance and development. Topics for discussion include advances and changes in technology, the global economy and governance as well as risk management and destinations' response to disruptions. Within a rapidly changing world, emphasis is given on resilient thinking and strategic management techniques in order to unlock the inner potential of destinations to respond and adapt positively to economic, environmental and social changes.

This is valuable reading for tourism students and researchers, destination managers and policy makers.

Elisa Innerhofer, Eurac Research, Center for Advanced Studies, Bozen.

Martin Fontanari, International School of Management (ISM), Cologne.

Harald Pechlaner, Eurac Research, Center for Advanced Studies, Bozen; Catholic University of Eichstätt-Ingolstadt, Chair of Tourism, Eichstätt.

Contemporary Geographies of Leisure, Tourism and Mobility

Series Editor: C. Michael Hall,

Professor at the Department of Management, College of Business and Economics, University of Canterbury, Christchurch, New Zealand

The aim of this series is to explore and communicate the intersections and relationships between leisure, tourism and human mobility within the social sciences.

It will incorporate both traditional and new perspectives on leisure and tourism from contemporary geography, e.g., notions of identity, representation and culture, while also providing for perspectives from cognate areas such as anthropology, cultural studies, gastronomy and food studies, marketing, policy studies and political economy, regional and urban planning, and sociology, within the development of an integrated field of leisure and tourism studies.

Also, increasingly, tourism and leisure are regarded as steps in a continuum of human mobility. Inclusion of mobility in the series offers the prospect to examine the relationship between tourism and migration, the sojourner, educational travel, and second home and retirement travel phenomena.

For a full list of titles in this series, please visit www.routledge.com/series/SE0522

The series comprises two strands

Contemporary Geographies of Leisure, Tourism and Mobility aims to address the needs of students and academics, and the titles will be published in hardback and paperback. Titles include:

Routledge Studies in Contemporary Geographies of Leisure, Tourism and Mobility is a forum for innovative new research intended for research students and academics, and the titles will be available in hardback only. Titles include:

Destination Resilience

Challenges and opportunities
for destination management
and governance

**Edited by Elisa Innerhofer, Martin
Fontanari and Harald Pechlaner**

LONDON AND NEW YORK

First published 2018 by Routledge

2 Park Square, Milton Park, Abingdon, Oxon OX14 4RN
605 Third Avenue, New York, NY 10017

Routledge is an imprint of the Taylor & Francis Group, an informa business

First issued in paperback 2022

Publisher's Note

The publisher has gone to great lengths to ensure the quality of this reprint
but points out that some imperfections in the original copies may be apparent.

British Library Cataloguing-in-Publication Data
A catalogue record for this book is available from the British Library

Library of Congress Cataloging-in-Publication Data
A catalog record for this book has been requested

ISBN: 978-1-138-57268-3 (hbk)
ISBN: 978-1-03-233925-2 (pbk)
DOI: 10.4324/9780203701904

Typeset in Times New Roman
by Apex CoVantage, LLC

Contents

Figures

Tables

Contributors

Authors	Institution/organisation
Mareike Bentfeld	Globale Initiative Katastrophenrisikomanagement, Deutsche Gesellschaft für Internationale Zusammenarbeit (GIZ) GmbH
Philipp Corradini	Eurac Research, Center for Advanced Studies, Bozen
Siarhei Danskikh	Yanka Kupala State University, Grodno
Timm Ewald	Berge & Meer, Rengsdorf
Martin Fontanari	International School of Management (ISM), Cologne
Trevor Girard	Karlsruhe Institute of Technology, Center for Disaster Management and Risk Reduction (CEDIM)
Georgi Gribov	Belarusian Association of Rural and Ecotourism "Country Escape"
Stefan Hartman	European Tourism Futures Institute, Stenden University, Leeuwarden Young Wadden Academy, Leeuwarden
Georg Hechenberger	ecKing-group, scl-projekte, Kitzbühel
Stephan Huppertz	Globale Initiative Katastrophenrisikomanagement, Deutsche Gesellschaft für Internationale Zusammenarbeit (GIZ) GmbH
Elisa Innerhofer	Eurac Research, Center for Advanced Studies, Bozen
Germann Jossé	Hochschule Worms, University of Applied Studies,
Bijan Khazai	Karlsruhe Institute of Technology, Center for Disaster Management and Risk Reduction (CEDIM)
Andreas Koler	Lo.La Peak Solutions GmbH, Trins
Dirk Kredinger	SWT – Stadtwerke Trier, Trier
Stefan Ortner	alpS GmbH, Innsbruck
Harald Pechlaner	Eurac Research, Center for Advanced Studies, Bozen Catholic University of Eichstätt-Ingolstadt, Chair of Tourism, Eichstätt
Mike Peters	University of Innsbruck, Department of Strategic Management, Marketing and Tourism
Christof Pforr	Curtin University, School of Marketing/Curtin Business School, Perth
Veronika Rakitskaja	Brest State Technical University, Brest
Dirk Reiser	Rhine-Waal University of Applied Sciences

Authors	Institution/organisation
Bernd Schabbing	International School of Management (ISM), Dortmund
Knut Scherhag	Hochschule Worms, University of Applied Studies
Anna Scuttari	Eurac Research, Center for Advanced Studies, Bozen
Anastasia Traskevich	Belarus State Economic University (BSEU), Minsk
Lauren Ugur	University of Heilbronn, Faculty for International Business
Michael Volgger	Curtin University, School of Marketing/Curtin Business School, Perth
Daniel Zacher	Catholic University of Eichstätt-Ingolstadt, Chair of Tourism, Eichstätt

Part I

Definition and conceptual framework

1   Linking destinations and resilience – challenges and perspectives

Harald Pechlaner & Elisa Innerhofer

1. Introduction

One of the challenges destination managers and tourism organizations responsible for the governance of destinations are facing is the management of the risks and impacts globalization as well as global economic, environmental and social changes have on tourism. They are forced to give support in the recovery from crisis, to cope with complex interrelated changes and to implement systems of crisis management, which are aimed at reducing the impact of crisis. The ongoing intensity and overlapping of various global structural changes and economic turmoil require adaptation and transformation processes not limited on single and medium-term initiatives, but asking for adaptability and the organizational ability to change. Tourism needs new strategies to cope with complex and interrelated change impacts (Luthe & Wyss, 2014). In the future, successful destinations will have to concentrate more and more on their ability to adapt to changing conditions and circumstances. In order to describe this ability, researchers in natural as well as in social sciences and psychologists are more and more referring to the concept of resilience. Among different resources and capabilities for dealing with such a situation of change, "resilience is the concept that is gaining currency". Resilience is the capacity of a system (a social system like a group, a community, an organization or the society) to absorb disturbance and reorganize while undergoing change (Holling, 1973; Walker, Holling, Carpenter, & Kinzig, 2004). Concepts aimed at resilience are taking into account insecurities, uncertainties and unexpected events and are trying to turn these challenges into opportunities (Meyen, 2015). The management of unforeseeable and unpredictable situations is one of the "strategic issues", which lies within the responsibility of the top management of a destination.

The main objective of the following chapter is to link the concept of destinations to those of resilience and thus to introduce the concept of resilience to the destination dialog. This objective is based on the assumption that resilience has much explanatory power for destinations coping with changes (Luthe & Wyss, 2014). Changes, disturbances and crisis in tourism are diversifying and not only connected to climate and natural environment, but next to economic disturbances, they increasingly include phenomenon such as terrorism, internal turmoil, digital economy and profound social changes. Thus, the topic requires more attention in tourism research (Fabry & Zeghni, 2016; Calgaro, Dominey-Howes, & Lloyd, 2013; Hall, Prayag, & Amore, 2017). Existing tourism studies on resilience mainly focus on ecological and environmental resilience of tourism systems (Becken, 2013). However, in the last two decades, the analysis of tourism in times of crisis and conflict arose as a new area of tourism research studies (Paraskevas, Altinay, McLean, & Cooper, 2013). In order to deal with the deterioration of natural, social and economic environments and to manage and handle crisis as well as the challenges arising from them, the introductory article will discuss the terms "destination" and "resilience" and describe the link between the two concepts. This complex and important link cannot be fully analyzed and explained on the few pages of this chapter. But it should contribute to the scientific discussion and point out some key and important approaches and ideas.

2. Global changes in the context of tourism and destinations

Traditional economic and political ideologies erode. There is something new in today's political belief system and in the contemporary ideological landscape (Steger, 2008). The contemporary social-political change exerted by globalization and going on a global level does not depend any more on traditional notions of politics and economics alone but on more factors which are mutually interdependent and characterized by a high level of complexity (Benedikter, 2013a). Global change and developments are co-shaped by the "cultural turn of civilizations" and "the renaissance of religions" and by the less embedded and less controllable forces of transformation, which are technology and demography (Benedikter, 2013b). Demographic trends influence political stability or instability, the economic potential for development and the development of a society (De Souza, 2015), while technology, and mainly digitalization and digital data, are causing unprecedented change on a global scale (Benedikter, 2013b). This contemporary global change process, the increasing uncertainty and insecurity as well as economic and environmental shocks and the growing awareness of the negative implications of naturally or human induced developments have led to a higher sense of sensitivity for the ability or capacity of a system to deal with sudden and unexpected changes (Sheppard & Williams, 2016).

The system, whose resistance to crisis and adaptability to change is focused within this edited volume, is the tourism system defined as an interrelated social-economic-ecological system (Nelson, Adger, & Brown, 2007). Talking about tourism and tourism and destination development and the vulnerability of destinations to shocks, stressors and sudden changes is a rising concern for researchers and industry stakeholders. Tourist destinations and actors are facing various governance and management challenges arising from global phenomenon, such as climate and demographic change or economic turmoil (Luthe & Wyss, 2014). Despite these challenges and the rising concern, knowledge on the causal factors and processes that create vulnerability as well as on strategies to handle and manage it is limited. Most of the investigations and studies published focus on a single cause or a few selected factors but fail to capture the whole complexity of vulnerability in tourist destinations (Calgaro, 2011). The resilience perspective is one approach to deal with the complexity of tourism and destination governance and management catching more and more the attention of researchers from different disciplines (see e.g. Tyrrell & Johnston, 2008; Davoudi & Porter, 2012; Sheppard & Williams, 2016; Hall et al., 2017). Studies and analysis focus on the capacity of tourism systems to deal with challenges and to maintain the stability of the tourism-related regional economy, politics and social life and at the same time to guarantee flexibility to react to changes and to ensure innovation and development (Luthe & Wyss, 2014). Even if for the term "resilience" a generally accepted definition doesn't exist, the general assumption that it is good to be resilient is widely accepted (Davoudi & Porter, 2012).

In the light of contemporary global change, good destination governance and management or good tourism systems' governance and management will require an understanding of complex global trends and the ability to develop farsighted and strategies (i.e. Khanna, 2017). In addition, destination management faces the challenge to help their destinations to adapt and thus to coordinate its change management. Taking action on change is challenging not only because it requires a new and sophisticated set of methods and toolkits able to handle high complexity, but because it overcomes the boundaries of scientific disciplines and requires interdisciplinary as well as transdisciplinary thinking. A more problem- and challenge-oriented research is needed (Schneidewind, 2016).

Despite the high degree of complexity of change and the lack of clarity regarding the term "resilience" and its inconsistent usage, there is a growing number of organizational, governmental and non-governmental initiatives which aim to develop toolkits for resilience-assessment and resilience-building (e.g. Calgaro et al., 2013). This volume follows the same purpose working in the same direction.

3. Concept of resilience

Discussing and analyzing the term "resilience" often leads to the initial question of what distinguishes resilience from the concept of sustainability. Since the Brundtland Report issued by the World Commission on Environment and Development for the United Nations in 1987, sustainable development has been the leading framework for future development. The Brundtland Report was the global agenda to deal with the disturbances of natural and social environments. It defines sustainability as a development that meets the needs of the present without compromising the ability of future generations to meet their own needs.[1] Although the concept of sustainable development is still the preferred development paradigm (for the majority of developed countries), the non-sustainable world with the environmentally damaging emission of greenhouse gasses, biodiversity losses, income disparities and social inequities remains reality (Lew, 2012).

However, it appears that currently resilience replaces the concept of sustainability in some scientific discourses. Several researchers discuss the equivalence of resilience and sustainability. Therefore, Holling and Walker (2003) state that a resilient socio-ecological system is synonymous with a region that is ecologically, economically and socially sustainable. Even if some authors describe sustainability as the desirable outcome of resilience and thus resilience as a necessary precondition for sustainability (e.g. Lebel et al., 2006; Perrings, 2006), the concept of resilience has a great variety of definitions and interpretations (Derissen, Quaas, & Baumgärtner, 2011). The disciplines of evolutionary biology and ecology refer to the concept of adaptation when defining resilience (Davoudi & Porter, 2012). Resilience as applied to integrated systems of people and natural resources refers to the ability of a system to undergo change and disturbance and to still retain the same controls on its structure as well as to the ability to re-organize after a shock or disturbance and to build and increase the capacity for learning and adaptation (Holling & Walker, 2003). In this sense, resilient systems have the adaptive capacity to re-organize and re-configure to retain their functions and structures (Walker et al., 2004). Other authors, such as Adger (2000), state that resilience is the "ability of groups or communities to cope with external stresses and disturbances as a result of social, political and environmental change." And Zolli and Healy (2013) refer to the capacity of a system (enterprise, person, etc.) to maintain its core purpose and integrity in the face of dramatically changed circumstances.

Here the authors adopt what seems to be a very general but at the same time a widely accepted understanding of resilience. Based on different definitions (some of them mentioned above), resilience is understood as the capacity of a system to absorb disturbance without collapsing into a qualitatively different state and to re-organize itself to maintain structures and functions while allowing change and development. In addition, resilience always refers to a positive transformation, requiring structural and individual change (Hall et al., 2017) and helps systems to emerge stronger from shocks and stresses.

Following this, the aim of a system's management and governance is to keep the system within a particular configuration of states that allow it to deliver the desired outcomes and to prevent the system from moving into an un-desirable configuration from which it is difficult or impossible to recover (Hartman, 2016; Fabry & Zeghni, 2016).

3.1 Destination resilience

This chapter as well as the entire volume discuss resilience in the context of tourism. The focus is on the ability of tourism as a social, economic and ecological system to recover from stresses as well as on the link between destination and resilience. The concept of resilience was initially applied to ecological systems. When talking about tourism, the application of the theory to social-ecological systems occurs. Tourism is a good example of a social-ecological system (Cochrane, 2010), in which people are considered part of the system and which requires integrative, interdisciplinary analysis methods and approaches (Pechlaner & Volgger, 2014; Pechlaner & Volgger, 2017).

A social-ecological system can be an entity, an enterprise, an organization or a person. In the context of organizations, the term "operational resilience" is used. It describes the organization's ability to adapt to and manage risks that arise from day-to-day operations (Caralli & Losi, 2007; Lee, Vargo, & Seville, 2013). Psychologists, psychiatrists and sociologists deal with individual-focused resilience, which is the capacity for successful adaptation and positive functioning of a person despite high risk, stress or trauma (Egeland, Carleson, & Sroufe, 1993).

Applied to tourism, the term destination resilience may be used. A tourist destination can be defined as an "amalgam of tourism products offering an integrated experience to consumers" (Buhalis, 2000). In a regional context, a tourist destination can be described as a geographical region with common cultural and environmental characteristics, designed by a management or governmental organization, where tourists make intensive use of diverse resources, products and services that have been specifically (but not exclusively) intended for tourists. A destination of this type may comprise different independent stakeholders, which can be privately owned businesses such as hotels or public companies and organizations, all linked by cooperative networks (Leiper, 2008). Hence, destinations are complex systems articulating various stakeholders, which try to develop a set of natural, cultural, built and intangible resources within physical and administrative boundaries (Fabry & Zeghni, 2016). Talking about destination resilience, tourism researchers often refer to the concept of community resilience which is "the ability of a place to maintain a normal level of service in the face of periodic or unpredictable external shocks or system failures" (Lew, 2012). Resilience helps the local actors to plan the touristic development and to organize the transition towards sustainable development (Fabry & Zeghni, 2016). With the concept of resilience in mind, a successful destination is here defined as a system which is commercially viable and offers its stakeholders and tourism actors sustainable access to resources and equally distributes benefits while minimizing or preventing negative impacts on the environment (Cochrane, 2010). Destination resilience requires resilient businesses and organizations or in other words "organizational resilience", which provides organizations with comparative advantage (Parsons, 2010). Destination resilience and organizational resilience are thus interdependent and organizational resilience contributes to the speed and success of destination resilience (McManus et al., 2008).

Tourist destinations can face a range of change pressures, which may be environmentally induced, such as changing natural resources, socially induced, like changing cultural resources, or economic in nature, such as changing economic conditions or the loss of tourist markets, skilled employees or tourism facilities and services (Lew, 2012). Tourist destinations completely change if the ecosystem collapses below a certain state of environmental quality or if attraction points lose attractiveness, meaning that previous tourism is no longer viable. These negative impacts may arise when a certain amount of tourism is reached. The destination may experience a shift from luxury to budget or from budget visitors to no visitors anymore (Tyrrell & Johnston, 2008).

3.2 Features/characteristics and abilities of resilient destinations

A wide variety of multiple and dynamic variables and factors, such as geographical exposure, specific regional development characteristics, social structures, cultural norms and governance processes, influence the resilience of a tourist destination. These factors and the disturbances from which they may be affected, cannot only be attributed to ecology, climate and natural environment, but are more and more diversifying. Academic literature generally use three categories to describe and discuss the resilience of a destination: ecological-environmental dimension, economic-fiscal dimension and social-cultural dimension (Calgaro et al., 2013; Fabry & Zeghni, 2016). The ecological environmental dimension includes the biophysical characteristics of a destination, its natural settings and natural resources, such as wildlife, mountains, beaches or walking tracks, while the economic-fiscal dimension refers to industrial risks, the effects of the digital economy, fiscal imbalances or economic crisis. The social-cultural dimension includes the strengths and weaknesses of the social system, cultural norms, culturally induced risk perceptions as well as residents' attitudes towards tourism (Calgaro et al., 2013). The interrelationships between these dimensions and the influencing factors of a destination's exposure to shocks and disturbances are important drivers for destination resilience (Tyrrell & Johnston, 2008).

These categories imply that the context of the destination and its developmental history play an important role in determining resilience. Thus, the pre-existing economic, social, political and ecological conditions shape the anticipatory and immediate response capabilities of destinations (Calgaro et al., 2013). Next to the developmental history, the speed of recovery of a destination from a shock or a destabilizing event depends on the destination's adaptive capacity (Cochrane, 2010). Adaptive refers to the capacity of a destination to respond and adjust to market changes as a mean to maintain or improve its performance (Axelrod & Cohen, 2000). Hence, the adaptive capacity is the ability to adapt to persistently changing situations and is strongly related to the degree of diversity in terms of products, experiences, organizations and businesses. Diversity means to have more options to choose from and more chances to find development possibilities that result in better performance (Hartman, 2016).

According to Cochrane (2010), a resilient destination as a socio-ecological system consists of three principal elements and three abilities, which can be described as the factors of destination resilience: the elements are harness market forces, stakeholder cohesion and leadership, whereas the abilities are flexibility, adaptability and learning. Since successful engagement with the market is essential, resilient destinations need to know how to harness market forces. Second, private and public stakeholders with different strengths and weaknesses need to cooperate and develop in a coordinated way. In addition, destinations need a strong and consistent leadership, which is able to resolve conflicts, to bring together stakeholders and to drive forward change and development. Next to the principal elements, flexibility is an important capability of destinations to handle unpredictable situations and to adapt to variability and uncertainty (Hall et al., 2017). This includes the second essential ability "adaptability", which is significant for the system as it moves between different states and as it has to adapt to an ever-changing world. To successfully deal with change, the third essential ability is needed, which is the ability to learn from a disturbance to be better prepared for future shocks (i.e. Lew, 2012). Learning is important to identify the impacts of changes. So for example, the analysis of lifestyle changes and demographic dynamics may draw attention to emerging types of tourism and may inspire new business concepts (Hartman, 2016).

4. Conclusion and outlook

When analyzing the term "destination resilience", the question of what distinguishes a resilient destination from a sustainable destination arises. Is there an interface between the two concepts? For some researchers, sustainability and resilience are slightly nuanced perspectives on the same phenomenon. For others, the perspectives are different, because the sustainability's conservation goals are in opposition to the adaptation goals of resilience (Lew, Ng, Ni, & Wu, 2016). According to Lew et al. (2016) there are two reasons for this confusion. The first one is that for both concepts different definitions exist, and both are used to achieve political goals that may not reflect the core definitions. The second reason is that sustainability and resilience share similar goals and approaches, like for example the focus on climate change and the goal to reach a balance between human and nature.

Many destinations have strategies and plans in place to promote sustainable tourism. They use tourism to combat poverty and conserve natural and cultural heritage, for example, through the creation of monuments, National Parks and protected areas. In this sense, the promotion of sustainable tourism is the application of sustainability principles to tourism development (Hall & Lew, 1998). For the definition of sustainability principles it is generally referred to the Brundtland Report's widely quoted definition of sustainable development as development that ensures the well-being of people, today and in future generations (Lew et al., 2016).

Sustainable development and the adoption of sustainable principles in destination management and governance means that through the use of an inclusive approach and the implementation of a well-conceived strategy, shared prosperity can be reached, while a destination's sense of place and corporate interests of different stakeholders (residents, entrepreneurs, guests etc.) can be protected. According to Krippendorf, sustainable tourism and thus also sustainable destination management means that there is less mass tourism, tour operators have less power, there is local control and tourists are partnering with locals (Krippendorf, 1984). Similar elements and aspects are mentioned from other authors when describing and analyzing sustainable destinations. In a sustainable destination, tourists are forced to enhance and protect cultural heritage and traditions, local jobs are supported by tourism, the residents and locals are engaged in deciding the role of tourism in their region and community, a destination's authenticity is preserved and negative impacts on the environment are mitigated (Bramwell & Lane, 1993; Buckley, 2012).[2]

The aim of sustainable destination management and governance is to channel the benefits of tourism into environmental and cultural conservation and into host communities by helping the industry to look to the long term and to become more responsible for its actions and impacts (Krippendorf, 1984).

The discussion on resilience builds on these already developed approaches of sustainability. However, as already mentioned above and as other chapters in this volume will show, resilience goes beyond sustainability. It is more than a situation or a state and more than an outcome. It is the process of or the capacity for successful adaptation despite challenging or threatening circumstances (Masten, Best, & Garmezy, 1990). Due to the dynamic nature and complexity of this concept, many challenges are linked with studying it. However, the continuation of scientific work in this field is of great importance. The key challenge here is the scientific approach necessary to understand and analyze an issue with such a high degree of complexity. Research on resilience requires inter- and transdisciplinary research methods and cross-disciplinary thinking. Resilience as a crossfield between traditional subjects and disciplines requires a strong and excellent disciplinary research as a precondition to go beyond and apply inter- and transdisciplinarity. Thus, to advance research on resilience, the collaboration of different disciplines is needed. One precise way to describe resilience, which builds upon these considerations, is Clark's (2007) definition of sustainability science. Based on Clark (2007), who describes sustainability science "as a field defined by the problems it addresses rather than by the disciplines it employs", resilience may be described as a field with the same character.

Based on the considerations developed in this chapter, tourism appears to be an appropriate field for applied research on resilience. Tourism literature shows that there is a disagreement in tourism research regarding the question of whether tourism is an academic discipline or not. For some academics, tourism is not an accepted field of research as a standalone academic discipline, because researchers from different disciplines approach tourism studies. Other academics emphasize the efforts in developing holistic and integrated theories evolving tourism studies into its own discipline (Pechlaner & Volgger, 2014; Pechlaner, Volgger, & Zehrer, 2017; Echtner & Jamal, 1997). This "weakness" of tourism studies becomes a strength when talking about resilience studies. The destination appears to be an appropriate level to observe resilience and one way to put into practice a resilience-based governance.

The goal of the chapter as well as the volume is to stimulate debate regarding the potential role of resilience and resilience theories and approaches in guiding tourism systems, such as destinations, hotels or organizations. In addition, it gives insights for the development of real-world solutions. The fact, that the destination's specific character as well as its history play a fundamental role for its resilience allows one, by analyzing and observing different destinations, to make empirical and theoretical conclusions regarding the characteristics of a destination and its resilience level. Based on this comparative analysis, real-world solutions may be developed.

However, this book can only be a contribution to the discussion of resilience and its concept as it is still an emerging approach.

Notes

1 *Report of the World Commission on Environment and Development: Our common future.* Retrieved from www.un-documents.net/our-common-future.pdf (Accessed 26 June 2017).
2 Mullis, B.T., *Destination sustainability.* Retrieved from www.destinationsustainability. com/blog/ (Accessed 18 September 2017).

References

Adger, N. (2000). Social and ecological resilience: Are they related? *Progress in Human Geography, 24*, 347–364.

Axelrod, R., & Cohen, M. (2000). *Harnessing complexity: Organisational implications of a scientific frontier.* New York: Basic Books.

Becken, S. (2013). Developing a framework for assessing resilience of tourism sub-systems to climatic factors. *Annals of Tourism Research, 43*, 506–528.

Benedikter, R. (2013a). Global systemic shift: A multidimensional approach to understand the present phase of globalization. *New Global Studies, 7*(1), 1–15.

Benedikter, R. (2013b). Understanding contemporary change. What is the global systemic shift of our days- and how does it work? *Transcience: The Journal of Global Studies of Humboldt University Berlin, 4*(1).

Bramwell, B., & Lane, B. (1993). Sustainable tourism: An evolving global approach. *Journal of Sustainable Tourism, 1*(1), 1–5.

Buckley, R. (2012). Sustainable tourism: Research and reality. *Annals of Tourism Research, 39*(2), 528–546.

Buhalis, D. (2000). Marketing the competitive destination of the future. *Tourism Management, 21*, 97–116.

Calgaro, E.L. (2011). *Building resilient tourism destination futures in a world of uncertainty: Assessing destination vulnerability in Khao Lak, Patong and Phi Phi Don, Thailand to the 2004 Tsunami.* Australia: Macquarie University.

Calgaro, E.L., Dominey-Howes, D., & Lloyd, K. (2013). Application of the destination sustainability framework to explore the drivers of vulnerability and resilience in Thailand following the 2004 Indian Ocean Tsunami. *Journal of Sustainable Tourism.* Retrieved from www.tandfonline.com/doi/abs/10.1080/09669582.2013.826231 (Accessed 20 July 2017).

Caralli, R.A., & Losi, S. (2007). *Adapting to changing risk environments: Operational resilience.* Carnegie Mellon University, CERT, Software Engineering Institute, University, Pittsburgh. Retrieved from www.cert.org/podcasts/podcast_episode.cfm?episodeid=34722 (Accessed 19 July 2017).

Clark, W.C. (2007). Sustainability science: A room of its own. *Proceedings of the National Academy of Sciences, 104*(6), 1737–1738.

Cochrane, J. (2010). The shere of tourism resilience. *Tourism Recreation Research, 35*(2), 173–185.

Davoudi, S., & Porter, L. (2012). Resilience: A bridging concept or a dead end? *Planning Theory & Practice, 13*(2), 299–333.

Derissen, S., Quaas, M.F., & Baumgärtner, S. (2011). The relationship between resilience and sustainability of ecological-economic systems. *Ecological Economics, 70,* 1121–1128.

De Souza, R.M. (2015). Demographic resilience: Linking population dynamics, the environment, and security. *SAIS Review of International Affairs, 35*(1) Winter–Spring, 17–27. Retrieved from https://muse.jhu.edu/article/582524 (Accessed 30 June 2017).

Echtner, C.M., & Jamal, T.B. (1997). The disciplinary dilemma of tourism studies. *Annals of Tourism Research, 24*(4), 868–883.

Egeland, B., Carleson, E., & Sroufe, L.A. (1993). Resilience as a process. *Development and Psychopathology, 5,* 517–528.

Fabry, N., & Zeghni, S. (2016, June). *Resilience, tourist destination and governance: An analytical framework.* Paper presented at the meeting of the 32nd Journées du développement ATM 2016, Lille, France.

Hall, C.M., & Lew, A.A. (Eds.). (1998). *Sustainable tourism: A geographical perspective.* London: Addison Wesley Longman.

Hall, M.C., Prayag, G., & Amore, A. (2017). *Tourism and resilience: Individual, organisational and destination perspectives.* UK: Channel View Publications.

Hartman, S. (2016). Towards adaptive tourism areas? A complexity perspective to examine the conditions for adaptive capacity. *Journal of Sustainable Tourism, 24*(2), 299–314.

Holling, C.S. (1973). Resilience and stability of ecological systems. *Annual Review of Ecology and Systematics,* 1–23.

Holling, C.S., & Walker, B.H. (2003). Resilience defined. In International Society of Ecological Economics (Eds.), *Internet encyclopedia of ecological economics.* Retrieved from http://isecoeco.org/pdf/resilience.pdf (Accessed 17 July 2017).

Khanna, P. (2017). *Jenseits von Demokratie. Regieren im Zeitalter des Populismus.* Rüschlikon and Zürich: GDI Gottlieb Duttweiler Institute.

Krippendorf, J. (1984). *Die Ferienmenschen: Für ein neues Verständnis von Freizeit und Reisen.* Zürich: Orell Füssli Verlag.

Lebel, L., Anderies, J.M., Campbell, B., Folke, C., Hatfield-Dodds, S., Hughes, T.P., & Wilson, J. (2006). Governance and the capacity to manage resilience in regional social-ecological systems. *Ecology and Society, 11*(1), 19.

Lee, A.V., Vargo, J., & Seville, E. (2013). Developing a tool to measure and compare organizations' resilience. *Natural Hazards Review, 14,* 29–41.

Leiper, N. (2008). Why the "tourism industry" is misleading as a generic expression: The case for the plural variation, tourism industries. *Tourism Management, 29,* 237–251.

Lew, A.A. (2012, October 21). Creative resilience: The next sustainability for tourism? *TG Journal's Tourism Place.* Retrieved from http://tourismplace.blogspot.com/ (Accessed 26 June 2017).

Lew, A.A., Ng, P.T., Ni, Ch., & Wu, T. (2016). Community sustainability and resilience: Similarities, differences and indicators. *Tourism Geographies, 18*(1), 18–27.

Luthe, T., & Wyss, R. (2014). Assessing and planning resilience in tourism. *Tourism Management, 44,* 161–163.

Masten, A., Best, K., & Garmezy, N. (1990). Resilience and development: Contributions from the study of children who overcome adversity. *Development and Psychopathology, 2,* 425–444.

McManus, S., Seville, E., Vargo, J., & Brunsdon, D. (2008). Facilitated process for improving organizational resilience. *Natural Hazards Review, 9,* 81–90.

Meyen, M. (2015). Resilienz als diskursive Formation: Was das neue Zauberwort für die Wissenschaft bedeuten könnte. *Resilienz.* Retrieved from http://resilienz.hypotheses.org/365 (Accessed 22 September 2017).

Mullis, B.T., *Destination sustainability*. Retrieved from www.destinationsustainability. com/blog/ (Accessed 18 September 2017).

Nelson, D., Adger, W.N., & Brown, K. (2007). Adaptation to environmental change: Contributions of a resilience framework. *Annual Review of Environment and Resources, 32,* 395–419.

Paraskevas, A., Altinay, L., McLean, J., & Cooper, C. (2013). Crisis knowledge in tourism: Types, flows and governance. *Annals of Tourism Research, 41,* 130–152.

Parsons, D. (2010). Organisational resilience. *The Australian Journal of Emergency Management, 25*(2), 20–22.

Pechlaner, H., & Volgger, M. (2014). Can tourism qualify for interdisciplinary research? A European view. In H. Pechlaner & E. Smeral (Eds.), *Tourism and leisure: Current issues and perspectives of development* (pp. 3–21). Wiesbaden: Springer Gabler.

Pechlaner, H., & Volgger, M. (2017). Tourismus als Wissenschaft – Prädestiniert für interdisziplinäres Forschen? Eine europäische Perspektive. In H. Pechlaner & A. Zehrer (Eds.), *Tourismus und Wissenschaft. Wirtschaftliche, politische und gesellschaftliche Perspektiven* (pp. 25–42). Wiesbaden: Gabler Verlag.

Pechlaner, H., Volgger, M., & Zehrer, A. (2017). Tourismus und Wissenschaft oder Tourismuswissenschaft? Ein (weiterer) Erklärungsversuch. In H. Pechlaner & A. Zehrer (Eds.), *Tourismus und Wissenschaft. Wirtschaftliche, politische und gesellschaftliche Perspektiven* (pp. 245–252). Wiesbaden: Gabler Verlag.

Perrings, C. (2006). Resilience and sustainable development. *Environment and Development Economics, 11,* 417–427.

Schneidewind, U. (2016). The need for more transdisciplinary research. In A. Martinuzzi & M. Sedlacko (Eds.), *Knowledge brokerage for sustainable development: Innovative tools for increasing research impact and evidence-based policy-making* (pp. 49–54). UK: Greenleaf Publishing.

Sheppard, V.A., & Williams, P.W. (2016). Factors that strengthen tourism resort resilience. *Journal of Hospitality and Tourism Management, 28,* 20–30.

Steger, M.B. (2008). *The rise of the global imaginary: Political ideologies from the French Revolution to the Global War on Terror.* Oxford and New York: Oxford University Press.

Tyrrell, T.J., & Johnston, R.J. (2008). Tourism sustainability, resiliency and dynamics: Towards a more comprehensive perspective. *Tourism and Hospitality Research, 8*(1), 14–24.

Walker, B., Holling, C., Carpenter, S., & Kinzig, A. (2004). Resilience, adaptability and transformability in social-ecological systems. *Ecology and Society, 9*(2), 5.

Zolli, A., & Healy, A.-M. (2013). *Resilience: Why things bounce back.* New York: Simon & Schuster Paperbacks.

2 Risk- and resilience-awareness. An empirical analysis of the basic supply in regions and on the demand side

Martin Fontanari & Dirk Kredinger

1. Introduction

Globalization, increasing technical interconnections and a rising sensitivity for environmental concerns due to changed climatical conditions do nowadays represent the framework which provides orientation for systems. With this comes a higher vulnerability to crisis. However, the more complex, global and interconnected these new economic, technical and political structures become, the more complex will be the governance and the smaller will be the ability to react when it comes to maintaining superregional and global systems in a steady state during unsecure and disruptive times. This requires us to deal with structures and approaches which make the survivability respectively performance of systems, that is to say enterprises and regions, a subject of discussion.

"Resilience" is described as a strength and ability which enables societies to maintain their social and ecological balance in times of crisis and failure. Bürkner has created an interesting overview on the topic of resilience and vulnerability in science and defines vulnerability as follows:

- the vulnerability of a system vis a vis existing hazardous events, risks, crisis, stress, shocks or harmful events which have already taken place.
- as a rule, the damage means that important functions are constrained or do not exist anymore.

(Bürkner, 2010, p. 24)

In this context, the trigger of a disorder or of a systemic crisis which leads to serious impairments of existential sub-systems and supply systems may be of secondary importance. In case of system malfunctions disposing of adequate resilience, the high mutual interdependence and connectivity of the sub-systems will lead to a domino effect. Starting from this point of view, more thought was given over the last few years on how society and sub-systems on the supply side can increase their ability for resilience in order to resist such an existential crisis (Osztovics, Kovar, & Mayrbäurl, 2012).

In the context of developing tourism destinations, resilient destinations are spaces which are most widely disconnected of such dependences, put an increased focus on internal strengths, existing resources and authentic potentials, and thus, contribute more to added value and the creation of value on a global level (Fontanari & Kredinger, 2017, p. 5). A corresponding ability for resilience exists the more one breaks away from fragile superregional dependencies with supply and disposal, and the more one focusses on self-sufficient regional or local supply systems resp. systems for recycling management. The following article will show to what extent there is a consciousness of resilience and a certain manifestation of resilience with the agents on the supply and disposal side of a selected region and with citizens in general.

2. Supply security from the point of view of the supply side

The supply security of a region comprises sub-areas, especially sectors like, for example, securing vital basic needs (drinking water, nutrition, medical support) as well as securing minimum public services (postal services and telecommunication, data storage and data processing, cash supply, waste disposal and sewage disposal). Add to this transport and traffic with the provision of fuel and the supply of energy as cross-sectional tasks (BMI, 2016, p. 42ff.). Peterman et al. regard these as the essential spheres of influence on the supply security of a region and, hence, for the practicability of tourism in a region (Petermann et al., 2010, p. 59).

2.1 Supply security and resilience

From a technical point of view as well as in the context of critical infrastructures, supply security is equally important as energy security. Once the energy supply is interrupted, there will be severe disorders with regard to supply and functions. The fragility of energy supply is particularly given when there is an unequal feed-in and consumption, which can bring about under-frequency or excessive frequency with line voltage and, hence, lead to severe disorders (BBK, 2014, p. 100 f).

Various research has led to the conclusion that depending on the length of a disruption, exogenous or endogenous power interruptions can lead to multi-billion-dollar damages, and the longer electric power is provided sufficiently, the more supply security is likely to be sustained (Fontanari & Kredinger, 2017, p. 7). Supply security, thus, is the main factor of influence when it comes to assessing the resilience of individual critical infrastructures. In the context of evaluating technical infrastructures, according to Holling, resilience is defined as follows: "[. . .] the measurement of resilience is the magnitude of disturbance that can be absorbed or accommodated before the system changes its structure by changing the variables and processes that control system behavior" (Holling & Meffe, 1996, p. 330). This definition is also referred to as ecological resilience, where several tolerable system states exist. A system, hereby, is subject to a dynamic stability if it can maintain its system integrity in case of malfunctions (Borgert, 2013, p. 10 f).

This approach is apt to be applied in a regional economic context, because it includes the possibility for interaction between a region and potential triggers (Wink, 2011, p. 114) and contributes to the complexity of inter-operability of systems.

Given the scenario of a multi-day power cut, we can talk about a resilient state, if the population can be provided with the most important resources, and if communication between population and administration is still possible. In order to evaluate the total resilience of the border region of Trier-Saarburg, the rating scale which is displayed in Table 2.1 (Fontanari & Kredinger, 2017, p. 8) and which refers to the survey model of resilience by Hagmann (Hagmann, 2012, p. 10) will be applied:

Table 2.1 Rating scale for resilience

Degree of resilience	*Comments*
100%	The sector/the total system disposes of total resilience vis-a-vis the scenario
75%	The sector/the total system disposes of high resilience vis-a-vis the scenario
50%	The sector/the total system disposes of partially resilient structures vis-a-vis the scenario
25%	The sector/the total system disposes of hardly any resilient structures vis-a-vis the scenario
0%	The sector/the total system disposes of no resilient structures vis-a-vis the scenario

Source: Fontanari and Kredinger (2017, p. 8)

2.2 *Evaluation of resilience of the region of Trier*

The city of Trier (114,914 inhabitants)[1] and the administrative district of Trier-Saarburg (142,940 inhabitants)[2] dispose of a total population of almost 258,000 inhabitants. The major part of the 25,900 professional commuters (incl. Eifelkreis Bitburg-Prüm) work in the Grand Duchy of Luxemburg.[3] In the city of Trier as a regional center, jobs for many bread-winners of the surrounding area are predominantly provided in the field of public services; the tertiary sector disposes of a corresponding 76.9 percent dominance with the gross value added of the city of Trier;[4] one out of ten jobs depends on tourism. The region of Mosel/Saar alone counts for two million guests representing approx. 26 percent of all guests visiting Rhineland-Palatinate, and with 6.2 million overnights, it represents a share of 28 percent of all overnights in this state. Tourism income and regional creation of value are based on a high degree of mobility.

The survey of the supply side of the region was carried out by relying on two methodical instruments. On the one hand, an online-questioning was carried out based on a previously established written contact with the suppliers and other agents (main sectors).[5] On the other hand, important figures, data and facts on the field of survey were compiled in order to evaluate the individual sectors.

Evaluation of resilience of the sector of transport and traffic

The determination of the resilience of the sector of transport and traffic was carried out under the premise that in case of emergency, nobody will block the fuel reserves. Assuming that at the time of a power cut, the fuel depots are filled to capacity, then a depot capacity of approx. 33.7 million liters of diesel and 1.1 million liters of gas were identified as a multiple quantity of supply for the region; even by taking into account that in the context of a catastrophe the used equipment of firefighters, ambulances, technical assistance, etc., will be put into action more often as usual.

In the context of this scenario, the stock of fuel isn't the problem, but the necessary power supply through emergency power aggregates for pumping fuel out of the depots. There are only two secured locations which, however, do not guarantee the minimum mobility in the region in an emergency situation. After the inventory, the sector of transport and traffic will be attributed a resilience degree of approx. 61 percent (cf. Fontanari & Kredinger, 2017, p. 12).

Evaluation of resilience of the health sector

This sector comprises hospitals, medical and dental offices, pharmacies, old-age homes, foster homes and dialysis centers. The city of Trier disposes of 1,654 registered beds; the administrative district of Trier-Saarburg disposes of 388 registered beds. At the same time, more than 491 doctors, 10 dialysis centers, 74 pharmacies as well as 49 old-age homes and foster homes are registered. Hospitals can maintain emergency power supply for 24 hours – depending on the season of the year where the scenario takes place. With hospitals a breakdown of operational services between the 24th and 48th hour is assumed to be very realistic. A similar situation is likely to arise with medical offices and dental offices. In case the sector of transport and traffic breaks down due to the lack of fuel, then private means of transport for employees and patients will be restricted drastically (Fontanari & Kredinger, 2017, p. 13). With the loss of mobility, a medical office cannot be sustained. A similar situation arises with pharmacies, dialysis centers as well as old-age homes and foster homes (decreasing mobility of the staff and decreasing availability of medication, breakdown of the buildings' internal infrastructure, etc.). After the inventory the sector will be attributed a resilience degree of approx. 16 percent. The sector hardly disposes of any resilient structures:

Table 2.2 Evaluation of the degree of resilience of the health sector

Sector	Health	Resilience
Sub-sectors	Hospitals	21%
	Medical offices	7%
	Pharmacies	7%
	Old-age homes and foster homes	21%
	Dialysis centers	21%
	Total sector	16%

Source: Fontanari and Kredinger (2017, p. 14)

Evaluation of resilience of the sector of water supply and sewage disposal

The city of Trier and the surrounding communalities which are supplied by the public utilities of Trier have an annual consumption rate of approx. 10 million cubic meters of drinking water. In order to distribute the water the city disposes of 23 pumping stations, 22 depots with approx. 33,000 cubic meters of storage volume, 460 km of drinking water networks and 220 km of networks for private household water service connections.[6] Given the German average, the supply of drinking water (125 liters/person/day) can be maintained quite safely for 2 to 3 days. With the underlying scenario one can, however, assume a restricted consumption of water (38 liters/person/day) as, for example, due to electricity cuts many water loads will not function any more (e.g. dish washers). Once an electricity cut has happened, one can generally not assume a continued filling of water towers without functioning pumps. Assuming a distinct reduction of water consumption upon the cut of electricity supply, water towers will then create a buffer of 5 to 10 days – in exceptional cases even up to 13 days. Such a long storage period is hygienically sound. Assuming that the water towers in the administrative district of Trier-Saarburg are filled up to 75 percent at the beginning of an electricity outage, one can conclude the following buffer calculated in days:

Table 2.3 Determination of buffer functions of water towers in the association of municipalities of the administrative district of Trier-Saarburg

Administrative district	Served population	Volume of water towers (m³)	Water supply storage, if filled up to 75% (m³)	Need for drinking water of the population (m³)	Buffer (days)
VG Ruwer	17,912	8,830	6,623	672	9.86
VG Trier-Land	21,566	10,000	7,500	809	9.27
VG Schweich, w/o city of Schweich	19,430	13,200	9,900	729	13.59
VG Hermeskeil	14,477	6,850	5,138	543	9.46
VG Saarburg	21,987	10,000	7,500	825	9.10
VG Konz	31,108	12,000	9,000	1,167	7.72
VG Kell am See	9,448	6,200	4,650	354	13.12

Source: Kredinger (2014, p. 121)

Given the same constraints, a supply via the water towers can be maintained for about 5 to 6 days for the city of Trier. The main water utility disposes of an emergency power aggregate and can guarantee the operating of the water utility for approx. 20 hours without fuel replenishment. Talking about the sewage disposal, functionality over the entire time span of the scenarios can be possible for a partial area. The sector of water supply and sewage disposal will be attributed a resilience degree of approx. 86 percent.

Table 2.4 Evaluation of the degree of resilience of the water supply/sewage disposal sector

Sector	Water supply and sewage disposal	Resilience
Sub-sectors	Water supply Trier	100%
	Water supply VF Saarburg	70%
	Water supply VG Hermeskeil	68%
	Water supply VG Ruwer	70%
	Water supply ZV Trier-Land	66%
	Water supply VG Schweich	97%
	Water supply VG Konz	55%
	Water supply Kell am See	94%
Weighing	**Population**	**Resilience**
Water supply Trier	46%	100%
Water supply administrative district Trier-Saarburg	54%	74%
Total sector		86%

Source: Fontanari and Kredinger (2017, p. 16)

Evaluation of resilience of the financial services and food supply sector

Information on the amount of cash on hand at the financial institutes in the city of Trier and at the administrative district of Trier-Saarburg as well as on the amount of cash on hand at individual private households are difficult to diagnose in an empirical way. Since a substantial part of transactions in retail is done with cash, cash remains an important factor. An outage of electronic money transfers would lead to a shutdown of the majority of food supply via discounters and supermarkets within 24 hours. In September 2011, the city of Trier disposed of 28 pure food businesses, while the administrative district of Trier-Saarburg disposed of 26 such businesses with a minimum sales area of 600 m2. Only 5.2 percent of the private households surveyed by Gardemann and Menski disposed of in-house stocks of food, which would have lasted for more than 8 days in case of need (Menski & Gardemann, 2005, p. 73). This feeling of security is based on the assumption that in Germany only, very few widespread damaging events take place. Should the logistics in the field of food supply crack, the central warehouses will quickly be emptied. Subsequently, the branches of big markets will just as well be empty only four days later. According to the authors, only about 13,000 people (5.2 percent of 248,969 inhabitants) in the surveyed region would weather well served. The remaining 235,000 people would face hunger sooner or later. According to the affected inventory, the sector of food supply will be attributed a degree of resilience of 25 percent (Fontanari & Kredinger, 2017, p. 17).

Evaluation of resilience of the fields of information technology and telecommunication

A crackdown of infrastructure will for the greater part take place immediately after the occurrence of an electricity outage. A few hours later, major parts of this sector will be out of service. The highest level of resilience is displayed by Mobile Switching Centers (MSC) with approx. 4 days. Likewise, land-based telephone switches dispose of a high level of resilience, which are able to resist electricity outages for about 3 to 4 days relying on their emergency electricity supply. Data centers for the provision of internet as well as data storage will crack down after one week at the latest, as there will be a lack of fuel with the supply of emergency electricity (Hiete et al., 2010, pp. F26–F31). Due to the planned conversion of land-based telephone to IP-telephone (phone calls via internet) scheduled for 2018 by Deutsche Telekom, no telephone connection would be working any more in the case of an electricity outage. Only radio broadcasting is attributed a resilience which will crack down only after a few weeks (Petermann et al., 2011, p. 92). According to the affected inventory, this sector will be attributed a degree of resilience of 25 percent and, thus, disposes of hardly any resilience vis-à-vis the scenario.

Evaluation of resilience of the tourism sector

A resilience evaluation of this sector shall sensitize on the issue of which further considerations on the sustenance of guests have to be included. The number of overnights in Rhineland-Palatinate in the year 2011 was taken as the basis of calculation:

Table 2.5 Overnights and guests in the administrative district of Trier-Saarburg and the city of Trier in 2013

Area	Number overnights 2013	Thereof foreigners	Number guests	Thereof foreigners
Administrative district of Trier-Saarburg (without camping sites)	1,216,439	517,644	344,725	109,757
City of Trier (without camping sites)	733,679	195,500	385,653	101,942
Administrative district of Trier-Saarburg (camping sites)	261,195	110,747	61,109	22,183
Administrative district of Trier-Saarburg (without camping sites)	1,216,439	517,644	344,725	109,757
City of Trier (camping sites)	no data			

Source: Statistisches Landesamt Rheinland-Pfalz (2014b, p. 15ff.)[7]

Given the data in Table 2.5 and other analyses concerning overnights and the number of foreign guests, we find that on an average day in September, about 8,900 overnights took place. Not every guest would have arrived by his or her own car. Hence, in the case of a crisis/catastrophe, the resulting additional bottlenecks with the sustenance and mobility of overnight guests as well as the increased dependence of overnight guests on local and regional supply structures have to be taken more into consideration with any thought on resilience and capacities for the destination – probably with an even higher factor of sustenance and support.

In the context of this online survey, a bunch of questions for the tourism sector were set up, and their formulation was adapted to the subject group like, e.g.: "What is the percentage of your employees who can roughly reach their work place by walking with a maximum length of walking of 40 minutes (approx. 3 km) between residence and work place?", "Is there a possibility to communicate via an analogous telephone connection in your house/ your office?", "Is it possible to operate your house/ your office with daylight (without electrical lighting)?" or "For how long do your food and water stocks last under normal conditions?". On total, 7 propositi at least partially answered the questions. A total of 131 enterprises were addressed in written form. The analysis of the responses leads to the following results:

- About 58 percent of employees can reach their workplace if it is within 3 km of walking distance.
- Two out of seven propositi indicated that they possessed an emergency power generator. One did not know this function, and another one indicated to use it for operating emergency lighting.
- On average, the range of food and water under regular operation is 8 days. Here, the lowest indication was 3 days and the highest one was 20 days, with a standard deviation of 5,1.

On the whole, from the point of view of the suppliers, the overnight industry assumes an important role should there be an emergency situation lasting for several days – not only because of the more intensive sustenance and support of its guests but also as a direct sustainer for the greater environment (overnight capacities, facilities, equipment of restaurant, function of business premises, etc.). For the tourism sector it is, thus, recommendable to not merely meet the requirements of the federal government for private households to provide stocks in case of emergency, but above that to file and take into account the provisions for stocking, the self-cultivation of available land, the use of emergency electricity aggregates and the provision of emergency shelters according to their local and regional importance for resilience. A hotel should be equipped with the appropriate means to provide its guests and the surrounding neighborhood, if necessary, for a minimum of 10 days with the most important necessities. Overnight providers could moreover be more actively involved in self-cultivation and self-sustainment. This could probably even have positive effects on the creation of tourism products. It was not possible to evaluate the degree of resilience of this sector on the basis of the data available.

Evaluation of total resilience

The underlying study has defined the degrees of resilience for the individual sectors. The specific degree of resilience for each sector is displayed in the following chart.

Table 2.6 Overview of results – degree of resilience of analyzed sectors

Sector	Degree of Resilience
Transport and traffic	61%
Health	16%
Water supply and sewage disposal	86%
Financial services	0%
Food supply	25%
Information technology and telecommunication	25%
Tourism	-

Source: Kredinger (2014, p. 143)

Forming the arithmetic mean of the individual degrees of resilience, one gets a total degree of resilience of about 33 percent. As the total system also disposes of partially resilient structures, it would be appropriate to define a maximal degree of resilience of 50 percent according to the established scale.

Further research should be carried out concerning the weighing of individual sectors. Thus, aspects like food and water supply seem to be more important than financial services, IT and telecommunication. Likewise, the sectors of transport and traffic as well as health have to be regarded as important. Without the necessary fuel reserves, most of the sectors stated here are, however, are incapable of acting by almost 100 percent, so that the factor of fuel attributes more weighing to the sectors of transport and traffic.

3. Risk awareness of citizens and attitudes towards security of supply

In 2014, an empirical investigation on the topic of "emergency situations and precautionary measures" was carried out in Germany in the context of an internal university project of eufom University with the goal of detecting the sensitivity for crisis of the German population. At the same time, it should be shown how far there is awareness for emergency situations, what people do to possibly prepare to emergency situations and extreme situations and how they react in an emergency.

Electricity supply

Since electricity is a central lifeline of modern societies, outages of electricity supply differ in the intensity of effects on households regarding the length and kind of an outage. The initial question was, "Have you already experienced a longer-lasting outage of electricity supply?" aimed at analyzing the range of experience of the German population:

Table 2.7 Question "Have you already experienced a longer lasting outage of electricity supply?"

Experienced an electricity outage?	Number of participants
Yes	45%
No	55%
Grand total	**100%**

Source: Fontanari & Kredinger: 22

The relatively high degree of experience with an electricity outage indirectly hints at the fact that there is a relatively high risk. The finding that such experiences are deeply marked in the conscience of the people questioned is interesting. If you cross this finding with the question on when people have experienced an electricity outage, 29.8 percent of those who have experienced an electricity outage remember that it has happened within the last four years at the point of questioning. Another 33.3 percent indicated this memory for a period of 5 to 10 years, while 26.3 percent remembered a former electricity outage which had taken place more than 20 years ago.

The potential of a threat is put into perspective with the length of an electricity outage. Thus, 77.4 percent indicated that it lasted about 1 to 3 hours; 18.5 percent experienced an electricity outage over a length of 4 to 12 hours and merely 0.6 percent indicated the length of an electricity outage with half a day to a full day, and 2.3 percent indicated the length of 2 to 3 days, while 1.2 percent experienced an electricity outage of more than 3 days. When asked "Do you think you were prepared for an electricity outage lasting several days?" 74.9 percent said no, while 25.1 percent said yes. It is remarkable that interventions into the power supply operation have increased from two in 2003 to 990 in 2011 (Popp, 2012).

Experiences of citizens in and with emergency situations

The kind and size of personal experiences with an emergency situation have a substantial impact on the question of consequences and attitudes towards preparing for a crisis. Specifically, experiences with flood waters, earthquakes, landslides, severe weather or outage of electricity supply were asked for. Thereby, "severe weather in general" and "flood waters" were stated most frequently, whereas it was suitable to provide several answers.

A continued questioning on the size and extent of personal experiences with emergency situations analyzed the evaluation of the probability of such emergency situations with respect to the occurrence of such an event.

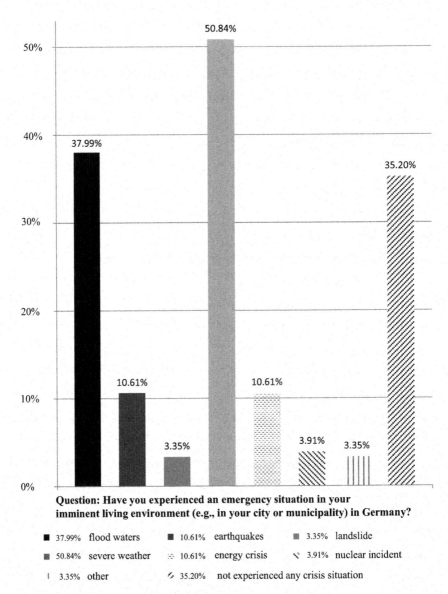

Question: Have you experienced an emergency situation in your imminent living environment (e.g., in your city or municipality) in Germany?

- ■ 37.99% flood waters
- ■ 10.61% earthquakes
- ■ 3.35% landslide
- ■ 50.84% severe weather
- ⋮ 10.61% energy crisis
- ᵛ 3.91% nuclear incident
- | 3.35% other
- ⧄ 35.20% not experienced any crisis situation

Figure 2.1 Experienced emergency situations
Source: Fontanari and Kredinger (2017, p. 24)

Probability of the occurrence of crises in Germany

Summarizing the categories "most probably" and "probably", the respondents most likely view themselves confronted with the danger of a natural catastrophe (56%), terrorism (36%) and the outage of water supply and electricity supply

(18%) as well as a nuclear catastrophe (18%). Least likeliness is attributed for the next 5 years to the danger of war in Germany (64%) and the danger of food shortages (62%):

Table 2.8 Question "According to you, how likely is the occurrence of this crisis in your region in Germany within the next five years?"

	Most likely	Likely	Rather not	Not within the next five years	Total
Natural catastrophes (generally)	17%	39%	31%	13%	100%
Outage of electricity and water	1%	17%	47%	35%	100%
War in Germany	1%	4%	31%	64%	100%
Terrorism	4%	32%	42%	23%	100%
Epidemics	2%	14%	44%	40%	100%
Nuclear catastrophe	3%	15%	45%	38%	100%
Food shortages	1%	4%	32%	62%	100%
Other	8%	17%	33%	42%	100%

Source: Fontanari and Kredinger (2017, p. 24)

Specifying the question on current personal and preventive preparations for a crisis, the result is that the majority of both the rural and the urban population (80% and 79%) is not prepared for a catastrophe, should there be the occurrence of a danger right now. A majority in both groups justify this by stating that they have never considered the occurrence of a crisis (49% in urban area – 45% in rural area):

Table 2.9 Attitudes towards preparing for a catastrophe

Would you be prepared for the occurrence of one of the catastrophes (natural catastrophe, energy crisis, war, and nuclear catastrophe) mentioned before?	Area of high population density	No area of high population density
That would depend on the kind of crisis.	2%	3%
Yes, I am prepared and could leave my apartment at any time.	9%	11%
Yes, I am prepared and could sustain myself at home at any time.	9%	7%
No, I have not yet reflected on such kinds of catastrophes.	49%	45%
No, I have already thought about it, but not taken any preparations, yet.	31%	34%
Grand total	**100%**	**100%**

Source: Fontanari and Kredinger (2017, p. 26)

Asking for the specific intention to personally prepare for a crisis, 48 percent of all respondents stated that preparing for a crisis does not make sense to them, because there is nothing to worry about (20%) or they do not believe in a useful preparation (28%). More than a quarter (27%) stated that they have never thought about precautions, while 11 percent want to deal with this issue in the future. A solid core of 14 percent has already internalized this issue and has carried out specific precautionary measures:

Table 2.10 Attitudes towards personally preparing for a crisis

Question 13: personal preparation for a crisis	*Number of Participants*
a) I make provisions.	14%
b) I intend to start with it in the near future.	11%
c) I have not made provisions, because I am convinced that nothing will happen.	20%
d) I have not made provisions, because I do not believe in a useful preparation.	28%
e) I have never thought about making provisions.	27%
Grand total	**100%**

Source: Fontanari and Kredinger (2017, p. 26)

The question on specific measures of making provisions for the most probable crisis event is answered by the majority of the respondents with the provision of sustainable food (91% think this is very important or important) and the provision of water (90% very important/important). Two-thirds of the respondents also prioritize access to financial means/ cash and the provision of hygiene products (82% very important/important). Securing mobility is also given high priority – 63 percent regard this to be very important/ important.

Crossing the question on the probability of the occurrence of a natural catastrophe with the intentions on a personal crisis preparation, you receive an interesting and differentiated statement: among those who see the highest probability for the occurrence of a natural catastrophe, 19.35 percent already actively make provisions, while 26.7 percent intend to do so in the near future; compared with this, there are also 22.22 percent who think that it is not possible to make meaningful provisions, and there are almost 9 percent who have never thought about it.

As expected, the highest approval among the respondents who make provisions can be found within the group of those who also see the occurrence of a natural catastrophe within the next 5 years to be probable (51.61%). After all, there is also a "careful" core of respondents who actively make provisions, although they do not expect such a crisis event within the next 5 years (16.3%). The majority of all respondents behave like this: "As long as there is no threat of immediate and confrontative danger, I do not worry or do not make provisions". Thus, there are 43.24 percent

Table 2.11 Question "Now think about the most probable occurrence of a crisis. In case you make provisions: how do your preparations look like or how would they look like?"

	Very Important	Important	Not so Important	Not important
Arrange for insurances	25%	19%	20%	35%
Water supply	77%	13%	5%	4%
Sustainable food	74%	17%	6%	4%
Money and other financial means	22%	44%	23%	11%
Hygiene	43%	39%	11%	6%
Clothes	22%	39%	28%	11%
Mobility	23%	40%	25%	11%
Escape plan/getaway spot	34%	32%	19%	15%
Self-defence /securing premises	19%	32%	28%	21%
Practical preparations	19%	38%	25%	18%
Mental preparations	20%	34%	27%	19%
I would not prepare anything	16%	12%	16%	56%

Source: Fontanari and Kredinger (2017, p. 27)

in the group of "I have not made provisions", who think that a natural catastrophe is probable and another 35.14 percent are in this group, who do rather not expect a crisis.

The most likely probability of the occurrence of a crisis through an outage of electricity supply and water supply – after all 18 percent of all respondents deem this "very probable/ probable" – leads to the following figure concerning the question on personal provisions: the one percent who see the occurrence of this danger with the highest probability has at least thought about it but are not prepared adequately for it at home. Around 17 percent of all respondents who deem this probable have for the greater part thought about it (35.9%) or have not at all thought about what will happen (38.46%), should this case occur.

Many of the respondents have in fact experienced severe weather or flood waters. Yet, this experience does not predominantly lead to the taking of preventative measures. Even the probability of a far more devastating emergency (e.g., a spacious and lasting electricity outage which could lead to a food shortage) is predominantly ignored, and the probability of its occurrence is considered to be minimal. Only for people who are already making provisions can it be said that they do so, because they are afraid of being taken by surprise by catastrophes.

A clear crisis-oriented awareness can at least be ascribed to the respondents when they learn about an immediate threat in their region from the news. Around

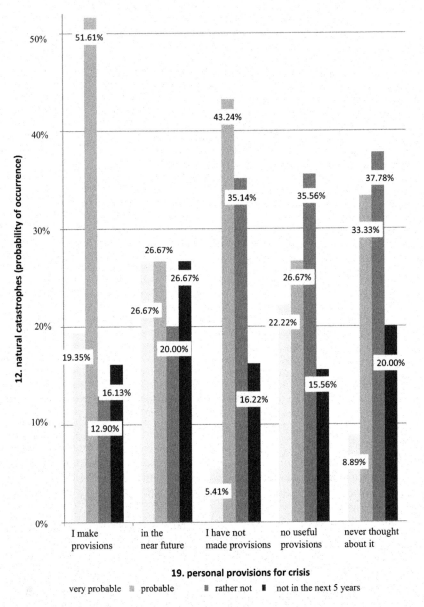

Figure 2.2 Probability of occurrence of natural catastrophes and attitudes towards personal
      provisions

Source: Fontanari and Kredinger (2017, p. 28)

90 percent of the respondents would actively search for more information to get
actual hazard warnings. Furthermore, the survey shows that people only become
sensitive to making provisions for a crisis when a crisis is imminent or has already
taken place. Independence from a stable infrastructure is very rare. The degree of
resilience among the respondents, therefore, is rather small.

Even if there is still a long way to go for the average citizen and society to develop an awareness of crisis and resilience which is adapted to the real situation of danger, one can see that a stronger thematization in media would increase public awareness.

4. Interpretations on the awareness of resilience from the part of supply and demand and implications for destination management

The empirical reflection of the analyzed sectors showed a first status quo. Modern management theory provides links for regional management or destination management based on resilience. Notably, the model of viable systems (Malik, 2006, p. 75f.) which was the first to describe organization-related minimum requirements for the viability of systems in the 1970s by relying on a model of set-theory by Beer (Hummelbrunner, Lukesch, & Baumfeld, 2002, p. 48). A regional management which is basically resilience-oriented has the advantage of effectuating a resilience-oriented distribution of resources in the region by linking and coordinating many supply enterprises and strong agents (Fontanari & Kredinger, 2017, p. 35). The question of how to design the legal, formal and technical regional co-ordination of structures for information and communication as well as their adequate mechanism seems solvable. So far, concluding thoughts will relate to the content-wise orientation and development of the ability for resilience of a region or destination.

Via internal marketing, tourism destinations have access to opinion and identity formation of citizens and agents. The embedding of a stronger (higher) orientation towards resilience through, e.g., developing a mission statement of a destination or through concrete tourism projects can particularly be achieved through a participative approach via public information design and communication design.

Based on this, concrete projects, activities and measures can be derived which focus on stronger tourism profiling and the alignment and integration of measures for increasing resilience at the same time. This consideration can be taken as a transformational approach and can be designed and implemented by regional agencies for tourism (or DMOs – destination management organizations), as is shown with Figure 2.3:

Resilience-oriented destination management with respect to regional management should be organized on the basis of some established destination management or as an enlarged approach for regional development. Apart from a complete assessment and evaluation of all critical infrastructures and supply structures on the procurement side, it will in a first phase address stronger awareness-raising on the procurement and demand side. In a second phase, more resilient infrastructures and more resilient regional value creation processes should be created in a participative way with citizens and agents. They should have a high degree of autonomy and be based on the principles of regional circular economy on a compartmentalized and small-area level. Incorporating and using these structures for tourism-oriented product development assures creative, innovative, and differentiating approaches for tourism marketing.

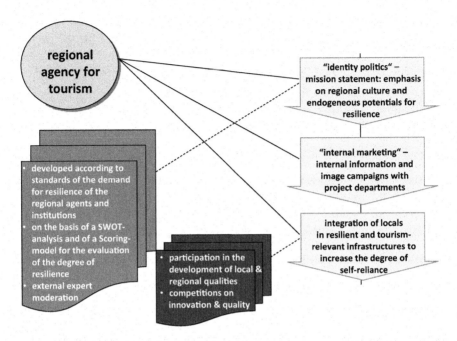

Figure 2.3 Transformational model for designing resilience within internal tourism marketing

Source: Based on Fontanari and Fontanari (2001, p. 71)

Notes

1 cf. Statistisches Landesamt Rheinland-Pfalz (2016). Retrieved from www.statistik.rlp. de/index.php?id=2818&tx_ttnews%5Btt_news%5D=2024
2 cf. Statistisches Landesamt Rheinland-Pfalz (2011). Retrieved from www.statistik.rlp. de/no_cache/staat-und-gesellschaft/bevoelkerung-und-gebiet/tabellen/verbandsgemeinden-nach-groessenklassen/
3 cf. Statistisches Landesamt Rheinland-Pfalz (2010). Retrieved from www.statistik.rlp. de/fileadmin/dokumente/monatshefte/rubriken/rlpkarte/201112.pdf
4 cf. Statistisches Landesamt Rheinland-Pfalz (2014a). Retrieved from www.statistik.rlp. de/veroeffentlichungen/statistische-berichte/
5 In total, 1.456 agents and suppliers have been invited to participate in the online survey.
6 cf. Stadtwerke Trier (2014). Retrieved from www.swt.de/swt/Integrale?SID=6F6C831A EB96C66D40FC42E0E72A1846&MODULE=Frontend&ACTION=ViewPageView& PageView.PK=5&Document.PK=2814&_p_Menu.PK=2815
7 Statistisches Landesamt Rheinland-Pfalz (2014b, p. 9, 13). Retrieved from www.statistik. rlp.de/fileadmin/dokumente/berichte/G4013_201300_1j_G.pdf

References

BBK [Bundesamt für Bevölkerungsschutz und Katastrophenhilfe]. (2014). *Stromausfall. Grundlagen und Methoden zur Reduzierung des Ausfallrisikos der Stromversorgung.* Wissenschaftsforum, Bd. 12, Bonn. Retrieved from www.bbk.bund.de/SharedDocs/

Downloads/BBK/DE/Publikationen/Wissenschaftsforum/Bd12_Stromausfall.pdf;jsessi onid=E6763837EE9BE77E5CF898B16C96D7B9.1_cid330?__blob=publicationFile (Accessed 24 May 2014).

BMI [Bundesministerium des Innern]. (2016). *Konzeption Zivile Verteidigung (KZV)*. Retrieved from www.bmi.bund.de/SharedDocs/Downloads/DE/Broschueren/2016/ konzeption-zivile-verteidigung.html (Accessed 4 July 2017).

Borgert, S. (2013). *Resilienz im Projektmanagement*. Wiesbaden: Springer Gabler.

Bürkner, H.-J. (2010). *Vulnerabilität und Resilienz – Forschungsstand und sozialwissenschaftliche Untersuchungsperspektiven*. IRS Leibnitz-Institut für Regionalentwicklung und Strukturplanung. Working Paper, No. 43. Retrieved from http://d-nb. info/1028582749/34 (Accessed 12 February 2017).

Fontanari, M., & Fontanari, M. (2001). Die Rolle des Tourismus als Instrument zur ganzheitlichen Regionalentwicklung – Regionale Integration, Regionale Identität & ökonomische Regionalentwicklung. In M. Fontanari & M. Fontanari (Eds.), *Tourismus im Europa der Regionen* (ETI-Studien, Bd. 4) (pp. 59–80). Trier: ETI-Eigenverlag, S.

Fontanari, M., & Kredinger, D. (2017). *Risiko- und Resilienzbewusstsein. Empirische Analysen und erste konzeptionelle Ansätze zur Steigerung der Resilienzfähigkeit von Regionen*. Working Paper, No. 9. Dortmund and Münster: Readbox Unipress. Retrieved from http://unipress.readbox.net (Accessed 24 May 2017).

Hagmann, J. (2012). *Factsheet Risiko, Verwundbarkeit, Resilienz: Neue Gefahrenkonzepte in der internationalen Sicherheitsanalyse*. Retrieved from www.files.ethz.ch/isn/164454/ Factsheet-Risiko-Verwundbarkeit-Resilienz.pdf (Accessed 24 May 2017).

Hiete, M. et al. (2010). *Krisenmanagement Stromausfall – Krisenmanagement bei einer großflächigen Unterbrechung der Stromversorgung am Beispiel Baden-Württemberg*. Langfassung, Stuttgart. Retrieved from www.bbk.bund.de/SharedDocs/Downloads/ BBK/DE/Publikationen/PublikationenKritis/Krisenhandbuch_Stromausfall_ Kurzfassung_pdf.pdf?__blob=publicationFile (Accessed 12 February 2017).

Holling, C.S., & Meffe, G. (1996). Command and control and the pathology of natural resource management. *Conservation Biology*, *50*(2), S. 328–337.

Hummelbrunner, R., Lukesch, R., & Baumfeld, L. (2002). *Systemische Instrumente für die Regionalentwicklung*. Retrieved from www.bka.gv.at/DocView.axd?CobId=3381 (Accessed 02 June 2014).

Kredinger, D. (2014). *Der Begriff der Resilienz und Aspekte des Regionalmanagements im Kontext von Systemkrisen oder dem Katastrophenfall. Implikationen auf die Stadt Trier und den Landkreis Trier-Saarburg*. Master-Thesis, IIS FOM Luxemburg.

Malik, F. (2006). *Strategie des Managements komplexer Systeme. Ein Beitrag zur Management-Kybernetik evolutionärer Systeme*. Bern: Haupt.

Menski, U., & Gardemann, J. (2005). *Auswirkungen des Ausfalls Kritischer Infrastrukturen auf den Ernährungssektor am Beispiel des Stromausfalls im Münsterland im Herbst 2005*. Empirische Untersuchung im Auftrag der Bundesanstalt für Landwirtschaft und Ernährung (BLE).

Osztovics, W., Kovar, A., & Mayrbäurl, C. (2012). *Arena Analyse 2012 – Resilienz oder Katastrophe*. Wien: Kovar & Köppl Public Affairs Consulting GmbH. Retrieved from www.publicaffairs.cc/arena-analyse-2012/ (Accessed 12 February 2017).

Petermann, T. et al. (2010). *Gefährdung und Verletzbarkeit moderner Gesellschaften – am Beispiel eines großräumigen Ausfalls der Stromversorgung* (TAB-Arbeitsbericht, Bd. 141). Berlin: TAB - Büro für Technologiefolgenabschätzung des Deutschen Bundestages. Retrieved from http://www.tab-beim-bundestag.de/de/pdf/publikationen/ berichte/TAB-Arbeitsbericht-ab141.pdf (Accessed 30 January 2017).

Petermann, T. et al. (2011). *Was bei einem Blackout geschieht – Folgen eines langandauernden und großräumigen Stromausfalls*. Berlin: Edition Sigma.

Popp, M. (2012). *Was geschieht bei einem längeren Stromausfall?* Retrieved from www. energie-fakten.de/html/black-out.html (Accessed 30 January 2017).

Stadtwerke Trier Versorgungs-GmbH. (2014). *Trinkwasserversorgung – Aufbereitung*. Retrieved from www.swt.de/swt/Integrale?SID=6F6C831AEB96C66D40FC42E0E72A 1846&MODULE=Frontend&ACTION=ViewPageView&PageView.PK=5&Document. PK=2814&_p_Menu.PK=2815 (Accessed 16 April 2014).

Statistisches Landesamt Rheinland-Pfalz. (2010). *Statistische Monatshefte Rheinland-Pfalz – Auspendler in andere Bundesländer bzw. nach Luxemburg am 30. Juni 2010*. Retrieved from www.statistik.rlp.de/fileadmin/dokumente/monatshefte/rubriken/ rlpkarte/201112.pdf (Accessed 18 April 2014).

Statistisches Landesamt Rheinland-Pfalz. (2011). *Verbandsgemeinden nach Größenklassen, Bevölkerungsdichte und Anzahl der Gemeinden am 31. Dezember 2011*. Retrieved from www.statistik.rlp.de/no_cache/staat-und-gesellschaft/bevoelkerung-und-gebiet/ tabellen/verbandsgemeinden-nach-groessenklassen/ (Accessed 19 April 2014).

Statistisches Landesamt Rheinland-Pfalz. (2014a). *Bruttoinlandsprodukt, Bruttowertschöpfung in den kreisfreien Städten und Landkreisen Deutschlands – Reihe 2 Kreisergebnisse, Bd 1*. Retrieved from www.statistik.rlp.de/veroeffentlichungen/statistische-berichte/ (Accessed 26 April 2014).

Statistisches Landesamt Rheinland-Pfalz. (2014b). *Statistische Berichte – Gäste und Übernachtungen im Tourismus 2013*. Retrieved from www.statistik.rlp.de/fileadmin/ dokumente/berichte/G4013_201300_1j_G.pdf (Accessed 26 April 2014).

Statistisches Landesamt Rheinland-Pfalz. (2016). *Anzahl der Einwohner in den Kommunen am 31. Dezember 2015*. Retrieved from www.statistik.rlp.de/index.php?id=2818&tx_ ttnews%5Btt_news%5D=2024 (Accessed 12 February 2017).

Wink, R. (2011). Evolution regionaler Resilienz: Theoretischer Rahmen und Messkonzepte. In C. Dreger, R. Kosfeld & M. Türck (Eds.), *Empirische Regionalforschung heute* (pp. 111–124). Gabler: Wiesbaden, S.

3 Multidisciplinary approaches to resilience in tourism destination studies

A conceptual framework

Anna Scuttari & Philipp Corradini

1. Introduction

The increasing popularity of the concept of resilience led to the elaboration of a wide array of different approaches, theoretical frameworks and possible applications, which endeavor to conceptualize and apply the notion. The multidisciplinary nature of the concept – applied in engineering, natural science, management and regional development studies – has led, over more than two decades, to a scattered panorama of resilience studies. These seem to rely on different conceptualizations of resilience according to the discipline they relate to. The natural science perspective on resilience is dominant in tourism research: resilience is commonly addressed as "the capacity of a system to absorb disturbance and reorganize while undergoing change so as to still retain the same function, structure, identity and feedbacks" (Walker, Holling, Carpenter, & Kinzig, 2004). This definition is taken over from *revised ecosystem ecology* (Farrell & Twining-Ward, 2004), addressing complex adaptive ecosystems, their structure, function and behavior, as well as their interface to human systems. The predominance of the ecological perspective in tourism research is presumably related to the emergence of resilience within the tourism research agenda in relation to sustainability studies (Espiner, Orchiston, & Higham, 2017), with a series of contributions regarding sustainable tourism development (McDonald, 2009; Tyrrell & Johnston, 2008), sustainable tourism indicators (Schianetz & Kavanagh, 2008), or natural hazard management partially related to climate change (Calgaro & Cochrane, 2009; Cochrane, 2010). At the same time, there is some evidence of lacking in-depth analyses of social dimensions of resilience (Calgaro, Lloyd, & Dominey-Howes, 2014), with reference for example to multi-scaled socio-political processes, power relations and cultural norms.

In brief, if resilience is a multidisciplinary concept, its application to tourism still seems to be bound mostly to one discipline. The attempt of this paper is to offer a framework to understand resilience in tourism destinations from multiple and complementary perspectives, across the disciplinary boundaries of the concept and the possible scales of analysis. We aim to crystallize one definition for tourism resilience that takes into account the existing discipline-specific literature and builds on it, to stimulate new applications of resilience to tourism destination research.

2. Resilience: definitions from multiple disciplinary perspectives

Among the most comprehensive definitions of resilience is the one of the UN International Strategy for Disaster Reduction: hereby resilience is defined as "the ability of a system, community or society exposed to hazards to resist, absorb, accommodate to and recover from the effects of a hazard in a timely efficient manner, including through the preservation and restoration of its essential basic structures and functions" (UNISDR, 2009). Even though it makes reference to just one type of risk (hazards), this definition implicitly accepts at least two of the existing conceptualizations of resilience: engineering resilience and ecological resilience. Nevertheless, an additional approach has been recently introduced to assess resilience in social sciences: evolutionary resilience. To understand the shadings of these different approaches and comprehend their relationship to destinations as complex systems, an initial disciplinary approach is necessary.

2.1 Engineering resilience

Resilience originated in the realm of materials sciences, within which it is one of the elements of stability analysis in terms of elasticity, describing the capacity and velocity of a system or material to return to its equilibrium after a displacement (Bodin & Wiman, 2004). The measure of resilience in these domains relates to the total strain energy which can be stored in a given volume of material and can be released after unloading, without permanent deformation. The temporal interval within which the system is able to return to its initial state is a relevant aspect of engineering resilience, because it focusses on stability. (Folke, 2006; Adger, Hughes, Folke, Carpenter, & Rockström, 2005; Pimm, 1984) Hereby the idea of stability is referred to as the maintenance of the efficiency of function (Holling & Gunderson, 2002): the reduction, elimination or resistance to immanent variability, disturbance and change, as well as the provision of measures of rapid recovery in case of perturbation are its main features. Engineering resilience therefore plays a major role within structural engineering, where it is defined as "a function indicating the capability to sustain a level of functionality or performance for a given building, bridge, lifeline networks, or community, over a period defined as the control time" (Cimellaro, Reinhorn, & Bruneau, 2010, p. 3640).

The introduction of the concept of resilience to ecosystem ecology was undertaken by Holling (1973, 1996), according to which resilience was initially acknowledged as the ability of a system to resist disturbance and to return to a steady-state near an equilibrium. Nevertheless, the notion of steady state and static equilibrium would change very soon in the framework of *revised ecosystem ecology*, giving birth to the concept of *ecological resilience*.

2.2 Ecological resilience

The concept of ecological resilience was introduced by Holling, defining it as "the magnitude of disturbance that can be absorbed before the system changes its structure" (Holling, 1996). This definition acknowledges the engineering concept of maximum strain energy applicable before irreversible changes occur and nevertheless considers a change in structure as a possible new situation of equilibrium. Therefore, the concept of "limit" is progressively substituted by the one of "threshold". Indeed, acknowledging that a system can change its structure implies the acceptance of the possible presence of multiple stable states or equilibria, as well as an adaptive capacity to reach and maintain them. The possible outcome after a shock or stressor occurs, therefore, is either a "bounce back" to the system's state as to before the disturbance occurred, or a "bounce forth" towards a new system depending on the adaptive capacity of the system by supporting diversity and complexity (Davoudi, 2012; Bergen, Bolton, & Fridley, 2001). Conferring to ecological resilience also a certain degree of pursuit of stability, it has to be acknowledged that while within engineering resilience the idea of stability means the maintenance of the efficiency of function, within ecological resilience the focus is set towards the maintenance of the existence of function (Holling & Gunderson, 2002). Therefore, a resilient system in its adaptation phase after a shock might not be working efficiently, but must be somehow still operating.

2.3 Evolutionary resilience

A further step towards the conceptualization of resilience diverging from the concept of steady states is evolutionary resilience. Evolutionary resilience distances itself from the notion of equilibrium (or multiple equilibria) by considering the continually changing nature of complex adaptive systems and defining resilience as a dynamic process (Davoudi, 2012; Martin, 2012). Throughout this process, the functionality of the system is maintained or even improved by continuous adaptation and transformation. Hereby the system focuses not only on resistance and recovery but on re-orientation and renewal (Boschma, 2015; Wink, 2014). Based on the concept of revolutionary economics and the evolutionary perspective in economic geography, this conceptualization of resilience focusses on the "dynamic process of transformation to a more desirable trajectory" (Davoudi, Brooks, & Mehmood, 2013; Boschma & Martin, 2007), accepting continuous "permanent deformations" of the systems and going beyond the concepts of limit and threshold. Therefore, resilience, which in its origins was measured as a characteristic of the disturbance (maximum magnitude of a strain energy below which no permanent transformation of material occurs), now is described as a property of a system (the capacity to proactively strive towards a desirable development trajectory). Instead of preventing the disturbance of equilibrium and ensuring efficiency of function, evolutionary resilience stands for the process of managing inevitable disturbances towards a desirable and unsteady development path.

The adaptive cycle and the panarchy heuristics

Resilience in its evolutionary interpretation can be conceptualized by the adaptive cycle (or "Holling Loop"), developed by Holling (2001). The four phases inherent to adaptive cycles, comprise exploitation, conservation, release and reorganization. The phases of exploitation and conservation represent the front loop of the cycle and are characterized by stability and prosperousness, within which resources are accumulated and bound within the system (Gotts, 2007; Walker & Salt, 2006). The back loop comprises the release phase, during which, due to internal or external events, the system itself declines, releasing the resources utilized within the previous phases. Within the subsequent reorganization phase, the system restructures itself, and the previously released resources as well as the structure of the system are reoriented towards a new configuration. Within a socio-economic system, this new configuration is often characterized by the entrance of new subjects, such as entrepreneurs approaching the current state of apparent chaos by grasping new opportunities, contributing to innovation, an important element for the successful reorganization of the system itself (Lew & Cheer, 2018; Pelling & Manuel-Navarrete, 2011; Gotts, 2007; Lewis & Green, 1998). Walker and Salt (2006) add for consideration that the process of the adaptive cycle is not fixed, but implicates the possibility of a diverse sequence of the occurrence of the different phases. A cycle, for instance, can move from an exploitation phase directly to a release phase. The different adaptive cycles, which in terms of linked sets are conceptualized as panarchy, function at different scales in space and time (Gotts, 2007). While lower levels of adaptive cycles operate at a higher speed and are more vulnerable to small-scale disturbances, the higher levels move slower and are oftentimes unaffected by lower-level stresses. Nevertheless, also small-scale disturbances can have cross-scale and cascading effects on the different nested sets of adaptive cycles, and therefore on the overall panarchy (Walker & Salt, 2006; Farrell & Twining-Ward, 2004).

3. Tourism destinations as complex adaptive systems: risks and capacities

In recent years tourism destinations are increasingly interpreted as Complex Adaptive Systems, particularly for the analysis of transformational processes (Correia, 2009; Farrell & Twining-Ward, 2004; Scuttari, Volgger, & Pechlaner, 2016). While system thinking is not new to the tourism academic body of literature (Leiper, 1990; Kaspar, 1998), complexity science was introduced later on, in relation to the emergence of sustainability issues (McDonald, 2009), as well as governance network studies (Baggio, 2011). To introduce a multidisciplinary perspective to tourism resilience, some preliminary considerations on Complex Adaptive Systems, their capacities and their application to tourism destinations is needed.

3.1 Complex adaptive systems

A system is "an integrated whole whose essential properties arise from the relationships between its constituent parts" (Hall, 2005, p. 57). Based on this definition, systems comprise a certain amount of constituent parts: basic elements or units, relationships between these elements and some interactions with the surrounding environment. Units and relationships are analyzed in a context which is defined by the scale of analysis and the boundaries designed for the system itself. The system can be tagged as "complex" in case it has the following characteristics: a) a large amount of elements in a dynamic interaction, b) multiple layers and hierarchies among elements, c) perpetual novelty and self-organization without external organizing principle (Ottino, 2003), d) a non-linear path of development and cascading system effects, e) development dynamics far from a condition of stable equilibrium, and finally f) path dependency (McDonald, 2009).

Adaptability emerges as a characteristic of complex systems in relation to the "capacity to evolve, learn, and work towards adjusting to the surroundings" (Farrel & Twining-Ward, 2004) given the uncertainty, non-linearity and unexpected changes in non-linear development paths.

3.2 Tourism destinations as complex adaptive systems

By applying this conceptualization of Complex Adaptive Systems to the destination scale, it becomes clear that tourism destinations no longer are simple (linear) compositions of the entities constituting them (Baggio, 2011), but rather organic life-like systems, with multiple layers of stakeholders and relational connections, as well as multiple infrastructural, natural and social elements within the destination space (Pechlaner, Pichler, & Herntrei, 2012). Destinations as Complex Adaptive Systems have the following characteristics: a) they involve a large number of co-producing actors delivering a variety of products and services (Gunn, 1994; Haugland, Ness, Gronseth, & Aarstad, 2011; Pearce, 1989), with no unique organizing principle; and b) they tend to rather evolve and adjust according to the territorial socio-economic context and to tourism markets. Tourism destinations as Complex Adaptive Systems comprise at least four subsystems (Scuttari et al., 2016): the social-ecological subsystem, the socio-technical system, the socio-political subsystem and the tourism subsystem. The constituent elements of these subsystems include both human and nonhuman units. For instance, components of the social-ecological systems are the local population, the guests and the natural and cultural resources; those of the socio-technical subsystem include a tangible set of infrastructures (transport, hospitality, sport facilities, etc.), as well as a portfolio of services (commercial, cultural, transport-related, booking-related, etc.) and their providers; the socio-political system includes both decision-makers, as well as rules and regulations, norms and practices. Finally, the tourism system encompasses parts of the tangible and intangible elements of the other subsystems, and exists as a cross-cutting element among the other systems in relation to tourists' activities on site. Human elements of the subsystems interact with natural ones in a non-linear way (Correia, 2009; Farrell & Twining-Ward, 2004, 2005; Folke, 2006; McDonald, 2009), and they also relate to existing infrastructures and technical facilities on site. The complex interaction of human, nature and infrastructure in space and time determines a new concept of dynamic evolution: linear models such as the Butler's tourism destination life cycle (Butler, 1980) are re-interpreted through a complexity science approach to explain unpredictable changes in the destination development path (Russell & Faulkner, 1999). Within this new approach to destination development, the concepts of risk, vulnerability, as well as absorptive coping, adaptive and transformative capacity emerge.

3.3 Risks and vulnerability in complex systems

Tourism destinations as complex systems face a multitude of internal and external risks at various scales (Calgaro et al., 2014). Risks can develop into either gradually emerging stressors (slow onset) or originating shocks (rapid onset), in relation to the vulnerability of the system (Lew, 2014; Walker et al., 2012; Sharpley, 2005). Looking into sustainability science, vulnerability is assessed as "the degree to which an exposure unit [e.g. a destination] is susceptible to harm due to exposure to a perturbation or stress, and the ability (or lack thereof) of the exposure unit to cope, recover, or fundamentally adapt" (Kasperson, Turner, Schiller, & Hsieh, 2001, p. 7). Vulnerability is therefore "place- and system-specific, contextualized, highly scaled, dynamic and differential" (Calgaro et al., 2014, p. 343). Risks, in form of stressors or shocks, are on the other hand different in their magnitude, frequency and duration and can occur also simultaneously, generating multiplicative effects (Lew, 2014; Becken, 2013; Walker et al., 2012). Typical external shocks for tourism destinations are terror attacks, natural hazards and health epidemics, while stressors often refer to human-environment interactions, such as anthropogenic climate change, water shortage, environmental degradation and reduction of biodiversity (Calgaro et al., 2014). Internal risks comprise sudden or incremental variations in tourism demand and prices, as well as policy-driven reorganisation in the tourism management system. These drivers of change induce the tourism destination to apply different strategies in order to cope with increasing uncertainty, change and complexity (Espiner et al., 2017; Strickland-Munro, Allison, & Moore, 2010).

3.4 The capacities inherent in complex systems

Strategies to cope with risks are different according to the scale and rate of change, the exposure and sensitivity of the system, as well as different capacities of the destination system to reduce and counter vulnerability (Lew, 2014; Hudson, 2009; Nelson, Adger, & Brown, 2007). These capacities encompass the absorptive coping capacity, the adaptive capacity and the transformative capacity (Béné et al., 2012). Through absorptive coping, adaptive or transformative capacities a destination system and its subsystems address change leading to persistence, incremental adjustments or transformational responses (Bec, McLennan, & Moyle, 2016; Béné, Headey, Haddad, & von Grebmer, 2016).

Absorptive coping capacity relates to the ability of a system to prepare for, reduce, absorb or mitigate the impact of shocks and stresses while maintaining its state and continuing to persist in its original form, focusing on the *stability* of the system (Sansavini, 2017; OECD, 2014; Béné et al., 2012; Holling, 1973). For instance, examples for absorptive coping capacity within the tourism destination context include price management across seasonal fluctuations in the hospitality industry, as well as recovering capacity of infrastructure stocks after a natural hazard. In the face of shocks, such as natural disasters and the subsequent crises, the retention of a system's state is oftentimes perceived as an ideal outcome (Norris, Stevens, Pfefferbaum, Wyche, & Pfefferbaum, 2008). Indeed, the intensity of the pursuance of stability and retention of the system's state, its adaptation to the changed environment or its transformation is connected of the overall perception of its desirability as a social construct (Engle, 2011; Robards, Schoon, Meek, & Engle, 2011).

If the magnitude of the disturbance exceeds the absorptive coping capacity or if the system's coping responses are insufficient, the necessity of exerting its *adaptive capacity* emerges (Cutter et al., 2008). Going beyond the notion of a stable, unchangeable state of a system and the overall goal of its persistence, adaptive capacity refers to the ability of a system, to learn and adjust, in order to either anticipate disturbances and change or adapt to effects deriving from disturbances, through incremental adjustment. Furthermore, the adaptive system is able to modify its characteristics while avoiding major qualitative changes within its structure and functionality (Béné et al., 2016; Béné, 2013; Smit & Pilifosova, 2001; Gunderson, 2000). As an example within the context of tourism destinations, the study of Cellini and Cuccia (2015) identified destinations which were able to mitigate the demand decrease during the "great recession" by substituting their domestic target market with foreign markets.

If the magnitude of the disturbance within the social, economic or ecological dimension exceeds the absorptive coping as well as the adaptive capacity of a system, a major transformation might have to be pursued to avoid a system failure. Hereby the *transformative capacity* encompasses the creation of an essentially new system, which necessitates a profound change of its structure and nature, by the deliberate initiation of transformational changes (Béné et al., 2016; Folke et al., 2010; Walker et al., 2004). For example, if the essential subsystem of snow activities of a year-round destination ceases to exist due to climate change, the destination system's structure could shift towards a summer destination (Becken, 2013).

The capacities – *absorptive coping, adaptive and transformative* – have to be considered as complementing each other. This is exemplified by the argument that the three capacities often are used simultaneously in order to address the vulnerability of systems to multiple disturbances or the diverse effects of a shock or stressor within the different scales of the hierarchy of a system. Furthermore, considering that the main focus of absorptive coping capacities is the preservation of stability of the system, the interconnectedness of the capacities is underlined by the fact that one of the prerequisites for the generation or renewal of adaptive and transformative capacities is a certain amount of stability (Béné et al., 2012; O'Brien et al., 2004; Fiksel, 2003).

4. A framework to conceptualize the resilience of tourism destinations

Tourism destinations necessitate a holistic framework to interpret resilience, given the complex and dynamic nature of their structure. Indeed, system's components, as stated before, are both human and nonhuman, and their interactions cause no-linear, but rather complex, unpredictable, multilevel and often self-organized development patterns. On the one hand, acknowledging these features, the evolutionary approach to resilience seems to be the most appropriate to grasp the complexity of tourism destinations. In fact, this approach allows the coexistence of absorptive coping, adaptive and transformative capacities and assumes constant and unpredictable change and transformation, often in response to the unpredictable nature of tourism itself (McKercher, 1999). On the other hand, we argue that, by focusing on dynamic trends and not on equilibrium states, this approach seems to lack emphasis on the *stability* and *elasticity* of the system towards coping with stressors and shocks, on the *time* necessary to recover from them, and on the *existence and role of thresholds* across the development phases. Therefore, it seems that the evolutionary approach to resilience as conceptualized in literature is necessary but not sufficient to explain destination resilience in its complexity. A combination of different approaches – including also engineering and ecological ones – might be more appropriate and comprehensive to assess the complex tourism development dynamics (Lew, 2014).

Destination resilience should therefore focus not only on transformational patterns and processes *beyond* an equilibrium but also on the multiple equilibria *underneath* these transformations, as well as on system stability and elasticity *around* each equilibrium state. The context of analysis determines which of these three aspects of resilience is more prominent in resilience analysis, and which is less relevant for the specific case. The context of analysis can be conceptualized according to at least three key aspects: the characteristics of the destination system (its vulnerability and the types of subsystems affected by the disturbance); the characteristics of the shock or stressor (its magnitude, frequency and duration) and, subsequently, the scale and time extension of the disturbance's effects on the system as a whole (cross-scale and cascading effects).

4.1 Disturbances' and systems' characteristics and approaches to destination resilience

As far as disturbances are concerned, we argue that the more extensive the magnitude of the disturbance is and the longer the duration, the higher the probability to focus on dynamic development trends, rather than on system stability and elasticity towards a stressor or shock. In fact, if the disturbance is intense and long-lasting, it is supposed to break equilibria and act as a driver of system change and subsequently either adaptation or transformation in the destination. Conversely, in case of minor disturbances, which do not necessarily imply significant reorganizations of the destination system, a threefold focus on transformative and evolutionary dynamics as well as system stability and elasticity might be necessary. Predictability of the risk of disturbances would give to the destination the time advantage to organize its capacities, so it might possibly increase its transformative, adaptive or absorptive coping capacity, depending on the nature of the disturbance.

Shocks' or stressors' characteristics have to be considered not only on their own, but also in relation to systems' characteristics, with a particular focus on vulnerability. Indeed, if a system is particularly vulnerable towards a certain disturbance, the reaction that will unfold after its occurrence will be transformational – either abrupt or gradual in its nature (Gallopín, 2006). This occurs because the system, due to its vulnerability, is easily harmed by the force exercised by the shock or stressor, and its ability to "bounce back" is reduced if not impeded. Vulnerability is not a constant characteristic through the development phases of a complex system. It can also emerge due to an excessive pursuit of stability: for example in the late K phase of the adaptive cycle, within which the preservation of the conservation phase is deemed beneficial, the flexibility of the system is reduced, becoming locked up and resulting in a higher vulnerability which leads to a higher probability of system failure (Davoudi et al., 2013; Walker & Salt, 2006). If disturbances occur in this phase, the system is more likely to be harmed, resulting in successive changes during the release phase of the adaptive cycle.

The type of subsystems affected by the disturbance also affects the assessment of resilience. The more infrastructural elements are affected by the disturbance (e.g. non-human elements of the socio-technical or social-ecological subsystem), the more likely the engineering approach will be prominent within the response. Indeed, tangible infrastructural elements of the destination system such as accommodation and transport facilities as well as natural and cultural heritage structures are subject to limited possibilities of undergoing changes in function and tend to be rather restored to their pre-disturbance phase (Proag, 2014). On the other hand,

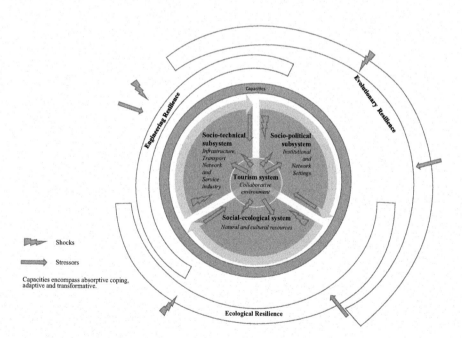

Figure 3.1 Tourism destination subsystems and approaches to resilience

Source: Based on Scuttari et al.(2016)

the more human units are affected by the shock, the easier it is to apply ecological or evolutionary approaches to resilience, as a proactive orientation towards desirable trends and processes towards them might be suitable. In case a disturbance affects more elements of different destination subsystems, there might be different types of reactions starting simultaneously. For instance, in the case of natural disasters, the actors of the socio-technical system might focus on rebuilding the affected infrastructures, while at the same time the governance system might introduce policies, rules or regulations which proactively contribute to strengthen the future engineering resilience of the affected infrastructures towards this disturbance (Lew, 2014), by, at the same time, exercising an adaptive capacity from a governance perspective.

4.2 Scale and time of disturbances' effects and approaches to resilience

Focusing on disturbances' effects on the destination, we consider scale and time variables. Scale in our interpretation is connected to the amount of systems' units affected by one disturbance, as well as to the centrality of these units to the destination system as a whole. The more units are affected by one disturbance, at the same time, the higher the probability that multiscale cascading effects will occur. The development of cascading effects all across the system implies an increased complexity in governing resilient behavior and necessarily suggests focusing on the ecological or evolutionary approach to measure resilience. Moreover, the role of units in the network is central, as well: the more central these units are in the

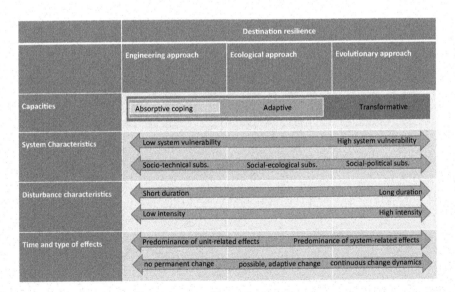

Figure 3.2 A framework to assess approaches to resilience in tourism destinations
Source: Own illustration

destination network, the more cascading effects are likely generated if these units are harmed or affected by the disturbance. The interaction between the number of units affected by the disturbance, their centrality and the time necessary to react, recover, adapt or transform might be a field where all approaches to resilience could be integrated and build additional knowledge. Conversely, a focus on engineering resilience and more simple "bounce back" dynamics might be necessary with less central units, or – in a panarchy framework – within the lower levels of the overall hierarchy of the system.

Reaction time might also have an influence on reaction dynamics and the activation of absorptive coping, adaptive or transformative responses to disturbance. The longer the recovery time, the higher the probability to generate cascading effects, and subsequently to involve multilevel and non-linear reactions.

Finally, the evolutionary approach to resilience seems to be more suitable in case disturbances generate significant multiscaled system effects, i.e., when the effects on the system as a whole prevail in relation to those on its units. Conversely, when unit-related effects prevail on system effects, an engineering or ecological approach might be prominent.

5. Conclusion

Ecological and evolutionary approaches to resilience from a natural science perspective are the most common approaches to assess the concept in destination studies (Espiner et al., 2017). These studies often relate to the measurement of sustainability in destinations and have the advantage to introduce a novel, process-oriented and system-based approach. Process-orientation and system-based approaches have somehow advanced the interpretation of sustainability in destinations, moving beyond the idea of a stable, pre-defined tourism carrying capacity (Middleton & Hawkins, 1998; Chamberlain, 1997) and towards the interpretation of sustainability as a process (Nordman, Christopher, & Jakobcic, 2017). Indeed, tourism carrying capacity was originally defined as "the maximum number of people that may visit a tourist destination at the same time, without causing destruction of the physical, economic, socio-cultural environment and an unacceptable decrease in the quality of visitors' satisfaction" (UNWTO, 1981). This interpretation of carrying capacity recalls the engineering resilience concept of maximum strain energy which can be stored in a given material without permanent deformation. Conversely, ecological approaches to resilience, introducing the concept of threshold, recall the concept of "limits of acceptable change", developed as a critical response to carrying capacity in tourism research (McCool, 2013).

By acknowledging this parallel development process both within resilience studies and in sustainability science applied to destinations, this chapter aimed at critically reflecting upon how comprehensive and how multidisciplinary this approach effectively is. We argue that evolutionary approaches to resilience might grasp complexity and long-term development, but they lack the capacity to understand limits of acceptable change in tourism destinations and to assess the absorptive coping capacity of a system and its units to cope with disturbance. Therefore, we propose a broader interpretation of destination resilience, which acknowledges the presence of dynamic development and transformational capacities, but also assesses stability and flexibility of systems. According to this more comprehensive approach, the different disciplinary perspectives of resilience are not mutually exclusive, but rather complementary in destination resilience assessment. The more the system is complex, the more intense the disturbance, the higher the hierarchy level and the longer the time frame of resilience assessment, the more it is necessary to combine evolutionary approaches with engineering approaches to understand the resilience of the whole system. We thank the editors of this book and Ingrid Kofler, Senior Researcher at the Center for Advanced Studies at Eurac Research, for assistance with the conception of this research, and for comments that improved this paper.

References

Adger, W.N., Hughes, T.P., Folke, C., Carpenter, S.R., & Rockström, J. (2005). Social-ecological resilience to coastal disasters. *Science, 309*(5737), 1036–1039.

Baggio, R. (2011). Collaboration and cooperation in a tourism destination: A network science approach. *Current Issues in Tourism, 14*(2), 183–189.

Baggio, R., Scott, N., & Cooper, C. (2010). Improving tourism destination governance: A complexity science approach. *Tourism Review, 65*(4), 51–60.

Bec, A., McLennan, C., & Moyle, B.D. (2016). Community resilience to long-term tourism decline and rejuvenation: A literature review and conceptual model. *Current Issues in Tourism, 19*(5), 431–457.

Becken, S. (2013). Developing a framework for assessing resilience of tourism sub-systems to climatic factors. *Annals of Tourism Research, 43*, 506–528.

Béné, C. (2013). *Towards a quantifiable measure of resilience.* Institute for Development Studies Working Paper, No. 434.

Béné, C., Headey, D., Haddad, L., & von Grebmer, K. (2016). Is resilience a useful concept in the context of food security and nutrition programmes? Some conceptual and practical considerations. *Food Security, 8*(1), 123–138.

Béné, C., Wood, R.G., Newsham, A., & Davies, M. (2012). *Resilience: New utopia or new tyranny? Reflection about the potentials and limits of the concept of resilience in relation to vulnerability reduction programmes.* Institute for Development Studies Working Paper, No. 405.

Bergen, S.D., Bolton, S.M., & Fridley, J.L. (2001). Design principles for ecological engineering. *Ecological Engineering, 18*, 201–210.

Bodin, P., & Wiman, B. (2004). Resilience and other stability concepts in ecology: Notes on their origin, validity, and usefulness. *ESSN Bulletin, 2*(2), 33–43.

Boschma, R. (2015). Towards an evolutionary perspective on regional resilience. *Regional Studies, 49*(5), 733–751.

Boschma, R., & Martin, R.L. (2007). Constructing an evolutionary economic geography. *Journal of Economic Geography, 7*, 537–548.

Butler, R.W. (1980). The concept of a tourist area cycle of evolution: Implications for management of resources. *The Canadian Geographer/Le Géographe canadien, 24*(1), 5–12.

Calgaro, E., & Cochrane, J. (2009). *Comparative destination vulnerability assessment for Thailand and Sri Lanka: Sustainable recovery and resilience building in the tsunami affected region.* Stockholm Environment Institute.

Calgaro, E., Lloyd, K., & Doniney-Howes, D. (2014). From vulnerability to transformation: A framework for assessing the vulnerability and resilience of tourism destinations. *Journal of Sustainable Tourism, 22*(3), 341–360.

Cellini, R., & Cuccia, T. (2015). The economic resilience of tourism industry in Italy: What the "great recession" data show. *Tourism Management Perspectives, 16*, 346–356.

Chamberlain, K. (1997). *Carrying capacity*. UNEP Industry and Environment 8. Paris: UNEP.

Cimellaro, G.P., Reinhorn, A.M., & Bruneau, M. (2010). Framework for analytical quantification of disaster resilience. *Engineering Structures, 32*, 3639–3649.

Cochrane, J. (2010). The sphere of tourism resilience. *Tourism Recreation Research, 35*(2), 173–185.

Correia, F. (2009). *Parks, people and processes: Rethinking sustainable tourism in protected areas through complexity approaches*. PhD Thesis, Leeds Metropolitan University.

Cutter, S.L., Barnes, L., Berry, M., Burton, C., Evans, E., Tate, E., & Webb, J. (2008). A place-based model for understanding community resilience to natural disasters. *Global Environmental Change, 18*, 598–606.

Dahles, H., & Susilowati, T.P. (2015). Business resilience in times of growth and crisis. *Annals of Tourism Research, 51*, 34–50.

Davoudi, S. (2012). Resilience: A bridging concept or a dead end? *Planning Theory & Practice, 13*(2), 299–333.

Davoudi, S., Brooks, E., & Mehmood, A. (2013). Evolutionary resilience and strategies for climate adaptation. *Planning, Practice & Research, 28*(3), 307–322.

Engle, N.L. (2011). Adaptive capacity and its assessment. *Global Environmental Change, 21*, 647–656.

Espiner, S., Orchiston, C., & Higham, J. (2017). Resilience and sustainability: A complementary relationship? Towards a practical conceptual model for the sustainability-resilience nexus in tourism. *Journal of Sustainable Tourism, 25*(10), 1–16.

Farrell, B.H., & Twining-Ward, L. (2004). Reconceptualizing tourism. *Annals of Tourism Research, 31*(2), 275–295.

Farrell, B.H., & Twining-Ward, L. (2005). Seven steps towards sustainability: Tourism in the context of new knowledge. *Journal of Sustainable Tourism, 13*(2), 109–122.

Fiksel, J. (2003). Designing resilient, sustainable systems. *Environmental Science & Technology, 37*, 5330–5339.

Folke, C. (2006). Resilience: The emergence of a perspective for social-ecological systems analyses. *Global Environmental Change, 16*, 253–267.

Folke, C., Carpenter, S.R., Walker, B., Scheffer, M., Chapin, T., & Rockström, J. (2010). Resilience thinking: Integrating resilience, adaptability and transformability. *Ecology and Society, 15*(4), 20.

Gallopín, G.C. (2006). Linkages between vulnerability, resilience, and adaptive capacity. *Global Environmental Change, 16*, 293–303.

Gotts, N.M. (2007). Resilience, panarchy, and a world-systems analysis. *Ecology and Society, 12*(1), 24.

Gunderson, L.H. (2000). Ecological resilience – In theory and application. *Annual Review of Ecology and Systematics, 31*, 425–439.

Gunn, C.A. (1994). Emergence of effective tourism planning and development. *Tourism: The State of the Art*, 10–19.

Hall, C.M. (2005). *Tourism: Rethinking the social science of mobility*. Essex: Pearson Education Limited.

Haugland, S.A., Ness, H., Gronseth, B.O., & Aarstad, J. (2011). Development of tourism destinations: An integrated multilevel perspective. *Annals of Tourism Research, 38*(1), 268–290.

Holling, C.S. (1973). Resilience and stability of ecological systems. *Annual Review of Ecology and Systematics, 4*, 1–23.

Holling, C.S. (1996). Engineering resilience versus ecological resilience. In P. Schulze (Eds.), *Engineering within ecological constraints* (pp. 31–44). Washington, DC: The National Academies Press.

Holling, C.S. (2001). Understanding the complexity of economic, ecological, and social systems. *Ecosystems, 4*(5), 390–405.

Holling, C.S., & Gunderson, L.H. (2002). Resilience and adaptive cycles. In L.H. Gunderson & C.S. Holling (Eds.), *Panarchy: Understanding transformations in human and natural systems* (pp. 25–62). Covelo, CA: Island Press.

Hudson, R. (2009). Resilient regions in an uncertain world: Wishful thinking or a practical reality? *Cambridge Journal of Regions, Economy and Society, 3*(1), 11–25.

Kaspar, C. (1998). Das System Tourismus im Überblick. *Tourismus-Management, 3,* 15–32.

Kasperson, R.E., Turner, B.L., Schiller, A., & Hsieh, W.H. (2001). *Research and assessment systems for sustainability: Framework for vulnerability.* Paper presented at the AIACC Project Development Workshop: Climate Change Vulnerability and Adaptation, Trieste, Italy.

Leiper, N. (1990). Tourist attraction systems. *Annals of Tourism Research, 17*(3), 367–384.

Lew, A.A. (2014). Scale, change and resilience in community tourism planning. *Tourism Geographies, 16*(1), 14–22.

Lew, A.A., & Cheer, J. (2018). Lessons learned: Globalization, change, and resilience in tourism communities. In J. Cheer & A.A. Lew (Eds.), *Tourism resilience, and sustainability: Adapting to social, political and economic* change (pp. 319–323). London: Routledge.

Lewis, R., & Green, S. (1998). Planning for stability and managing chaos: The case of Alpine ski resorts. In E. Laws, B. Faulkner, & G. Moscardo (Eds.), *Embracing and managing change in tourism: International case studies* (pp. 138–160). London: Routledge.

Luthe, T., & Wyss, R. (2014). Assessing and planning resilience in tourism. *Tourism Management, 44,* 161–163.

Martin, R. (2012). Regional economic resilience, hysteresis and recessionary shocks. *Journal of Economic Geography, 12,* 1–32.

McCool, S.F. (2013). Limits of acceptable change and tourism. In A. Holden & D.A. Fennel (Eds.), *Routledge handbook of tourism and the environment* (pp. 285–298). Oxon: Routledge.

McDonald, J.R. (2009). Complexity science: An alternative world view for understanding sustainable tourism development. *Journal of Sustainable Tourism, 17*(4), 455–471.

McKercher, B. (1999). A chaos approach to tourism. *Tourism Management, 20*(4), 425–434.

Middleton, V.C., & Hawkins, R. (1998). *Sustainable tourism: A marketing perspective.* Oxford: Butterworth-Heinemann.

Nelson, D.R., Adger, W.N., & Brown, K. (2007). Adaptation to environmental change: Contributions of a resilience framework. *Annual Review of Environment and Resources, 32,* 395–419.

Nordman, E.E., Christopher, N., & Jakobcic, Y. (2017). Sustainability as a university value: A journey from awareness to behavior change. In J.A. Arevalo & S.F. Mitchell (Eds.), *Handbook of sustainability in management education: In search of a multidisciplinary, innovative and integrated approach* (pp. 131–150). Glos: Edward Elgar Publishing Limited.

Norris, F.H., Stevens, S.P., Pfefferbaum, B., Wyche, K.F., & Pfefferbaum, R.L. (2008). Community resilience as a metaphor, theory, set of capacities, and strategy for disaster readiness. *American Journal of Community Psychology, 41,* 127–150.

O'Brien, K., Leichenko, R., Kelkar, U., Venema, H., Aandahl, G., Tompkins, H., Javed, A., Bhadwal, S., Barg, S., Nygaard, L., & West, J. (2004). Mapping vulnerability to multiple stressors: Climate change and globalization in India. *Global Environmental Change, 14,* 303–313.

OECD. (2014). *Guidelines for resilience systems analysis.* OECD Publishing.

Ottino, J.M. (2003). Complex systems. *AIChE Journal, 49*(2), 292–299.

Pearce, D. (1989). *Tourist development* (2nd ed.). Harlow: Longman.

Pechlaner, H., Pichler, S., & Herntrei, M. (2012). From mobility space towards experience space: Implications for the competitiveness of destinations. *Tourism Review, 67*(2), 34–44.

Pelling, M., & Manuel-Navarrete, D. (2011). From resilience to transformation: The adaptive cycle in two Mexican urban centers. *Ecology and Society, 16*(2), 11.

Pimm, S.L. (1984). The complexity and stability of ecosystems. *Nature, 307*(26), 321–326.

Proag, V. (2014). The concept of vulnerability and resilience. *Procedia Economics and Finance, 18,* 369–376.

Robards, M.D., Schoon, M.L., Meek, C.L., & Engle, N.L. (2011). The importance of social drivers in the resilient provision of ecosystem services. *Global Environmental Change, 21*(2), 522–529.

Russell, R., & Faulkner, B. (1999). Movers and shakers: Chaos makers in tourism development. *Tourism Management, 20*(4), 411–423.

Sansavini, G. (2017). Engineering resilience in critical infrastructures. In M.V. Florin & I. Linkov (Eds.), *IRGC resource guide on resilience* (pp. 204–210). Lausanne: EPFL International Risk Governance Center (IRGC).

Schianetz, K., & Kavanagh, L. (2008). Sustainability indicators for tourism destinations: A complex adaptive systems approach using systemic indicator systems. *Journal of Sustainable Tourism, 16*(6), 601–628.

Scuttari, A., Volgger, M., & Pechlaner, H. (2016). Transition management towards sustainable mobility in Alpine destinations: Realities and realpolitik in Italy's South Tyrol region. *Journal of Sustainable Tourism, 24*(3), 463–483.

Sharpley, R. (2005). The tsunami and tourism: A comment. *Current Issues in Tourism, 8*(4), 344–349.

Smit, B., & Pilifosova, O. (2001). Adaptation to climate change in the context of sustainable development and equity. In J.J. McCarthy, O. Canziani, N.A. Leary, D.J. Dokken & K.S. White (Eds.), *Climate change 2001: Impacts, adaptation and vulnerability* (pp. 877–912). Cambridge: Cambridge University Press.

Strickland-Munro, J.K., Allison, H., & Moore, S.A. (2010). Using resilience concepts to investigate the impacts of protected area tourism on communities. *Annals of Tourism Research, 37*(2), 499–519.

Tyrrell, T.J., & Johnston, R.J. (2008). Tourism sustainability, resiliency and dynamics: Towards a more comprehensive perspective. *Tourism and Hospitality Research, 8*(1), 14–24.

UNISDR. (2009). *Terminology: Resilience.* Retrieved from United Nations Office for Disaster Risk Reduction website: www.unisdr.org/we/inform/terminology#letter-r

UNWTO. (1981). *Saturation of tourist destinations.* Report of the Secretary General, Madrid, Spain.

Walker, B.H., Carpenter, S.R., Rockstrom, J., Crépin, A.S., & Peterson, G.D. (2012). Drivers, "slow" variables, "fast" variables, shocks, and resilience. *Ecology and Society, 17*(3), 30.

Walker, B.H., Holling, C.S., Carpenter, S.R., & Kinzing, A. (2004). Resilience, adaptability and transformability in social-ecological systems. *Ecology and Society, 9*(2), 5.

Walker, B.H., & Salt, D. (2006). *Resilience thinking: Sustaining ecosystems and people in a changing world*. Washington: Island Press.

Wink, R. (2014). Regional economic resilience: European experiences and policy issues. *Raumforschung und Raumordnung, 72*, 85–91.

Part II

Destination management and governance towards resilience

4 From resilience thinking to resilience practice – perspectives on destination development

Daniel Zacher

1. Introduction – resilience approach in a tourism context

Tourism is growing on a global scale (UNWTO, 2016, p. 3). More and more people have the opportunity to spend money on holidays. Keeping this in mind, there is really little reason for responsible political and industry representatives to be concerned about the future of tourism. Taking a national perspective, however, a more differentiated picture emerges. Examples from past years have shown that entire economies are experiencing economic and political crises, as in Tunisia, for example, where after a series of terrorist attack, the guests stayed away (Jeffrey & Bleasdale, 2017). At the same time, countries such as Spain and Greece, whose popularity as a tourist destination are the result of geopolitical development (Lane, 2017; Rappold, 2016), are benefiting. However, there are challenges with regard to sustainable tourism development, whether by the omnipresence of terrorist threats or by the burdens local inhabitants face, due to strongly increasing numbers of visitors. Similar logics could be discussed on a smaller scale for regions and individual firms. All these are, however, only momentary snapshots. Profiting from the problems of the competitors cannot be the main goal of tourism in the sense of a long-term positive development. The aim should rather be to decouple from the possible negative influences and make optimal use of resources, potentials and opportunities.

Discussions such as these contribute to the fact that the resilience approach is currently entering the field of tourism research (Butler, 2017; Cheer & Lew, 2018) . This takes place at a time when a universal understanding of resilience is not established either in scientific or practice-oriented environments (Renn & Klinke, 2015; Taubenböck & Geiß, 2014). At this point, we will examine the influence of the resilience approach on tourism. We ask the question on how a better understanding of resilience among different stakeholder groups could be a potential for tourism development, and how resilience thinking can contribute to the action-oriented consideration of questions to future tourism development.

2. Definition of resilience and entry into tourism research

The etymological background of resilience is of some relevance for the understanding of its diverse adaptation in different scientific disciplines. Here, we can only have a brief look at a few basic approaches that subsequently can be related to tourism-related issues. It is important to note that the conceptual blurring of the term is a major point of criticism with regard to the scientific value of the resilience approach (Duit, Galaz, Eckerberg, & Ebbesson, 2010; Reghezza-Zitt, Rufat, Dja-ment-Tran, Le Blanc, & Lhomme, 2012). However, in this *vagueness*, important voices see a quality, to bring research on future questions to an interdisciplinary level and to provide a frame for the description of complex problems (Brand & Jax, 2007; Strunz, 2012).

Resilience experienced a first deeper scientific use in material science. There, it is defined by the property of different materials being able to withstand stresses by either remaining unimpressed or returning to their initial state after a negative event occurs (Alexander, 2013; Smith et al., 2008). This way of thinking is based on the paradigm of an equilibrium state, which can be seen as the constant of the proper functioning of an object or a system, and to which the object or system needs to return (Nyström, Folke, & Moberg, 2000). Ecologists subsequently used the resilience approach for their research to describe the behaviour of an ecosystem after the occurrence of a catastrophic event. A new feature of their perspective was that resilience understanding is no longer related to a return to the state of origin. The focus was on achieving a new balance as a result of the ecosystem's recovery and internal reorganisation processes. The idea of multiple equilibria and adaptive cycles as a framework for evaluating the resilience of a system was born (Folke, 2006; Pendall, Foster, & Cowell, 2010).

Ecosystem research was essential for adapting the resilience approach in the context of social, economic and spatial sciences (Adger, 2000). In this way, the systemic understanding, pursued by many current studies on resilience, was developed. In the last few years, research into resilience in the context of organisations and regions has grown considerably (Christopherson, Michie, & Tyler, 2010; Vogus & Sutcliffe, 2007). This development is accompanied by two extensions of the resilience approach, which are characteristic for the current resilience understanding:

Organisational resilience is a popular approach to economic science, as here, it is not only described as a reactive resistance to crises, but also an active entrepreneurial process that parallels the logics of an innovation process (Vogus & Sutcliffe, 2007).

Research on resilience with regard to the regional level considers the region as a system that needs to adapt itself and to develop against the background of external crises and internal structural problems. The equilibrium paradigm of ecosystem research is replaced by an evolutionary understanding of resilience, which takes into account the politically demanded and socially desired growth targets of regional development (Boschma, 2015; Simmie & Martin, 2010). A stable state of equilibrium is not any longer the point of reference for the definition of resilience. It is replaced by a permanently prospering, evolutionary growth paradigm.

With regard to this understanding, psychology also plays an important role and must be mentioned prominently when we talk about the spreading of the concept of resilience in science and practice. Psychology has established resilience as a field of research since the 1960s and describes resilience of the human psyche against the background of difficult environmental conditions, such as poverty or shocking events, like the loss of a close relative (Masten, 2001).

As tourism can be discussed on different levels (individual/firm/destination/nation), it can be stated that regarding the complexity of tourism development issues, a comprehensive understanding of resilience is required, which takes into account the advantages and criticisms of the respective understanding traditions.

The investigation of destination resilience can be based on already existing discussions of resilience in tourism science. Tyrrell and Johnston (2008, p. 14) define tourism resilience "as the ability of social, economic or ecological systems to recover from tourism-induced stress." Here, a system is in danger of losing balance due to tourism development; resilience does not refer to tourism development itself, but rather to the space in which tourism takes place as a disturber of communities. Overall, a prevalent dominance of ecological and environmental resilience research can be observed in the tourism context (Becken, 2013; Strickland-Munro, Allison, & Moore, 2010). It is thus connected with the socio-ecological research tradition of resilience, as coined by Holling (1996) and Folke (2006).

Studies that deal with the evolutionary view of the resilience approach and with questions of a resilient development of the tourism industry at the regional level have so far mainly taken place in the context of developing countries (Dahles & Susilowati, 2015; Larsen, Calgaro, & Thomalla, 2011). Studies focusing on organisational aspects of tourism development and, for example, the role of Destination Management Organisations (DMOs) for a resilient tourism development, are focusing primarily on skills and competencies for crisis management from a post-crisis perspective (Orchiston, Prayag, & Brown, 2016). Few studies are attempting to address preventive planning issues in the context of tourism and resilience, focusing on specific problems such as the effects of climate change on winter sports tourism in a particular region (Luthe, Wyss, & Schuckert, 2012).

Which system or which scale the resilience approach in tourism should be referred to has only been addressed indirectly so far. In her article "Resilience to what? Resilience for whom?", Cutter (2016) states that the question of the reference level is crucial for the assessment of resilience and non-resilience. Speaking for tourism-specific units, for example, a resilient hotel business does not necessarily have to contribute to regional resilience if its strategy is at the expense of the competitors.

The tourist destination can be described as a spatial competition unit and a virtual service company (Raich, 2006). It represents a central identification space for the guest in the process of making a travel decision (Zehrer, Pechlaner, & Raich, 2007). With regard to the governance of the tourism offer, destinations are therefore to be seen as directed networks which are aimed at pursuing common goals (Raich, 2006). From a political, operational and social perspective, destinations are seen as units within which appropriate management can be undertaken to carry out sustainable tourism development against the background of ecological, economic and social issues (Ritchie & Crouch, 2003). Even if a dynamic competitive environment is necessary within the context of a changing environment and external crisis-inducing influences, it is to be assumed that a destination provides the framework for a viable business development (organisational resilience) on the one hand and resilience at the regional level (regional resilience) on the other hand.

Becken (2013) notes that the conceptualisation of a Tourist Destination Resilience requires interdisciplinary approaches, since destinations are always exposed to a variety of different, more or less visible stress factors. Furthermore, destinations are the product of human action in its environment. In this respect, a destination resilience can be seen in the tradition of socio-ecological approaches (Becken, 2013; Farrell & Twining-Ward, 2004; Lacitignola, Petrosillo, & Zurlini, 2010), and thus has direct links in resilience research (Folke, 2006; Holling, 1996). In this understanding, the destination provides a suitable framework within which the consistent build-up of resilience appears to be meaningful.

At this point, it is time to step back and ask which prerequisites have to prevail within a destination so that the building of resilience can be carried out. Subsequently, the idea of *resilience thinking* will be discussed. It is derived from socio-ecological resilience research and can provide valuable access to the understanding of resilience in a destination context.

3. Resilience thinking – from resilient destination to destination resilience

Resilience thinking is a concept that has attracted attention recently in the scientific and practice-oriented discussion of resilience (Berkes, 2007). This concept groups together research projects moving away from the consideration of specific, individual crisis events (against which a system can develop a specific resilience) towards a generalised view of the challenges of a system. The aim is to develop an understanding of the reasons for system changes and the appropriate handling of these changes. People as the central actors in this system adopt their passive victimhood and instead develop abilities to deal with the change taking place actively (Walker & Salt, 2012).

Starting from its original way of looking at social-ecological systems, for example in connections that consider specific human-environment relationships, resilience thinking has entered many research disciplines. Therein, issues in predominantly social systems have been playing a decisive role (Dwiartama & Rosin, 2014). Thus, resilience thinking has already been applied in the context of city planning (Eraydin & Tasan-Kok, 2013) or in regional economic cycles (Dawley, Pike, & Tomaney, 2010). Resilience thinking focuses on human thinking, politics and prevailing power relations (Bahadur & Tanner, 2014). It recognises change as something necessary and positive. By contrast, ignoring change would be equated to the increase in the vulnerability of a system. People are particularly good at identifying rapid changes and in developing solutions in reaction to them. They are worse at finding appropriate responses to challenges that are slow and gradual. This can also to be seen in connection with a perceived impotence of large-scale challenges such as, for example, climate change (Walker & Salt, 2012).

In summary, *resilience thinking* is understood as the sum of people's abilities in a system that enables them to raise awareness of emerging change processes and develop strategies that actively promote resilience building.

Biggs, Schlüter, and Schoon (2015) discuss seven approaches that provide an orientation on how the abstract requirement of resilience thinking could be implemented in practice (see figure 3.1). These approaches are also discussed by the Stockholm Resilience Center (2017), a prestigious institute in the area of resilience research. This institution played a major role in attracting public attention to resilience thinking. The insights result from empirical observations in different case studies that are sometimes also related to tourism. Hence, they require further research when it comes to a specific perspective on destination development. The approaches are briefly presented below, and a possible reference to questions of destination development is provided.

3.1 Maintaining diversity and redundancy

In a turbulently developing environment, reliable responses to change processes or disturbances are required. Diversity ensures alternatives for action in a critical phase. Redundancy avoids the total failure of the overall system and increases its reliability. The goal should ideally be a combination of both, the diversity of response possibilities to challenges while simultaneously redundancy of processes to maintain the performance of social-ecological systems. However, diversity can also increase the complexity and inefficiency of the system, which can lead to an increase in its vulnerability. Lietaer, Ulanowicz, Goerner, and McLaren (2010) warn of a decline in resilience at a high level of diversity. Efficiency and resilience are here in a possible trade-off. In that way, every system has to find a middle way.

Tourism literature is comprehensively discussing the concept of community-based tourism (e.g. Goodwin & Santilli, 2009; Reed, 1997). This is linked to the slogan of sustainable tourism development (Saarinen, 2006) and it is an object of discussion within the strategic management of destinations (Flagestad & Hope, 2001). At the same time, the heterogeneity of the actors is presented as a challenge for the coordinated development of products and services. Here, the advantages and disadvantages of diversified tourism structures are addressed explicitly. The role of the DMO, which coordinates the product development in the destination (Pechlaner, Beritelli, & Volgger, 2015; Timur & Getz, 2008), is seen as crucial.

3.2 Managing connectivity

Connectivity can present both an advantage and a drawback with respect to resilience. Connectivity is about the kind and the strength of the interlinkages of resources and actors in a system. High connectivity is conducive to recovery measures after major disturbances. At the same time, however, this connectivity increases the likelihood that negative disturbances will have a serious impact on the overall system, as the disturbance in a part of the system can directly affect the other parts.

Flexible networks at the interface of public and private actors and organisations which are connected by common interests can be seen as a success factor for innovative destinations (Nordin & Svensson, 2007). These cooperations present a prerequisite for adjustments to be made in relation to changing framework conditions. At the same time, a systemic leadership quality for destinations is demanded in the literature to tie together the actors in the context of the necessary adjustment measures (Beritelli & Bieger, 2014; Pechlaner, Kozak, & Volgger, 2014).

3.3 Managing slow variables and feedbacks

Socio-ecological systems are subject to variables which are sometimes gaining or losing in importance very slowly and continuously. These changes are therefore hardly perceptible. It is characteristic, however, that there are certain thresholds which, if exceeded, make a return to a resilient state possible only with very great efforts. Coordinating organisations must help to ensure that these thresholds are not exceeded. In addition, management must consider possible feedback loops, which become a negative process with its own internal dynamics.

Tourist destinations are subject to long-term changes, which can result, for example, in increasing overnight stays. In this context, the concept of the *carrying capacity* of destinations can be discussed, which represents a maximum of manageable guest arrivals for a sustainable destination development (Butler, 1996; O'Reilly, 1986). *Carrying capacity* should be respected in the sense of a resilient destination and, if necessary, be ensured through active measures.

3.4 Fostering complex adaptive systems thinking

Complex adaptive system thinking refers to the understanding of the complexity of the interrelations and recognises that certain decisions have to be made with uncertainty. This can also mean that sometimes unpopular decisions need to be taken to the disadvantage of a subgroup of stakeholders in order to keep the overall system resilient.

A destination can be seen as a complex adaptive system. The focus is on institutions and other controlling actors who face similar challenges as formulated in a complex adaptive systems framework, such as the difficulty of prediction and the need for adaptive management (Baggio, Scott, & Cooper, 2010).

3.5 Encouraging learning

System members must acknowledge that they are part of a continuous development process that requires a persistent desire to understand and desire to learn in the system. Cooperative learning processes of relevant system members can be a promising way to build the resilience of a system.

Knowledge and the further development of knowledge is seen as a central resource of destination development. Measurements to promote these are to be institutionalised at destination level (Svensson, Nordin, & Flagestad, 2005).

3.6 Broadening participation

A broad and functioning participation has a number of advantages. A community of well-informed and trusted people has the potential to build a common understanding of complex problems and challenges and can get collective action off the ground on the basis of a high level of acceptance.

Political legitimisation of tourism planning, a diversified tourism development or a high level of hospitality: participatory processes can contribute to an increasing acceptance of tourism in a region and also to product development directly (Bramwell & Sharman, 1999). The motivation for participation can be built up through experience from already existing resilience practices in other fields.

3.7 Promoting polycentric governance

State coordination, municipal coordination, coordination by lead firms and self-organisation are the best way to build resilience when they interlock appropriately. Decision-making must nevertheless be guaranteed. The key to successful polycentric governance is network resources such as communication and trust.

Notably, in publicly dominated destination management structures, different levels of governance prevail which are involved in the decision-making process for tourism policy issues (Bornhorst, Ritchie, & Sheehan, 2010). In a vertical view, clear counterparts are missed by tourist actors. They sometimes complain that information relevant to the target group is not passed on. In a horizontal view, decision-making as close as possible to the affected person while simultaneously ensuring a coordinated approach can be a key to more action orientation in the building of resilience (Lebel et al., 2006).

4. Resilience understanding in tourist destination practice

Even though references to challenges for tourism have been established so far, these aspects have not explicitly addressed the resilience term in questions of destination development. As a result, attempts are made to close this gap by presenting the opinions of tourist experts on perspectives of resilience in tourism.

The interviews were held with Bavarian destination managers and were transcribed and evaluated using the qualitative analysis method GABEK® and the referring software tool WinRelan (Zelger, 1999; Zelger & Oberprantacher, 2002). They result in an association graph which represents relationships in the context of resilience and destination development. Besides presenting the graph (see figure 4.1), the insights will be discussed and supported by direct quotations that have been translated from the German language.

Figure 4.1 Approaches to develop resilience thinking

Source: Own illustration based on Biggs et al. (2015)

4.1 Maintaining diversity and redundancy

The interview partners found that a monothematically structured tourism offer is generally more susceptible to crises. Resilience is achieved through diversification, not only with regard to a variety of different offers, but also with regard to the financial sources of tourism structures, such as DMOs. The basis for resilience is good planning and preparation through a strategic concept, which affirms the change processes and discusses alternative development possibilities consistently:

> *If a good concept exists, I am also resilient, [. . .] then I have my concept, my strategy, and if it does not work in one place, then I go a parallel path, which at first was not obvious, but can also be effective. The ability to change oneself is a core competency in tourism.*

4.2 Managing connectivity

This is regarded as a central task of destination managers. It is about setting up a culture of cooperation that leaves the single companies freedom in their development with simultaneous consideration of destination development goals:

> *I am the one who builds a network, charges it with new ideas and I have to ensure that this network works harmoniously but also critically. Ideas should further be developed in a relationship of trust between the network, myself and our company in order to develop products which can be marketed successfully.*

4.3 Managing slow variables and feedbacks

The interviewees also confirm that tourism is characterised by long-term trends and that a measurability or assessability of subtle change processes is a major challenge. Altogether, it is critically noted that many actors can only be moved to act when a crisis situation is just around the corner or has already arrived. Hard persuasive work is required. In the interest of a resilient destination development, personal skills are crucial for destination managers according to one interviewee:

> *Be on the pulse of time, be capable of self-reflection, keep track of all interest groups and take measurements to change.*

4.4 Fostering complex adaptive systems thinking

Foresighted thinking and acting is required in the sense of a resilient destination development.

> *I believe he has to foresee trends, he has to carry these developments to the respective agencies – politics, business and service providers. This is what the destination manager has to do.*

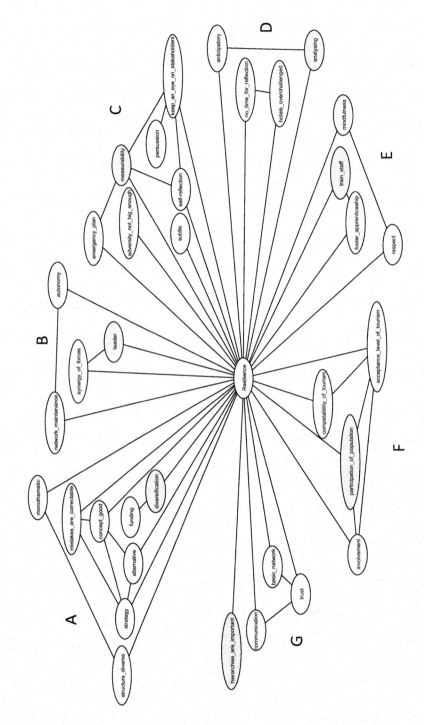

Figure 4.2 Association graph: Resilience in Destination Development

Source: Own illustration created with GABEK®/WinRelan

This is not easy, especially since planning horizons are relatively short and future developments are not easy to anticipate. In a complex governance structure of tourism, the interviewees seem to be already facing enough challenges. The discussion of scientific concepts such as resilience takes a backseat because of a wide range of practical questions.

4.5 Encouraging learning

From the point of view of destination managers, education and advanced training is seen as an essential resource for building resilience. This is particularly related to the learning ability within the DMO, by taking the existing human capital seriously:

The employees have to get the feeling that one counts on their input. [You have to] lure them, by asking: "You are close to the market, where could we do something? Or what does the market not want at all? [. . .] Such things must come, and I must be able to trust these messages and draw the appropriate conclusions.

4.6 Broadening participation

As far as the acceptance of tourism at the municipal level is concerned, early participation of the population is considered important:

[. . .] it is very important to make it clear already at the present time: What you think of tourism affects us, [. . .]. We want to inform you, we want to take you with us, maybe let you participate if you want to.

Broad participation is likely to be a key competence of Destination Resilience, in addition to developing a competence to actively move the population towards participation.

4.7 Promoting polycentric governance

Polycentric structures are seen as an obstacle in the development of the destination rather than as an opportunity. Different views, for example regarding the best strategy in destination marketing, are prevalent, and conflicts are bound to occur:

Of course, there are conflicts and there are always such and such people, so it would be presumptuous to say I'm friends with all those I work together; but I need a basic network where I have trust in people. So the term trust is also important.

Certain hierarchies and enforceability must be ensured to be able to consistently promote key strategic questions of destination development.

5. Conclusion

Summarizing the expert statements, the central role of a DMO for setting up destination resilience can be confirmed. Questions of planning, development and both interior and exterior marketing are directly connected to the resilience at the destination level. Considering the pre-existing variety (and partial overload) of tasks for many DMOs, the active and consistent engagement with the implementation of *resilience thinking* at a destination presumably poses an overburden. A resilient destination needs a DMO that is led by a person who proves to be himself resilient against the background of the various stresses in the tension field of different expectations and requirements.

However, this is not enough. Destination resilience also requires an understanding of the challenge of tourism development in a wider regional context by actively involving different stakeholders. Destination resilience is a part of regional resilience and vice versa. In this sense, the claim of a resilient destination development is located organisationally not only in DMOs, but also in the offices of regional development agencies and political-administrative institutions. In this image, the local population is not only a background artist having a positive attitude towards tourism but has to be involved actively in a creative way to co-create future-oriented tourism development topics.

The understanding of destination resilience is at the beginning of its conceptual development. Against the background of diverse reception of the parent concept of resilience in various disciplines, the result of this development is open. However, one crucial conclusion can already be drawn today. Destination resilience can raise issues of a crisis-proof and future-oriented tourism development at the destination level in the consciousness of those actors who are needed for the answers. From today's perspective, the way from *resilient thinking* to resilient practice has to be paved mainly by established organisational tourism structures. The implementation of methodological competences is required to encourage service providers and decision-makers to recognise the challenges specific to the destination. An interdisciplinary exchange with resilience initiatives at local, regional, organisational and personal level might be a promising path.

References

Adger, W.N. (2000). Social and ecological resilience: Are they related? *Progress in Human Geography, 24*(3), 347–364.

Alexander, D.E. (2013). Resilience and disaster risk reduction: An etymological journey. *Natural Hazards and Earth System Sciences, 13*(11), 2707–2716.

Baggio, R., Scott, N., & Cooper, C. (2010). Network science: A review focused on tourism. *Annals of Tourism Research, 37*(3), 802–827.

Bahadur, A., & Tanner, T. (2014). Transformational resilience thinking: Putting people, power and politics at the heart of urban climate resilience. *Environment and Urbanization, 26*(1), 200–214.

Becken, S. (2013). Developing a framework for assessing resilience of tourism sub-systems to climatic factors. *Annals of Tourism Research, 43*, 506–528.

Beritelli, P., & Bieger, T. (2014). From destination governance to destination leadership – Defining and exploring the significance with the help of a systemic perspective. *Tourism Review*, *69*(1), 25–46.

Berkes, F. (2007). Understanding uncertainty and reducing vulnerability: Lessons from resilience thinking. *Natural Hazards*, *41*(2), 283–295.

Biggs, R., Schlüter, M., & Schoon, M.L. (Eds.). (2015). *Principles for building resilience: Sustaining ecosystem services in social-ecological systems*. Cambridge: Cambridge University Press.

Bornhorst, T., Ritchie, J.B., & Sheehan, L. (2010). Determinants of tourism success for DMOs & destinations: An empirical examination of stakeholders' perspectives. *Tourism Management*, *31*(5), 572–589.

Boschma, R. (2015). Towards an evolutionary perspective on regional resilience. *Regional Studies*, *49*(5), 733–751.

Bramwell, B., & Sharman, A. (1999). Collaboration in local tourism policymaking. *Annals of Tourism Research*, *26*(2), 392–415.

Brand, F., & Jax, K. (2007). Focusing the meaning(s) of resilience: Resilience as a descriptive concept and a boundary object. *Ecology and Society*, *12*(1), Art. 23.

Butler, R.W. (1996). The concept of carrying capacity for tourism destinations: Dead or merely buried? *Progress in Tourism and Hospitality Research*, *2*(3–4), 283–293.

Butler, R.W. (Ed.). (2017). *Tourism and resilience*. Wallingford, Oxfordshire, UK: CABI.

Cheer, J.M., & Lew, A.A. (Eds.). (2018). *Tourism, resilience and sustainability: Adapting to social, political and economic change*. London: Routledge.

Christopherson, S., Michie, J., & Tyler, P. (2010). Regional resilience: Theoretical and empirical perspectives. *Cambridge Journal of Regions, Economy and Society*, *3*(1), 3–10.

Cutter, S.L. (2016). Resilience to what? Resilience for whom? *The Geographical Journal*, *182*(2), 110–113.

Dahles, H., & Susilowati, T.P. (2015). Business resilience in times of growth and crisis. *Annals of Tourism Research*, *51*, 34–50.

Dawley, S., Pike, A., & Tomaney, J. (2010). Towards the resilient region? *Local Economy*, *25*(8), 650–667.

Duit, A., Galaz, V., Eckerberg, K., & Ebbesson, J. (2010). Governance, complexity, and resilience. *Global Environmental Change*, *20*(3), 363–368.

Dwiartama, A., & Rosin, C. (2014). Exploring agency beyond humans: The compatibility of Actor-Network Theory (ANT) and resilience thinking. *Ecology and Society*, *19*(3).

Eraydin, A., & Tasan-Kok, T. (Eds.). (2013). *Resilience thinking in urban planning*. Heidelberg/New York/London: Springer.

Farrell, B.H., & Twining-Ward, L. (2004). Reconceptualizing tourism. *Annals of Tourism Research*, *31*(2), 275–295.

Flagestad, A., & Hope, C.A. (2001). Strategic success in winter sports destinations: A sustainable value creation perspective. *Tourism Management*, *22*(5), 445–461.

Folke, C. (2006). Resilience: The emergence of a perspective for social – Ecological systems analyses. *Global Environmental Change*, *16*(3), 253–267.

Goodwin, H., & Santilli, R. (2009). Community-based tourism: A success. *ICRT Occasional Paper*, *11*(1), 37.

Holling, C.S. (1996). Engineering resilience versus ecological resilience. In P. Schulze (Ed.), *Engineering within ecological constraints* (pp. 32–43). Washington: National Academies Press.

Jeffrey, H., & Bleasdale, S. (2017). *Tunisia: Mass tourism in crisis?* CABI.

Lacitignola, D., Petrosillo, I., & Zurlini, G. (2010). Time-dependent regimes of a tourism-based social-ecological system: Period-doubling route to chaos. *Ecological Complexity*, *7*(1), 44–54.

Lane, L. (2017, June 5). Despite economic problems, Greece's tourism looking good in 2017. *Forbes*. Retrieved from www.forbes.com/sites/lealane/2017/06/05/despite-economic-problems-greece-tourism-looking-good-in-2017-using-new-strategies/#430cf001541f (Accessed on 22 September 2017).

Larsen, R.K., Calgaro, E., & Thomalla, F. (2011). Governing resilience building in Thailand's tourism-dependent coastal communities: Conceptualising stakeholder agency in social-ecological systems. *Global Environmental Change*, *21*(2), 481–491.

Lebel, L., Anderies, J., Campbell, B., Folke, C., Hatfield-Dodds, S., Hughes, T., & Wilson, J. (2006). Governance and the capacity to manage resilience in regional social-ecological systems. *Ecology and Society*, *11*(1) Art. 19.

Lietaer, B., Ulanowicz, R.E., Goerner, S.J., & McLaren, N. (2010). Is our monetary structure a systemic cause for financial instability? Evidence and remedies from nature. *Journal of Futures Studies*, *14*(3), 89–108.

Luthe, T., Wyss, R., & Schuckert, M. (2012). Network governance and regional resilience to climate change: Empirical evidence from mountain tourism communities in the Swiss Gotthard region. *Regional Environmental Change*, *12*(4), 839–854.

Masten, A.S. (2001). Ordinary magic: Resilience processes in development. *American Psychologist*, *56*(3), 227–238.

Nordin, S., & Svensson, B. (2007). Innovative destination governance: The Swedish ski resort of Åre. *The International Journal of Entrepreneurship and Innovation*, *8*(1), 53–66.

Nyström, M., Folke, C., & Moberg, F. (2000). Coral reef disturbance and resilience in a human-dominated environment. *Trends in Ecology & Evolution*, *15*(10), 413–417.

Orchiston, C., Prayag, G., & Brown, C. (2016). Organizational resilience in the tourism sector. *Annals of Tourism Research*, *56*, 145–148.

O'Reilly, A.M. (1986). Tourism carrying capacity: Concept and issues. *Tourism Management*, *7*(4), 254–258.

Pechlaner, H., Beritelli, P., & Volgger, M. (2015). Introduction: Emerging landscape of destination governance. In H. Pechlaner, P. Beritelli, S. Pichler, M. Pichler & N. Scott (Eds.), *Contemporary destination governance: A case study approach* (pp. vii–xvi). UK: Emerald Group Publishing Limited.

Pechlaner, H., Kozak, M., & Volgger, M. (2014). Destination leadership: A new paradigm for tourist destinations? *Tourism Review*, *69*(1), 1–9.

Pendall, R., Foster, K.A., & Cowell, M. (2010). Resilience and regions: Building understanding of the metaphor. *Cambridge Journal of Regions, Economy and Society*, *3*(1), 71–84.

Raich, F. (2006). *Governance räumlicher Wettbewerbseinheiten: Ein Ansatz für die Tourismus-Destination*. Wiesbaden: Springer.

Rappold, E. (2016, July 20). Tourism boom in Spain. *Deutsche Welle*. Retrieved from www.dw.com/en/tourism-boom-in-spain/a-19408343 (Accessed on 22 September 2017).

Reed, M.G. (1997). Power relations and community-based tourism planning. *Annals of Tourism Research*, *24*(3), 566–591.

Reghezza-Zitt, M., Rufat, S., Djament-Tran, G., Le Blanc, A., & Lhomme, S. (2012). *What resilience is not: Uses and abuses*. Cybergeo: European Journal of Geography.

Renn, O., & Klinke, A. (2015). Risk governance and resilience: New approaches to cope with uncertainty and ambiguity. In O. Renn (Ed.), *Risk governance: Coping with uncertainty in a complex world* (pp. 19–41). London: Earthscan.

Ritchie, J.B., & Crouch, G.I. (2003). *The competitive destination: A sustainable tourism perspective*. Cambridge, MA: CABI.

Saarinen, J. (2006). Traditions of sustainability in tourism studies. *Annals of Tourism Research, 33*(4), 1121–1140.

Simmie, J., & Martin, R. (2010). The economic resilience of regions: Towards an evolutionary approach. *Cambridge Journal of Regions, Economy and Society, 3*(1), 27–43.

Smith, B.W., Dalen, J., Wiggins, K., Tooley, E., Christopher, P., & Bernard, J. (2008). The brief resilience scale: Assessing the ability to bounce back. *International Journal of Behavioral Medicine, 15*(3), 194–200.

Stockholm Resilience Center. (2017). *Applying resilience thinking: Seven principles for building resilience in social-ecological systems*. Retrieved from www.stockholmresilience.org/research/research-news/2015-02-19-applying-resilience-thinking.html (Accessed on 22 September 2017).

Strickland-Munro, J.K., Allison, H.E., & Moore, S.A. (2010). Using resilience concepts to investigate the impacts of protected area tourism on communities. *Annals of Tourism Research, 37*(2), 499–519.

Strunz, S. (2012). Is conceptual vagueness an asset? Arguments from philosophy of science applied to the concept of resilience. *Ecological Economics, 76*, 112–118.

Svensson, B., Nordin, S., & Flagestad, A. (2005). A governance perspective on destination development-exploring partnerships, clusters and innovation systems. *Tourism Review, 60*(2), 32–37.

Taubenböck, H., & Geiß, C. (2014). Vulnerability and resilience research: A critical perspective. *International Journal of Disaster Risk Science, 5*(1), 86–87.

Timur, S., & Getz, D. (2008). A network perspective on managing stakeholders for sustainable urban tourism. *International Journal of Contemporary Hospitality Management, 20*(4), 445–461.

Tyrrell, T.J., & Johnston, R.J. (2008). Tourism sustainability, resiliency and dynamics: Towards a more comprehensive perspective. *Tourism and Hospitality Research, 8*(1), 14–24.

UNWTO. (2016). *Tourism highlights* (2016 ed.). Madrid: World Tourism Organization. Retrieved from www.e-unwto.org/doi/pdf/10.18111/9789284418145 (Accessed on 22 September 2017).

Vogus, T.J., & Sutcliffe, K.M. (2007). *Organizational resilience: Towards a theory and research agenda*. ISIC. IEEE International Conference on Systems, Man and Cybernetics, pp. 3418–3422.

Walker, B., & Salt, D. (2012). *Resilience thinking: Sustaining ecosystems and people in a changing world*. Washington: Island Press.

Zehrer, A., Pechlaner, H., & Raich, F. (2007). Destination Alps and its communicated brand image. *Anatolia, 18*(2), 319–333.

Zelger, J. (1999). Wissensorganisation durch sprachliche Gestaltbildung im qualitativen Verfahren GABEK. In J. Zelger & M. Maier (Eds.), *GABEK: Verarbeitung und Darstellung von Wissen* (pp. 31–91). Innsbruck: StudienVerlag.

Zelger, J., & Oberprantacher, A. (2002). Processing of verbal data and knowledge representation by GABEK®-WinRelan®. *Forum Qualitative Sozialforschung, 3*(2).

5 Resilient tourism destinations? Governance implications of bringing theories of resilience and adaptive capacity to tourism practice

Stefan Hartman

1. Introduction

The tourism industry is a fast-evolving industry. Many places around the world are in the process of being developed as tourism destinations. This process is shaped by the actions of many firms, societal organizations and institutions that are dispersed over multiple governance levels and often have different ambitions, interests and worldviews regarding issues at stake (Milne & Ateljevic, 2001; Urry, 2002; Parra, 2010; Hartman & De Roo, 2013). For places to transition towards tourism, destination factors need to interlock and mutually reinforce each other in multiple systems or domains, such as the economy, culture, lifestyles, institutions, technology, ecology and belief systems (Loorbach, 2007).

As a socio-spatial phenomenon, tourism has been treated and managed in different ways. In general three dominant ways of thinking and acting can be identified. First, tourism is being treated as an intruder of space and/or in competition or incompatible with other functions and land uses such as forestry, agriculture, nature, build heritage and landscape quality. Second, tourism is seen as an economic opportunity and approached for instance in policies by means of quantitative goals in terms of number of visitors, number of jobs and boosting welfare. Whereas major cities such as Venice, Paris and Amsterdam are very successful in doing so and nowadays also face the issue of 'visitor pressure' or 'overtourism', other destination are, in contrast, struggling to be seen, found and selected by the visitors (compare to Butler, 1980, on Tourism Area Life Cycle and Doxey, 1975, on Irritation Index). Third, tourism is used as a means to achieve wider societal goals than economic only, following the ideas of sustainable development. For instance, as a means to maintain livability, as a source of income to pay for upkeep of heritage and nature, as part of integrated coastal zone management and many more applications.

Over time, rural and peri-urban landscapes that were once predominantly dominated by production (agriculture, forestry) have evolved and nowadays also face the challenge of conservation and increasingly move towards places of consumption. Also city centers are evolving nonlinearly from marketplaces via shopping centers to a décor for leisure activities such as events (Richards & Palmer, 2010). As many places undergo these transitions, the competition is increasing and visitors have a vast range of options to select from. This puts pressure on the tourism industry in various ways. First, to stand out from the competition and attract visitors, the emphasis shifts to offering experiences and value creation via meaning making and 'mattering' (creating e.g. 'memorable moments' – and resulting in 'blurring' of industry sectors). Second, due to the increasing competition and ensuing professionalization of the industry life cycles of concepts and activities are shortening, meaning renewal and innovation is of the essence. This can be approached on the level of individual businesses, on the level of destinations or regions but also on branch or industry level. Third, the industry needs to anticipate and adapt to perturbations that can range from sudden shocks (e.g. natural and environmental disasters, terrorism, macroeconomic shocks, new technologies) and 'slow burns' (e.g. demographic change, climate change, lifestyle changes) that bring industries and destinations out of balance (Lew, 2014). The act of continuously finding a new balance in response to and to anticipate (also continuously changing) contextual circumstances is a key challenge that should be further explored, via literature on resilience theories and theories of complex adaptive systems for instance, to go beyond reactive responses and develop proactive, anticipatory strategies instead.

Overall, the tourism challenge for destinations is to become robust enough to endure perturbations and flexible enough to recover or to re-develop/re-invent itself – contributing to its resilience. This implies a more evolutionary-adaptive perspective, considering and managing tourism destinations as complex adaptive systems. Taking this perspective allows us to identify conditions that contribute to the ability of systems to adapt and evolve and to building resilience. The governance and management issues and discussions that come with (building) resilient tourism destinations still remains under researched in tourism literature whereas it gains increasing attention in fields such as urban and regional planning and the management of ecosystems and protection of area with a special status (e.g. National Park, Geopark, UNESCO World Heritage Site). This chapter aims particularly to contribute to an enhanced understanding the governance implications that are related to bringing resilience theories to tourism practice – making use of results and lessons learned of research projects conducted by the author in the Netherlands. For this chapter results and insights are used from various studies in regions such as the Wadden Sea area, UNESCO Global Geopark *De Hondsrug*, various National Parks and studies on industry clusters such as the traditional sailing industry.

The remainder of this chapter consists of three sections. In the first section, theories on resilience are explored. After introducing the concept of resilience, it is explained how resilience can enhance tourism (studies). Then key conditions are highlighted that can be derived from literature that are seen as important for building resilience. In the second section, implications of bringing resilience theories to practice are discussed. A set of conditions is distinguished and elaborated on that is needed for resilient tourism destinations and/or building resilience. Each condition comes with implications for governance, management and strategic planning. Implications that often equal practical limitations – here a link is made to various type of 'traps' that are discussed in resilience literature. In the third section, conclusions are drawn and a discussion is provided on how to proceed, drawing attention to and raising awareness about the magnitude of the ambition of building resilient tourism destinations and the importance of building resilience step by step over time.

2. How to engage in building resilience

Why are resilience theories relevant to tourism studies? Elsewhere in Hartman (2016a) the author has explained how tourism areas can be viewed as complex systems with a potential to be adaptive. The point here is that tourism areas are, similar to complex adaptive systems, always in a process of responding to and anticipating both endogenous as well as exogenous shocks and stresses that influence their development and the development of agents or actors within these systems. Many of these factors are drivers of change that occur autonomously from the perspective of tourism destinations. In other words, influencing in the sense of command and control is rather impossible, whereas adapting to consequences has become a crucial capacity.

Resilience is generally understood as *the capacity of a system to absorb disturbance and reorganize while undergoing change so as to still retain essentially the same function, structure, identity, and feedbacks* (Walker, Holling, Carpenter, & Kinzig, 2004). Next to general understanding of resilience, different types of resilience are distinguished in literature. Engineering resilience describes the capacity to bounce back after perturbation to a modal state. This presumes there is a single or origin state to which systems return. Ecological resilience includes multiple system states between which systems can fluctuate whereby resilience concerns 'the magnitude of the disturbance that can be absorbed before the system changes its structure' (Holling, 1996, p. 33). In evolutionary resilience (Davoudi, 2012), system states are endless and systems are conceptualized as always in a particular restless state of becoming; through adaptation, as they co-evolve continuously due to interactions with other systems. The latter seems to best fit the context of socio-economic and spatial development as it is in general very hard to return to a particular state or situation of the past. Hence, for this chapter the perspective is adopted that places are always dynamic to a certain extent, always in a state of becoming (cf. De Roo & Boelens, 2015).

When discussing resilience, it is important to be explicit about the '*resilience of what*' and '*resilience to what*' (Sellberg, Wilkinson, & Peterson, 2015). The *resilience of what* in this chapter concerns tourism destinations. Destination are generally rather complex entities that consist of many interrelated products, sectors and institutions and their mutual interactions (Ma & Hassink, 2013). More specifically, in the words of Brouder and Eriksson (2013, p. 373) tourism destinations can be regarded as a '*bundle of many sources of evolutionary change' that is driven by 'multiple levels of agent interaction in the form of labour, firms, networks, technologies and institutions*'. The resilience of a tourism destination then depends on many different parts that together influence and determine the extent to which the capacity to adapt is suitable and sufficient to manage changing circumstances. For tourism destinations *resilience to what* involves a broad range of slow variable and fast variables (Lew, 2014). Slow variables that destinations need to anticipate include amongst others climate change, developments in the (macro)economy and demography and increasing flows of tourists. Fast variables include for instance changing weather conditions, natural disasters, geopolitical events, terrorism, changes in consumer preferences and new technologies.

Furthermore, the challenge is to better understand how to build resilience. What are conditions that enable tourism destination to adaptively respond and anticipate driving forces of change that continuously alter circumstances? A key aspect of resilience is the process of fostering a degree of diversity that enables systems to be both robust as well as flexible *at the same time* (Hartman, 2016a). A degree of diversity means that areas do not collapse when particular products, businesses or organizations are replaced or disappear for instance due to bankruptcy. On the scale of a destination, it becomes possible to manage changes in the economy, in demand, in competitiveness, etc. Alternatively, fostering a degree of diversity involves experimentation and room for innovations and provides a range of alternatives that make shifting development paths possible. As also discussed in Hartman (2016a), too much diversity or overstimulating diversity, on the one hand, and too little diversity, on the other, could be counterproductive and requires governing diversity. When aiming to govern diversity, which factors should be taken into account?

A review of literature on enhancing adaptivity and building resilience draws attention to various conditions and principles (compare Biggs, Schlüter, & Schoon, 2015; Djalante, Holley, & Thomalla, 2011; Folke, 2016; Hartman, 2016b). These findings are brought together in the set of key conditions introduced below. These conditions are discussed and further operationalized, and attention is drawn to implications that emerge when aiming to bring these conditions to practice.

- *Condition 1 – variety & redundancy.*

  As already discussed in the context of diversity, variety and redundancy are important to cope with shocks and disturbances. In the socio-economic and spatial context of tourism diversity/variety is not a given and requires to be actively supported and promoted by (assemblages of) entrepreneurs, governments and (branch) organizations to result in new initiatives, innovations and experiments. These are important ingredients for novelty (development of new niches in tourism, leisure, recreation and/or crossover with other sectors) and enable processes of self-organization (growth of niches, emergence of industry subsectors, emergence of structures and organizations). Moreover, blindly supporting initiatives for the sake of diversity could at the same time be counterproductive for instance when important spatial qualities and local identities are negatively affected. Implications for governments and tourism planners are multiple. These include to ensure there is a 'possibility space' in institutional and policy frameworks that is restrictive on the one hand to prevent negative impacts and enabling on the other to foster experiments and new initiatives that enhance diversity. Shaping possibility space is increasingly done in co-makership with entrepreneurs and industry organizations, in order to raise awareness and promote support and effective implementations. For entrepreneurs, an implication is to make use of this possibility space (agency, entrepreneurship). In practice it asks entrepreneurs to understand, accept and incorporate the institutional and policy frameworks that are created to guide their initiatives and investment choices. In the Netherlands, the large amount of (sectoral) rules and regulations makes such an understanding difficult and time consuming. Entrepreneurs are expected to understand the 'policy language'. There are various examples of intermediary and often semi-governmental agencies that have the task to ensure that this possibility space is taken (supportive organization that create bridges and bonds between actors). Such agencies serve as intermediaries and can be involved in early phases of planning and decision-making to steer and shape the initiatives of entrepreneurs so that they fit policy frameworks on the one hand, and ensure an effective process that eases the realization of ideas of the entrepreneur on the other hand.

- *Condition 2 – connectivity*

Quite too often actors within and between tourism destinations are not well connected due to absent interaction (moments) and the ensuing lagging behind of coalition building. Managing connectivity requires actors to devote some or even a substantial amount of their precious resources (time, money, capacity) to networking, meetings, building platforms which do not necessarily result directly in concrete results on the short term. Through connectivity and interaction actors enables themselves to share mutual or opposing perspectives, identify potentially shared urgencies, build trust and come to the conclusion that there is added value in building coalitions and to take collective action. Hence, this could be in the interest of local governmental agencies and industry associations and create an argument to invest in such crucial networking moments and coalition building. Connectivity is an important condition as destination development is a multi-actor, multi-domain and multi-scale undertaking. This presumes to involve many stakeholders and operate as inclusive as possible. Inclusiveness and broadening participation implies an enhanced possibility that support, motivation and commitment is sustained for ideas for a longer period of time. In this context leadership and the ability to tell credible and salient stories about trends and development, emergent (shared) urgencies, future visions and concrete actions is required. Such forms of *storytelling* and the ensuing dialogs between stakeholders stimulate the identification of (autonomous) development directions at the scale of the destination (Hartman, 2016b).

- *Condition 3 – promote polycentric governance systems.*

The complexity and dynamisms of today's society imply that no single actor is or should be in control. When responsibilities, resources and decision-making power are centered around one party, it can be very productive for destination development in the short term. At the same time, in the long run, this puts systems potentially at risk of rigidity and could result over time in a lock-in situation when such a party is for instance not open to change, does not promote experimentation or emphasizes one development trajectory that manifested itself in the past e.g. to protect sunk costs, vested interests, please the electorate, etc. Whereas monocentric governance systems are promoted to pursue effectiveness and efficiency, it might negatively influence diversity (see condition 1) as well as the capacity to adapt to changing (contextual) circumstances (see section on traps below). Alternatively, polycentric governance systems have the capacity to link multiple scales of government, spatial scales and (policy) domains, enabling the possibility to identify trends and development (also see condition 4) and evaluating how their implications can be address best at which scale and by which actors (private, public, societal organization, or coalition or consortium). Moreover, polycentrism implies there is a self-steering/self-correcting capacity that manifests itself through the process of negotiations and consensus building as multiple parties often in need of support from others or need to bring together resources to achieve individual as well as collective goals. An implication is that an extensive multi-sector, multi-actor and multi-level system of governance is needed (Hartman, Parra, & De Roo, 2016). This needs to be supported and actively pursued as investing in interaction and forging (new) connections can easily lose priority. Polycentric governance systems run the danger of becoming perceived as bureaucratic constructs, especially when actors get the feeling that the focus is put too much on the process instead of the content. Again, the factor of leadership and storytelling ability is important to guarantee an action-oriented approach that is salient to the actors involved.

- *Condition 4 – environmental sensitivity*

Forces that drive the change and development of tourism destinations frequently come from the "outside" contextual environment. They could be very diverse. Examples are climatic change, natural disasters, technological innovations, economic fluctuations and changes in society related to demography, travel behavior, tolerance, terrorism and many more. In general these factors can be categorized as fast variables ('shocks') and slow variables ('stresses') – compare to Lew (2014). Identifying, monitoring and analyzing the impacts of these factors is step one. Doing so requires, again, a multilevel system of actors. At the international, global scale, there are originations such as the UNTWO that gather information about trends and development, and many countries have installed statistical bureaus and research institutions to do the same for their territories. Also more regional and local level data is gathered. This is essentially a part of the earlier-mentioned multilevel system of governance that is needed for resilient destinations. Strategically important is the ability to collect key information about the diversity of forces driving change, to analyze findings and to filter the information so that it becomes supportive steering information in processes of decision-making.

For instance information is needed on the effect of trends and developments such as tourism flows, expenditures and behavior on diversity (e.g. via bankruptcies, emerging initiatives). Hence, step two is developing strategies to respond to and, better yet, anticipate to changes in order avoid and reduce negative impacts and seize opportunities that stem from positive outcomes. Approaches that are applied in practice relate to strategic foresight such as scenario-planning, transition management and adaptive planning (see also Hartman, 2016a). These approaches allow for a more emergent, evolutionary way of destination development as they share that they embrace uncertainty, promote experimentation and focus on multiple possible futures instead of the traditional, blueprint-style masterplans that are guided by a single perspective on the future and present an end-state, fixed vision on how a destination should be developed.

- *Condition 5 – learning & reflexivity*

As destinations are constantly affected by pressures from the outside that drive change and create urgencies to act, this implies that destinations are ways in the process of developing – adapting to threats and opportunities and in doing so co-evolving to other systems. Such a system is in a permanent state of becoming (De Roo & Boelens, 2015). Hence, the capacity to reflect and learn from feedback is important to timely adapt to changing (contextual) circumstances. Monitoring variables such as industry diversity, growth and decline, influences and impacts between systems, match between supply and demand, adequacy of possibility space as amongst the ways to gather information to learn from and to take action on. Here, learning is a major contributor to reflexivity, which concerns the ability to *"reflect on and confront not only the self-induced problems (. . .) but also the approaches, structures and systems that reproduce them"* (Hendriks & Grin, 2007, p. 335). Reflexivity is very much about a (company or organizational) culture of learning and requires that there are failures and successes to learn from – another argument for promoting diversity, and an argument to explore safe-to-fail strategies next to fail-safe (Ahern, 2011).

- *Condition 6: incorporate thinking in adaptive systems*

The conditions outlined above require adopting an *adaptive perspective* on how tourism destinations develop, evolve and can become resilient systems. This requires amongst others to accept that tourism destinations are seen and addressed as somewhat coherent systems that have the potential to be adaptive. Systems that are, moreover, nested systems as destination development is (often strongly and autonomously) influenced by dynamics in other systems such as discussed under condition 4. In this context, it is important to be aware that tourism development impacts on local societies (people), local economy (profit) and local environment (planet) which, consequently, drives the need to create synergies. Then, tourism development meets other interests and could/should be approached as a means and not as a goal on its own. Hence, an implication it that tourism professionals are to a certain extent conceptual thinkers. Moreover, a key implication is that adopting an adaptive perspective requires to embrace and "choose" for complexity. This complexity can in practice be the unfavorable option and runs the danger of being ignored due to the resources needed or particular strong (political or individual) preferences, interest or ambitions.

3. From theory to practice

In practice it seems to be hardly possible to meet all the conditions outlined above and take care of all the implications foremost due to the high amount of resources involved. Whereas major tourism destinations such as capital cities are able to cover many conditions, the more rural and remote destinations tend to struggle to mobilize resources. Nevertheless, tourism destinations always have the tendency and therefore capacity to adapt, albeit in a reactive and responsive manner (recovering from collapse, via muddling through or trial-and-error) instead of proactive and strategically adaptive manner. In this context, fundamental discussions about conditions run the danger of being avoided, neglected or even forgotten. Discussions that revolve around solving acute day-to-day issues and responses could be ad hoc being taken without a perspective or long-term vision from which choices are made.

Alternatively stated, a differentiation between so-called traps can be made to understand the issues that relate to conditions not being met in practice (Allison & Hobbs, 2004; Gunderson, Holling, & Allen, 2010). When systems are trapped, they face difficulties to escape a development trajectory. The figure outlines four traps. The rigidity trap is a situation wherein a system has become rigid and inflexible even though actors are highly connected and there is much capital. The point is that the attention and resources are geared towards one particular development trajectory which is (over)emphasized at the expense of others, as such making it quite resilient. However, a destination can be successful for a while but can face immense difficulties to redirect its chosen development trajectories for instance when demand plunges due to exogenous forces. This could apply to destinations that focus only on one type of (niche) tourism. A lock-in trap applies to a similar situation, although in this case there is no capital or potential to escape the situation. Hartman and de Roo (2013) show how lock-in traps can strongly relate to choices and decisions made in the past that shape and limit opportunities for tourism development now and in the future. A poverty trap describes the situation where there is a lack of many factors that could contribute to the condition outlined above such as resources, ideas, initiatives, leadership, etc. Help from outside of the destination might be the solution needed to be able to build conditions for resilience as these sources are not present or mobilized from within the system. An isolation trap is a situation wherein capital and potential are available but they are not mobilized in an effective manner from the perspective of destination resilience. This could be the case when initiatives are being developed as stand-alone projects, in isolation, whereby the wider destination and its actors do not benefit in any way.

Table 5.1 System traps

	Capital/Potential	Connectivity	Resilience
Rigidity trap	High	High	High
Poverty trap	Low	Low	Low
Lock-in Trap	Low	High	High
Isolation trap	High	Low	Low

Source: Gunderson et al. (2010, p. 436)

When bringing theories of resilience and adaptive capacity to practice, these traps are valuable for multiple reasons. First, as meeting conditions that are outlined above is rather difficult, it is likely that destinations are facing one (or more?) of the traps to a greater or lesser extent. There could be a (rather big) gap between the conditions that are proposed in the literature and what destinations are able to achieve given the actors, resources and capital that they have available. Then, it is quite likely that destinations can be positioned somewhere relative to the traps, and which that understanding and from that position onwards develop strategies to enhance conditions for adaptivity. This shows a second application of identifying traps. The traps provide a framework for destinations that can be used to reflexively learn from the situation wherein they find themselves or to identify situations towards they are heading. It could help destinations to better understand their situation and develop strategies accordingly.

To conclude, the resilience perspective provides an interesting and promising perspective to further enhance destination development and management. Whereas it is a challenging perspective to bring to practice, the advantages in the long run can make a difference between the destinations that are resilient to the ongoing dynamisms of society and those that are not. Whereas the topic of resilient tourism regions is gaining attention, it is still relatively young and therefore underdeveloped. More research is needed on the (closely related) themes of building resilience and adaptive capacity building, particularly under sub-optimal conditions for the (practical) reasons discussed above, to understand the resourcefulness of actors in the tourism industry (and those related and/or closely affiliated) in their quest to build more resilient tourism regions and learn from their successes and failures – to reflexively learn and adapt tourism literature to further our understanding.

References

Ahern, J. (2011). From fail-safe to safe-to-fail: Sustainability and resilience in the new urban world. *Landscape and Urban Planning, 100*(4), 341–343.

Allison, H.E., & Hobbs, R.J. (2004). Resilience, adaptive capacity, and the "Lock-in Trap" of the Western Australian agricultural region. *Ecology and Society, 9*(1), 3. Retrieved from www.ecologyandsociety.org/vol9/iss1/art3 (Accessed on 22 September 2017).

Biggs, R., Schlüter, M., & Schoon, M. (2015). *Principles for building resilience: Sustaining ecosystem services in social-ecological systems.* Cambridge: Cambridge University Press.

Brouder, P., & Eriksson, R. (2013). Tourism evolution: On the synergies of tourism studies and evolutionary economic geography. *Annals of Tourism Research, 43,* 370–389.

Butler, R.W. (1980). The concept of a tourist area cycle of evolution: Implications for management of resources. *Canadian Geographer, 24*(1), 5–12.

Davoudi, S. (2012). Resilience: "A bridging concept or a dead end?". *Planning Theory and Practice, 13*(2), 299–307.

De Roo, G., & Boelens, L. (Eds.). (2015). *Spatial planning in a complex unpredictable world of change: Towards a proactive co-evolutionary type of planning within the Eurodelta.* Groningen: InPlanning.

Djalante, R., Holley, C., & Thomalla, F. (2011). Adaptive governance and managing resilience to natural hazards. *International Journal of Disaster Risk Science, 2*(1). doi:10.1007/s13753-011-0015-6

Doxey, G.V. (1975, September). *A causation theory of visitor-resident irritants: Methodology and research inferences.* Travel and Tourism Research Associations Sixth Annual Conference Proceedings, San Diego, pp. 195–198.

Folke, C. (2016). Resilience (Republished). *Ecology and Society, 21*(4), 44. Retrieved from https://doi.org/10.5751/ES-09088-210444 (Accessed on 22 September 2017).

Gunderson, L., Holling, C.S., & Allen, C.R. (2010). The evolution of an idea – The past, present, and future of ecological resilience. In L. Gunderson, C.R. Allen & C.S. Holling (Eds.), *Foundations of ecological resilience* (pp. 423–444). New York: Island Press.

Hartman, S. (2016a). Towards adaptive tourism areas? A complexity perspective to examine the conditions for adaptive capacity. *Journal of Sustainable Tourism, 24*(2), 299–314. Retrieved from http://dx.doi.org/10.1080/09669582.2015.1062017 (Accessed on 22 September 2017).

Hartman, S. (2016b). *Leisure landscapes: On emergence, transitions and adaptation.* PhD Thesis, InPlanning, Groningen. Retrieved from http://dx.medra.org/10.17418/PHD.2015.9789036784238 (Accessed on 22 September 2017).

Hartman, S., & De Roo, G. (2013). Towards managing non-linear regional development trajectories. *Environment & Planning C: Government and Policy, 31*(3), 556–570. Retrieved from http://dx.doi.org/10.1068/c11203r (Accessed on 22 September 2017).

Hartman, S., Parra, C., & De Roo, G. (2016). Stimulating spatial quality? Unpacking the approach of the province of Friesland, the Netherlands. *European Planning Studies, 24*(2), 297–315. Retrieved from http://dx.doi.org/10.1080/09654313.2015.1080229 (Accessed on 22 September 2017).

Hendriks, C.M., & Grin, J. (2007). Contextualizing reflexive governance: the politics of Dutch transitions to sustainability. *Journal of Environmental Policy and Planning, 9,* 333–350.

Holling, C.S. (1996). Engineering resilience versus ecological resilience. In P.C. Schulze (Eds.), *Engineering within ecological constraints.* Washington DC: National Academy Press.

Lew, A. (2014). Scale, change and resilience in community tourism planning. *Tourism Geographies, 16*(1), 14–22. doi:10.1080/14616688.2013.864325

Loorbach, D. (2007). *Transition management: New mode of governance for sustainable development.* Zeist: AD Druk.

Ma, M., & Hassink, R. (2013). An evolutionary perspective on tourism area development. *Annals of Tourism Research, 41,* 89–109.

Milne, S., & Ateljevic, I. (2001). Tourism, economic development and the global – Local nexus: Theory embracing complexity. *Tourism Geographies, 3*(4), 369–393.

Parra, C. (2010). Sustainability and multi-level governance of territories classified as protected areas: The Morvan regional park case. *Journal of Environmental Planning and Management, 53*(4), 491–509.

Richards, G., & Palmer, R. (2010). *Eventful cities- Cultural management and urban revitalization.* St. Louis: Butterworth-Heinemann.

Sellberg, M.M., Wilkinson, C., & Peterson, G.D. (2015). Resilience assessment: A useful approach to navigate urban sustainability challenges. *Ecology and Society, 20*(1), 43. Retrieved from http://dx.doi.org/10.5751/ES-07258-200143 (Accessed on 22 September 2017).

Urry, J. (2002). *The tourist gaze.* London: Sage.

Walker, B., Holling, C.S., Carpenter, S.R., & Kinzig, A. (2004). Resilience, adaptability and transformability in social-ecological systems. *Ecology and Society, 9*(2), 5. Retrieved from www.ecologyandsociety.org/vol9/iss2/art5 (Accessed on 22 September 2017).

6 Cooperative approaches between health- and agro-tourism stakeholders in increasing rural destination resilience in Belarus

Siarhei Danskikh & Anastasia Traskevich

1. Introduction

The tourism industry in Belarus was developed in the Soviet Union period as a part of a system that preserved the social and ideological policy of the state. This implied a dominance of non-commercial social tourism enterprises in Belarus. After the fall of the socialist system, the main consequence was to cut all government subsidies for social tourism in the country, as well as for the tourism sector as the whole. As a result, a new wave of active commercial tourism has taken place in the last two decades in Belarus. This was mostly achieved by targeting the vast, traditional and relatively undemanding Russian outbound tourism market. At the same time, the domestic tourist demand, which developed for a long time under the conception of social tourism and was guaranteed by the government, has been neglected due to the lower tourism consumption capacity of the Belarusians.

Still, the basic system of tourism destinations and stakeholders in Belarus was established under the Soviet-era conception of social tourism, which has resulted in the following current specifics of the national tourism sector:

- a vast network of rural tourism destinations created within social demands, without consideration of the economic factors and resources for destination development;
- the operating of just one or several big state-owned stakeholders within rural destinations;
- an immense impact of these stakeholders in creating tourism receipts in the destination (55 to 65 percent of the total amount of tourism expenditures in Belarus are created by sanatoria);
- all the necessary infrastructure for the normal functioning of such stakeholders has been broadly ensured by the state institutions;
- the stakeholders do not have enough experience and often have low motivation to operate within the commercial tourism paradigm and within the tourism market.

The new trend in the development of rural tourism destinations is now emerging as the fastest-growing segment of small private (family-owned) stakeholders – rural farmsteads – and operates under the concepts of agro- and eco-tourism. This new shift in the tourism sector in Belarus was vastly promoted by the government as a part of a national policy that aimed to recover rural territories of the country. In 2006, there were only 34 farmsteads in Belarus. In 2016, their number reached 2,279, which marks an increase of 67 times in the last ten years. The number of tourists in sanatoria and similar recreational establishments in 2016 were 508,519 people, while the farmsteads in Belarus attracted 294,200 people.

Detailed analysis of the statistics and dynamics of the sanatorium segment of the tourism industry in Belarus has now been undertaken within a competitiveness assessment framework, that was targeted to analyse the aggregated measures for the meso-level of a branch of the tourism industry in a particular destination (Traskevich, 2015). The issues of farmsteads operating and the current trends of agro-tourism in Belarus were analysed within the context of the sustainable regional development of rural territories and the impact of agro-tourism in preserving the local cultural heritage and native way of life (Danskikh & Vitun, 2016).

In this case study the following dimensions and aspects of destination resilience are considered:

- a strong orientation on local resources, and assets in the destination;
- the functional and infrastructural autonomy of the destination, in terms of creating and marketing different sustainable tourism products, which are able to generate a range of touristic experiences;
- the independence in expanding tourism policy and targeting different markets;
- the character and influence of global connections in tourism development in the destination;
- the level of cooperation between tourism stakeholders within the destination, while creating a tourism value chain;
- the sociocultural resilience, which marks the ability of the destination to draw upon local knowledge, traditions and competencies in delivering USP tourism products.

2. Geographical network of rural sanatorium-centre destinations

As a result of a combination of historical and modern trends, the current geographical network of rural destinations in Belarus can be described as *sanatorium-centre destinations*. Referring to such a type of destinations – which is quite unique to Belarus – means that every sanatorium in the country creates an independent tourism destination, which can be classified as a *kurort*-type destination (since the main stakeholder operates under the paradigm of 'health and wellness' tourism, which was historically initiated in Belarus within the German *kurort* tradition). These sanatoria are now surrounded by agro-tourism farmsteads. There are 105 sanatoria and similar 'health and wellness' tourism enterprises in Belarus (that is, five enterprises per 10,000 km2 of the territory of Belarus). The average capacity of a sanatorium is 269 beds, with the leaders in this field reaching more than 600 beds: "Serebrjanye Kluchi" (966 beds), "Pridneprovskij" (859 beds), "Letsy" (697 beds), "Radon" (620 beds) (Traskevich, 2015).

Eighty percent of the sanatoria are situated in strongly rural territories, i.e. in the middle of the forest, 20 to 30 km away from cities. At the same time, one of the two biggest kurorts in Belarus – Zhdanovichi – with 11 big sanatoria in operation is already merging with the agglomeration Minsk.

The sanatoria in Belarus all belong to the forest landscapes. The 'health and wellness' tourism enterprises are actually situated in the types of forest in Belarus, which possess proven healing properties (i.e. by possessing phytoncide qualities of pine, birch, and oak forests). Ninety-eight percent of the sanatoria neighbour a river or lake. Fifty-four percent of the sanatoria have a mineral water deposit on the premises: chloride-sulphate (sodium, calcium, magnesium) waters prevail. Nevertheless, there is a lack of current geological exploration – the finding of new mineral springs is considered very probable (Pirozhnik & Yasoveev, 2005). Some of the sanatoria possess the deposits of waters with special properties, particularly radon waters, which have been exploited by sanatoria "Radon" and "Alfa-Radon". Many kurort territories of Belarus are rich in healing muds (sapropelic and turfen). However, many sanatoria still do not make full use of the local muds in their vicinity, since only 30 percent of the sanatoria currently use local muds. The benefits of these natural resources could be put to much more efficient use.

Most sanatoria in Belarus still belong to big state-owned enterprises and government institutions. The institutions to which the biggest number of sanatoria belong are the following:

- Federation of trade-unions of Belarus: 12 sanatoria (overall capacity of 4,933 beds);
- The administration of the President of the Republic of Belarus: four sanatoria (1,047 beds);
- Concern "Belneftehim" (oil production): 11 sanatoria and similar facilities (2,478 beds);
- The Ministry of Industry: 13 sanatoria and similar facilities (2,200 beds);
- The Ministry of Transport and Communication: 10 sanatoria and similar facilities (1,564 beds);
- The Ministry of Labour and Social Protection: four sanatoria (667 beds)

(Bolbatovskij & Polujanova, 2017)

These institutions are some of the most powerful in Belarus in terms of their access to natural, financial and human resources. This means that the destinations which these institutions are interested in can receive these resources, regardless of the commercial success of sanatoria and similar facilities, to create these destinations.

Sanatoria are surrounded on average by four or five agro-tourism farmsteads. The leader of the number of farmsteads operating in the vicinity of sanatoria is the kurort Naroch, which has eight sanatoria with a simultaneous capacity of 2,445 beds and 65 farmsteads (with the capacity from four or five up to 60 beds).

While the recreational network of sanatoria was determined by voluntary decisions of the state-owned stakeholders, the geographical network of farmsteads in Belarus reveals first of all the motivation of tourism-oriented entrepreneurship on the part of the local communities. People in the north of Belarus (Vitebsk region) rely more on agro-tourism, since agriculture-related rural activities are less productive there due to climatic conditions. Therefore, the Vitebsk region can boast the greatest number of farmsteads (480). At the same time, the function of exchangeability between sanatoria and farmsteads in rural destinations can be detected: the Mogilev region, which falls substantially behind the other regions in terms of its sanatoria network development (only eight enterprises are in operation there), receives a comparatively substantial number of tourists in farmsteads (there were 32,000 in 2016). Moreover, the geography of tourist flows in farmsteads also reveals the historical initiative of entrepreneurs from the local communities in the west of Belarus: the Grodno and Brest regions, which make up 25.7 percent of the population in Belarus, attract 33.5 percent of the total amount of the agro-tourist flows in the country.

It can be concluded that the suitable geographical conditions of the rural sanatorium-centre destinations in Belarus present favourable factors for destination resilience. These factors are: (i) the natural resources for diversified and complex healing treatments available at the direct disposal of the local stakeholders; and (ii) the current geographical model of the destination, which functions with a big and powerful stakeholder surrounded by small family-run highly adaptive and mobile businesses all together, and which operates remotely from the urban and global tourism structures.

3. Resilient value chain creating

The sanatoria and similar facilities are only governed by the enterprises and institutions they belong to. Therefore they are not very dependent on the frequent shifts in tourism policy created by the Ministry of Sport and Tourism. However, the operation of sanatoria in Belarus is still determined by rather strict and complicated regulations of the Ministry of Medicine, which is responsible for the license issues, the categorization of facilities, all the treatment procedures and their security. This leads to the fact that while the infrastructure and facilities of city tourism in Belarus is becoming quite an attractive object for international investment, the national sanatorium/'health and wellness' segment is of no real interest for international investors and global spa chains. There are currently only two sanatoria belonging to an international investor: "Alfa-Radon" (Russian owner) and "Nadezhda-XXI Century" (German investor). It can be concluded that a value chain for sanatorium (health and wellness) tourism products is currently not dependent in Belarus, either on any global production linkages or indeed under the current system of government policy in national tourism.

The owners once chose rural territories for the development of 'health and wellness' tourism (which, however, was then targeted only for their internal staff needs) and had at that time the capacity to ensure the continued development of the entire necessary infrastructure. This means that, unlike the typical practice of kurort as it functions worldwide, sanatoria do not share any common kurort infrastructure in Belarus; rather they enjoy the enclosed infrastructure of their own. The typical functional system of a sanatorium includes the following infrastructural components:

- *Accommodation facilities*, which currently provide an acceptable level of comfort (though with no real spa atmosphere) and which are often equipped for the needs of disabled people.
- *Catering facilities*, the competitive advantage of which is a strong emphasis on healthy nutrition and diet-therapy with a variety of diets developed for the special needs of people with nutrition-related diseases. Besides the normal staff (e.g. chefs, cooks, waiters), the facilities always operate under the control and support of a dietologist.
- *Spa and medical treatment infrastructure and medical staff*, who comprise the strongest competitive advantage for the sanatoria in Belarus. Sanatoria are well-equipped for the most science-dense treatments and wellness-assessments, e.g. magnetotherapy (93% of the sanatoria in Belarus), lasertherapy (87%), darsonvalis (85%), dry carbonic acid gas bath (68%), galvanisation (62%), electromud cure (61%), electrosleep (48%), FIR-sauna (38%), criosauna (23%), aeroionitherapy (14%); ultrasound and functional diagnostics (46%), laboratory diagnostics (12%), electrocardiography (64%), electropuncture diagnostics (5%), iridodiagnostics (1%), etc. Six hundred and thirteen doctors work in sanatoria in Belarus (equivalent to 5% of the staff) – this is on average six doctors per enterprise. Some leaders in this indicator ("Radon", "Serebrjanye Kluchi", and "Lepelski") have 10–11 doctors in their staff. Three hundred and thirty-three doctors of sanatoria are physiotherapists, and 223 are specialists within a particular sphere: e.g. stomatologists (11% of the doctors working in sanatoria, who are available at 74% of the sanatoria in Belarus), pediatricians (9% of the doctors, available at 55% of the sanatoria), gynaecologists (5%, and 31%), psychologists (5%, and 28%), urologists (2%, and 10%) and cardiologists (2%, and 10%). The number of middle staff therapists delivering the treatments in sanatoria in Belarus is 2,205 people, or 18.2% of the staff. This is on average 200 people per enterprise.

(Traskevich, 2015)

- *Basic infrastructure ensuring autonomous functioning*, which includes an autonomous power-supply, fresh water and sanitation facilities, canalization, disposal of wastes, sewage and telephone and internet connection.
- *Supporting tourism infrastructure*, which was considered of particular importance during the SU era and was used for delivering an ideological function of sanatorium tourism in the country. This type of infrastructure in Belarus includes dancing halls (at 100% of the sanatoria) cinema-halls (72%),

libraries (97%), tourist equipment renting facilities (85%) and conference-halls (28%).

- *Mineral waters and muds on the premises*: the sanatoria which have mineral water deposits on the premises (58% of the enterprises) actively and autonomously use this natural asset in creating the signature 'health and wellness' tourism products of the destination: balneoproducts (various treatment baths, mineral pools), drinking of mineral waters from specially equipped and new and beautifully designed well-rooms (50% of the enterprises), production of bottled drinking mineral waters ("Borovaya", "Naroch", "Letcy", etc.). The resources of local sapropelic and turfen muds still remain hardly used in creating sanatorium tourism products (with the exception of sanatorium "Radon", which actively exploits the muds of the neighbouring Lake Dzikoe and even produces the substantial quantity of packaging for sale to other sanatoria of the country). However, these natural assets present great potential in terms of 'health and wellness' product-development, both for peloidtherapy practices and aesthetic treatments. There is a potential to produce and retail local spa and beauty products based on the available natural resources of mineral waters and muds.

- *Territory available for gardening and healing herbs production*: this belongs to the rural type of destination, in that all the sanatoria have some territory on the premises available for gardening and growing of the healing herbs to be immediately used in their phytotreatments.

- *Transport*: the roads available at the destination were often built together and exactly for the needs of the local sanatorium. Moreover, sanatoria have a fleet of vehicles of their own, including tourist buses, minibuses, trailers and autos.

- *Apartments for the staff*, which are offered to those members of staff who would prefer to live permanently at the kurort.

From this brief description, it can be concluded that sanatoria in Belarus are able to create their value chain autonomously without being overly dependent on other national and indeed global connections. However, those functioning components were mostly introduced and developed at the time when social tourism prevailed in sanatoria. As a result, they are not modern, adaptive and mobile enough to match up to the current dynamic trends of the tourism market. To remedy this matter, a strong cooperative approach between sanatoria and farmsteads is needed to increase the resilience and competitiveness of this type of rural destination in Belarus.

In terms of creating a more resilient tourism value chain, farmsteads actually already demonstrate more flexibility than sanatoria. Unlike sanatorium products, with their strong emphasis on medically proven curing of particular diseases, tourism products of farmsteads target directly the current negative shifts in modern urban lifestyle (e.g. the complete disconnection from nature, artificial food, emotional and intellectual overload and low physical activity, etc.). Farmsteads provide a more profound and active rural and natural escape for city dwellers and stressed intellectuals. Furthermore, farmsteads also invite their tourists for a historical and holistic journey back to historical and cultural roots. And while creating these kinds of tourism products, farmsteads draw upon the core and traditional local resources and assets. A few of the diverse examples of their tourist offers include:

- beekeeping with a strong educational emphasis on the ancient national traditions of apiculture, as well as a chance to explain and experience the various healing effects of honey and the basics of apitherapy;
- fishing and cooking traditional dishes from the hunted fish, often on an open fire;
- authentic handicrafts, e.g. pottery, "vycinanka" (Slavic papercutting), "Belarussian salomka" (straw-weaving), blacksmith craft, double weaving, etc.) involving learning experiences for the guests at the workshops;
- production of healing plants, in which guests are explained the cultural meaning and healing properties of the plants, learn sustainable agriculture techniques of their growing and the ancient practice of harvesting and preparation of herbs. Guests also experience the authentic herbal tea culture of the Slavs and grasp the basics of Slavic phytotherapy traditions;
- indigenous healthy cuisine: tasting local gastronomic delights, understanding the advantages of the pure and nature-based nutrition, learning cooking techniques (e.g. Russian oven) and traditional recipes;
- authentic "*edu*tainment" based on the folklore traditions and indigenous calendar of events.

Within this context, farmsteads offer a strongly diversified set of tourism products for the rural sanatorium-centre destinations in Belarus, basing this diversification on individual approaches to various tourist needs (from national cuisine and hippotherapy to historical attractions and sacral places).

Moreover, Belarusian farmsteads reveal more cooperative behavior in the domestic tourism market. While sanatoria envision themselves as big stakeholders who are predestined to compete only and rely solely on their state owner-institution in terms of both supply and promotion, farmsteads act in a more flexible and cooperative manner. For example, sanatoria were unable to agree on the terms of operating their professional association. Therefore, the association was never found. Meanwhile, farmsteads cooperate actively under the guidance of the Belarusian Non-Government Agro- and Ecotourism Association "Country Escape". There are also successful examples of establishing territorial agro-tourism clusters in many rural destinations.

The additional motive of cooperation between sanatoria and farmsteads within rural destinations is determined by the fact that these stakeholders currently attract very diverging tourist segments. If greater cooperation could be secured, this would in turn lead to the establishment of cooperative approaches at different stages of creating tourism value chain, which can imply exchanging of tourist flows while increasing the added value of the products.

4. Actual and perspective cooperation between rural destination stakeholders

It can be assumed that sanatoria create a much greater infrastructural, organisational and overall tourism product centre for rural destinations. This means that all the other (peripheral) stakeholders are dependent on the overall success of this central stakeholder (i.e. from the perspective of infrastructure, tourism product development, demand, destination promotion and sustainability). Similarly, this sanatorium-centre is mostly responsible for resilience development of the whole destination: if a centre increases its resilience, it also expands this quality for all the peripheral stakeholders and the destination itself (and with the same mechanism, sanatoria share tourist receipts and transfer innovations and best practices over to the destination). This also establishes the motivation for other stakeholders (particularly farmsteads) to cooperate with sanatoria for overall increase of the destination resilience.

This cooperation includes cooperation on the following points:

- *By sharing infrastructure and facilities*: while sanatoria share the basic tourism infrastructure and superstructure, farmsteads can provide more authentic and comfortable accommodation options, which are targeted for the individual needs of the niche tourist segments, and which is particularly important in the high season when the occupancy rate of sanatoria reaches 100 percent.
- *Products and services supply*: sanatoria offer a wide choice of science- and technology-dense spa and medical treatments, as well as some entertainment and "*edu*tainment" options (e.g. concerts and cinema, open-airs, life-coaching, healthy-lifestyle trainings). At the same time, there is a lack of Traditional & Complementary Medicine and indigenous healing practices in the typical sanatorium package. This gap can be richly fulfilled by the corresponding offer of the farmsteads (e.g. authentic Russian *banya* with unique "*venik*" experiences, phytotherapy, api-puncture therapy, etc.). While sanatoria are capable of providing healthy nutrition and massive catering opportunities, farmsteads are much stronger in creating native and local cuisine experiences with authentic dishes and cooking technologies (e.g. cooking in a Russian oven). Moreover, farmsteads can practice organic food production and plant local healing herbs authentic to the region, to be able to share these products with sanatoria of the destination, which is essential for meeting the modern trends of health and wellness tourism. This further reflects the growing interest in traditional and complementary medicine and indigenous healing practices, and the importance of social corporate responsibility in creating tourism products (Cohen & Bodeker, 2009; Smith & Puczko, 2014).
- *Transferring of knowledge and best practices*: thanks to the competence of staff who are equipped with innovative treatment equipment and infrastructure, sanatoria in Belarus can transfer medical scientific knowledge to the other kurort stakeholders, which can in turn be applied to the more sophisticated product development targeting different niche segments of tourist

demand. At the same time, sanatoria currently lack the indigenous traditional knowledge base which has become so important in the modern 'health and wellness' tourism (Global Wellness Institute, 2017). Some illustrative examples of this could be *banya* and phytotherapy: farmsteads can communicate to sanatoria the authentic details and meaningful rituals of the practices. Meanwhile the sanatoria can give back the scientifically dense information on the overall impact of the practices on different parameters of health and wellness. This itself gives greater notice to the modern principles of adapting ancient practices within the trendy and competitive tourism product. The transferring of these two types of knowledge between the two different types of stakeholders within a rural destination can make it independent from other external sources of knowledge and expertise, thus increasing the resilience of the destination.

- *Joint tourism projects and events*: ethnic and religious tourism themes have already become an essential part of a sanatorium offer owing to the entertaining function of these events. But historically and traditionally, they can have a far more meaningful and unique impact: cognition of the national soul of the communities at the destination, together with a healing nature of many Slavic fests and rituals (e.g. sacral immersions in ice on the Orthodox fest of the Baptism of Jesus, ascetic traditions of the Great Fast, phytotherapy highlights of the legendary *Kupalje* – with many other unique examples available). There is a strong need for a thoroughgoing cooperative approach between the two main types of rural destinations stakeholders to provide authentic, meaningful (from a range of perspectives) and thus valuable tourism experiences for the visitors.
- *Marketing and USP*: the unique selling proposition of the sanatorium-centre rural destinations of Belarus is exactly the harmonious combination of two – at first glance contrasting – tourism themes: (i) the ethnic and agro-tourism theme concentrated within farmsteads; and (ii) the spa and wellness tourism theme with strong medical science presented at the sanatoria. The unique character of these products is created by authentically merging these two themes together – this cannot be found in similar kurort-type destinations in Lithuania, Poland, the Czech Republic, Hungary or Russia. Therefore, this USP relevance is very much dependent on not having any excessive, falsely innovative and unnatural intrusions to any of the two themes. On the contrary, the USP significance can be immensely improved by concentrating on local products and traditions, knowledge of the local communities and their indigenous practices. This means that USP characteristics and resilience both increase correspondingly with a cumulative effect, thanks to the cooperative approach to tourism-product development in the sanatorium-centre rural destinations of Belarus.

The aforementioned dimensions of cooperation between health- and agro-tourism stakeholders in Belarus provide an understanding of a specific aspect of rural destination resilience – *sociocultural resilience* – which is important in creating and marketing tourism products of the destination. The core tourism products based on the knowledge and beliefs which have survived centuries of Belarus' colourful history can contribute substantially to the overall resilience of the destination. This is due to the fact that these products stand in a way outside of time; they do not appeal to the values and assets attributed to the global mass culture of consumption, and therefore do not depend on global linkages, supply and consumer shifts. Moreover, rural destinations of Belarus preserve through centuries the immense intangible assets to draw upon. So if these assets are applied together with the basic functions and actual achievements of the sanatorium segment, much more than just competitive USP products can be created. This cooperative approach also provides the chance to shape an alternative lifestyle model which can be communicated to tourists at the destination through a complex of recreation activities designed to be further integrated into the overall lifestyle of a visitor. These changes of lifestyle imply the corresponding reevaluation of values and shifts in the pattern of consumption. They can also initiate a segment of devoted repeated visitors who will come back to the destination notwithstanding the possible external shocks.

5. Conclusions

The case of Belarus shows that cooperative approaches between stakeholders belonging to different sectors of tourism can immensely increase the overall resilience of a destination, especially a rural-type peripheral destination. These approaches begin with basic functional aspects (electricity, water supply, sanitation facilities), altering the value chain of a tourism product by making it more independent from external suppliers and linkages. Furthermore, the effective partnership of the stakeholders can lead to a merging of these touristic sectors and create completely new tourism products, which would serve as USPs for the destination. Moreover, an integrative cooperation approach creates a new diversified basis of knowledge and a best-practice framework for developing tourism products and destination management. Finally, socially and culturally oriented cooperation gives the chance to initiate favourable shifts in tourism demand, consumption behaviour and tourism-related lifestyles.

References

Bolbatovskij, G.N., & Polujanova, I.E. (2017). Sanatorno-kurortnoe lechenie i ozdorovlenie naseleniya v Respublike Belarus [Health resort treatment of the population in the Republic of Belarus]. *Meditsinskienovosti = Proceedings of Medicine, 7*, 26–29.

Cohen, G., & Bodeker, M. (2009). *Understanding the global spa industry: Spa management.* Oxford: Butterworth Heinemann.

Danskikh, S.U., & Vitun, S.J. (2016). Osobennosti razvitija agroturizma v Respublike Belarus [Features of agro-tourism development in the Republic of Belarus]. In M. Karpitskaya (Eds.), *Problemy sovremennoj ekonomiki: globalnyj, nacionalnyj i regionalnyj aspekty* [*Issues of modern economy: Global, national and regional aspects*] (Vol. 2, pp. 3–10). Grodno, Belarus: Yanka Kupala State University of Grodno.

Global Wellness Institute. (2017). *Global wellness economymonitor*. Retrieved from www.globalwellnessinstitute.org/industry-research/

Pirozhnik, I.I., & Yasoveev, M.G. (2005). *Kurortyirekreacija v Belarusi* [*Health resorts and recreation in Belarus*]. Mogilev, Belarus: Belorussko-RossijskijUniversitet.

Smith, M., & Puczko, L. (2014). *Health, tourism and hospitality: Spas, wellness and medical travel*. London: Routledge Taylor & Francis Group.

Traskevich, A.G. (2015). *Konkurentosposobnost' sanatorno-kurortnogo segmenta turisticheskoj industrii* [*The competitiveness of the sanatorium tourism segment in Belarus*]. Minsk: Chetyre chetverti.

7 Integrated destination governance

An evolutionary approach to open innovation and stakeholder engagement for resilient tourism destinations

Lauren Uğur

1. Introduction: adopting an evolutionary approach to resilience

In the most simplistic sense, resilient development infers the necessity to pursue development practices that seek to achieve sustainability through in-built mechanisms that assure the maintenance of stability within a system. In particular, this refers to ensuring an ability to regain control under circumstances of disturbance or disaster. The measure of resilience from this perspective would thus be the speed at which equilibrium – the stable, functional state – is regained (Holling, 1973, 1996). This "engineering" approach to the concept of resilience immediately poses two key challenges: First, setting the goal as the return to the former functional state post-disturbance implies that the most desirable state to achieve is that which previously existed. Second, the attempt to return to former stable levels of functionality does not account for or provide any means to recognise and/or make use of potential opportunities for improvement. Accordingly, fail-safe, *engineered* designs for resilience are traditionally embedded in processes determined by the assumed ability to predict all possible outcomes and likewise, the ability to maintain control over these outcomes. However, particularly within a global, highly networked industry such as tourism, the simplicity of this reductionist perspective on resilience simply doesn't cut it. In reality, within a networked society, influencing factors are immeasurable in number and uncertainty over outcomes is rife, thus making prediction and control a futile exercise. Consequently, traditional cause and effect-based master-planning becomes somewhat redundant, as such processes of planning simply cannot account for all the possible variables and resultant outcomes over which they attempt to elicit control.

With the development in discourses on defining resilience, the acknowledgement that the return to a singular state of equilibrium and former functionality as the core measure of success has been recognised as representing an underestimation of the complexity of the systems within which we operate. Moving beyond the engineering approach, the concept of ecological resilience, as also defined by Holling (1996), distinguishes adaptation as a key factor of resilience, whereby change beyond the former functional state is a necessary means by which to resist further shocks. The measure of resilience therefore shifts from the speed at which equilibrium can be regained to being "the magnitude of the disturbance that can be absorbed before the system changes its structure" (Holling, 1996, p. 33). The notion of ecological resilience thus asserts the consideration of both the ability of a system to persist in its current state as well as its ability to adapt in order to strengthen. In other words, it concerns the ability of a system to change and achieve different states of stable equilibrium in reaction to systemic disturbances. The common ground between engineering and ecological resilience therefore lies in "the belief in the existence of equilibrium in systems, be it a pre-existing one to which a resilient system bounces back (engineering) or a new one to which it bounces forth (ecological)" (Davoudi, Shaw, Haider, Quinlan, & Porter, 2012, p. 301).

In contrast to engineering and ecological notions of resilience, evolutionary resilience emerged as a direct challenge to the notion of states of desired equilibrium. Rather, evolutionary concepts of resilience promote the idea that "the very nature of systems may change over time with or without an external disturbance" (Davoudi, 2012, p. 302). The adoption of an evolutionary perspective therefore does not promote resilience as a "return to normality, but rather as the ability of complex socio-ecological systems to change, adapt, and, crucially, transform in response to stresses and strains" (ibid.). Essentially, an evolutionary approach to resilience recognises uncertainty and chaos on the basis of real-world complexity, shying away from traditional views that the world and social systems are orderly and predictable. The core objective when looking at resilience in an evolutionary way is thus not to achieve any state of stable equilibrium but rather to master processes of feedback, incorporate structural learning and assure adaptive change so as to attain constantly emerging states of [improved] functionality.

Overall, the concept of resilience is thus applied here strategically, rather than in a normative way. This approach is embedded in the argument that in order to be effective, resilient development must be explicitly guided and determined by multi-dimensional and multi-level factors integrated across the environmental, ecological, social and economic spheres present in any particular context (Ahern, 2011; Anderies, Folke, Walker, & Ostrom, 2013; Uğur, 2016b). The nature of this multi-level, multi-dimensional reality demands movement beyond the focus on prediction and control in terms of developing fail-safe engineered solutions towards not only acceptance, but an embracement of unpredictability and dynamic change, whereby control is a luxury limited to a mere fraction of influencing variables and where uncertainty and an inherent lack of control constitute the norm. This implies of course that traditional problem-solving and decision-making approaches need to be appropriately re-thought and adapted to accommodate the surety of uncertainty and a lack of control over outcomes. Moving resilience thinking beyond a "unitary construct" (Duit, Galaz, Eckerberg, & Ebbesson, 2010, p. 364) calls for the rejection of resilience as a linear concept and embraces social systems as both complex and adaptive. Such a position therefore embraces an evolutionary approach, whereby the resilience of a region or destination considers the long-term ability of destinations to develop new growth paths through adopting a "comprehensive attitude, merging industry-specific, network-based, institutional dimensions" (Boschma, 2015, p. 734). Coupled with this kind of an evolutionary approach to resilience, it is argued here that the social dimension of tourism as a networked services industry cannot be ignored and thus requires a second layer of understanding in terms of applying resilience as a means to develop successful tourism destinations. Any definition of resilience in the context of a highly networked services industry such as tourism needs to simultaneously consider the specificities of social networks. Resilience itself therefore likewise needs to be considered beyond systemic structure and processes and to incorporate social aspects of resilience as they relate to communities. A socially apt definition of resilience would therefore include aspects such as the capacity to adapt resource use to changing conditions (Comfort, 1999), as well as consider the required structural conditions (social, cultural and political) that would enable individuals to adapt as and when necessary, usually in the face of adversity (Ungar, 2003 as cited by Sheppard & Williams, 2016).

In essence, an evolutionary approach to resilience acknowledges that systems change regardless of any form of external disturbance and thus likewise require approaches to planning and governance that take a position of recognising constant change and unpredictability and follow a paradigm of designing structures and processes that enable an environment in which failure is not catastrophic; in other words an environment in which it is "safe to fail" (Taleb, 2007, 2012; Ahern, 2011; Mehaffy, 2013). Such a stance is argued here to be essential in the development of resilient tourism destinations.

2. Characteristics of the resilient destination

In recent discourses authors have asserted that tourism destinations require new strategies to cope with "complex interrelated change impacts" in a networked industry and have argued that resilience thinking indeed provides a useful framework on which to base such strategies (Luthe & Wyss, 2014, p. 161). However, it is the notion of sustainability that sets the benchmark of tourism development practice and that has evolved as an expected principle of tourism management (Fodness, 2016). The relationship between the resilient destination and the sustainable destination is thus one that requires clarity if discussions on destination governance and the development of resilient destinations is to progress (Espiner, Orchiston, & Higham, 2017). In essence, it is argued that tourism destinations must first be resilient if they are to be sustainable. It is in fact therefore the resilience approach, not sustainability per se, that recognises the need to acknowledge complexity and thus asserts the need for tourism planning and management to (re)focus efforts on coping with continually changing, uncertain conditions. Overall, the consensus is that it is on the basis of incorporating "elements of resilience into destination development and planning, that offers the most realistic foundation upon which the aspirational principles of long-term sustainability might be built" (ibid. p. 12). What remains, however, are the questions of what it is that characterises the resilient destination and how it is that such destinations can and should be managed.

In tackling these questions, steps have indeed been made towards examining what it is that characterises a resilient destination. For example, Ruiz-Ballesteros

(2011) outlines four key "resilience enhancing" factors in tourism development, namely: i) the ability to live with change and uncertainty, ii) nurturing diversity, iii) the importance of combining different kinds of knowledge and iv) creating the opportunity for self-organization. Hartman (2016) similarly underlines the need for tackling uncertainty and change through adaptive governance approaches, placing prominence on the management of diversity while Uğur (2016b) asserts the promotion of diversity through the enablement of spatial, economic and institutional access as fundamental to creating more inclusive, and thus also diverse, tourism destinations. Across the board, unanimity on the need to cope with uncertainty and dynamic change is clear, and regardless of the semantics or specific focus, adaptive approaches to organisational process are suggested as being a necessary feature of resilient development. In short, built-in, process-supported adaptation is key to enabling resilient practices, as it takes cognisance of uncertainty, enables responses to dynamic change and thus works to combat systemic fragility. To borrow from Nassim Taleb's (2012) conception of the "anti-fragile", perhaps the central indicator of a resilient destination is one that is managed to be anti-fragile whereby governance and organisational strategy seek to not only create a system where change is expected but where it is in fact embraced and thus viewed as a valued source of potential through which to elicit improved change. In thinking about how it is that such an approach could be pragmatically visualised, the remainder of this chapter expands on the need for an integrated development approach, which places focus on open innovation and dynamic stakeholder management as the means to support resilient development across the situational (spatial), institutional and social spheres in the highly networked industry that is tourism.

3. Open innovation and dynamic stakeholder management at the core of resilient destination development

The call for new approaches to governance and management practices that are better suited to modern global connectivity and the levels of complexity characterising the international trade and the provision of services is one not limited to tourism. As aptly put by Duit and colleagues (2010, p. 367), "In the bigger picture, the by now well-established transition from 'government' to 'governance' taking place in many countries is a prime example of how public steering and institutions is constantly being re-defined and re-invented in order to co-evolve with a dynamic environment." Likewise, in governance research the central commonality tends to be the assertion that it can no longer be about governance in terms of top-down command and control, as this represents an outdated approach to management, which is incapable of eliciting sustainable results, particularly at the societal level. At the same time, top-down approaches cannot altogether be eliminated as it would be impossible to govern any kind of societal change without them (Loorbach, 2010). The appeal is therefore for "an adaptive approach, rather than a rigid deterministic, authoritarian style", which may very well require the adoption of stringent rules but which will also require adequate flexibility to change any set rules dynamically in response to foreseeable as well as unforeseeable change. It is flexibility in the governance system which would enable quick reactions to the myriad of changes that may occur in the destination or in the external environment (Baggio, Scott, & Cooper, 2010, p. 55). What this means is that government steering and the modalities of structuring and managing destination development need to strike a balance between top-down guidance and self-organised organic [bottom-up] approaches, which are essential in terms of allowing space for localised, stakeholder-driven innovation to occur.

In conceptualising what this kind of governance process would entail, focus is placed here on an integrated approach where institutional process concerned with dynamic stakeholder management is placed at the core of building resilience and promotes an open innovation approach which fosters collaboration and self-organisation in defining, marketing and servicing the destination (Figure 7.1). The pursuit of integrated development and most particularly, adaptive capacities within [destination] management, however, inherently infer a loss of control. Arguably, it is the fear of losing control that makes the pragmatic application of integrated, adaptive management pursuits so tenuous, particularly in socially driven industries such as tourism. As is too often the case, despite existing discourses on the need for more flexible, adaptive approaches to tourism destination development and management, all too often reality demonstrates a return to traditional, linear modes of management where control is maintained at the expense of utilising adaptive potential. For this reason, it is important to remind ourselves that even within the most complex of systems, points of stability or robustness are always present. It is the identification of these points of robustness that is an important step in allowing for a more "secure" basis from which adaptive methods may be applied. The assertion is that, in order to be successful, integrated planning and management methods

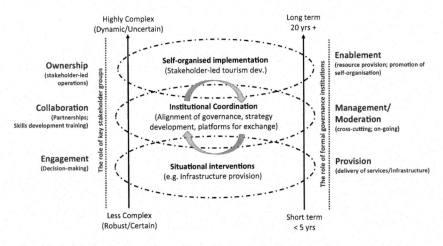

Figure 7.1 Integrated planning and development for the resilient destination – stakeholders and institutional roles

Source: Own illustration

are required and must consider a dynamic range of complexity in strategy implementation where the role of formal institutional governance transitions from that of provider in more robust situations where fundamental resources need to be allotted (i.e. necessary infrastructures) to that of a coordinating (or negotiating) entity across involved institutions and representative groups to that of an enabler where stakeholder engagement and self-organisation are promoted through strategic resource supply and the assurance of access across stakeholder groups (Uğur, 2014, 2016a). Here, the achievement of a balance between top-down control and bottom-up organic development on the basis of active citizenship and self-organised initiative is necessary (ibid.)

In the development of the tourist destination the need for on-going, broad-based stakeholder involvement in the development process is undeniable. Accordingly, the core point of robustness in this respect would be the establishment of a common vision for the destination towards which multiple stakeholders would be willing to contribute, while at the same time accepting the multiplicity of possible pathways which may lead to the successful achievement of any proposed outcome. This need for more effective, collaborative stakeholder engagement has likewise been reiterated in destination branding discourses, where authors have already demonstrated the importance of integrated coordination and more concentrated stakeholder collaboration in understanding destination identities and in the creation of destination image and branding approaches (i.e. Kavaratzis & Ashworth, 2008; Hanna & Rowley, 2011; Ashton, 2014; Line & Wang, 2017). This, however, is by no means achievable without the development of more *dynamic* methods of stakeholder management, which need to be placed at the centre of all strategic and operational processes involved in destination management.

Commitment to developing more dynamic approaches to stakeholder management likewise represents recognition for and the embracement of the complexity associated with the network and partnerships required to create and maintain successful destinations. Essentially, it is the locally based stakeholders who are best positioned to know what visitors wants, where challenges lie that need to be addressed and how it is that unexploited potential may be recognised and taken advantage of. The necessity is thus to move beyond static modes of stakeholder engagement common in traditional planning models and understand that, as destinations and tourism offerings develop, the interests and needs of stakeholders (including tourists themselves) change just as dynamically, all of which must be accounted for in the management set-up of a destination. Central to the means of achieving any kind of dynamic stakeholder management is the understanding of how social capital resources, particularly knowledge, are viewed and used. An open innovation approach (see Chesbrough, 2003; Gassmann, Enkel, & Chesbrough, 2010) whereby permeable management boundaries are allowed for is therefore purported as essential to enabling the acknowledgment and use of external resources that may otherwise not even be recognised, never mind effectively put to good use. Fluid boundaries of knowledge sharing, based on more active, on-going communication with stakeholders, would allow for the stimulation of innovation in terms of how a destination may be developed. At the same time, enabling the contribution and use of external resources inherently allows for the improved inclusion of different forms of knowledge, something already identified by authors such as Ruiz-Ballesteros (2011) as being essential to the promotion of resilience.

An evolutionary, integrated approach to resilience in tourism destinations thus infers that tourism management organisations are capable of merely providing a common vision and appropriate platforms for exchange, as it must be accepted that no single institution can wield control over or guide all elements of the multi-faceted businesses and service offerings that make up a tourist experience. The fundamental role is thus one of creating connections, establishing and guiding networked collaboration and ensuring appropriate forms of access to allow for participation across the diversity of stakeholder groups that exist. Furthermore, the suggestion is the pursuit of rolling processes of stakeholder engagement whereby institutional structures allow for more fluid communication, allowing for different groups of stakeholders to be more or less involved, as necessary at different phases of any given project/process. All too often on the ground participatory processes are set on the basis of static stakeholder identification, most often undertaken prior to a particular project being implemented, and very seldom consider how it is the needs and interests of stakeholders will develop over time as results are achieved or unforeseeable changes arise.

4. Concluding remarks

This chapter has engaged the concept of evolutionary resilience as an appropriate means through which to consider the governance requirements for developing and managing resilient destinations. The argument made is that an evolutionary approach recognises change as the only constant and asserts that more adaptive, flexible approaches to destination governance are required if the impacts and potential prompted through dynamic systemic change are to be either mitigated or made use of respectively. Furthermore, due to the social nature of tourism as a networked industry, the conceptualisation offered demonstrates the absolute necessity for open approaches to development and innovation so as to enable the use of resources beyond the bounds of traditional destination structures, which can only be leveraged through the development and implementation of more dynamic modes of stakeholder engagement.

To summarise, the most important factors associated with the approach outlined include:

- The need to pursue integrated development processes that enable flows of information across the situational, institutional and social spheres of development, which in turn stimulate more open processes of innovation.
- The requirement to pursue more adaptive management processes that allow the procedural flexibility required to react quickly and effectively to challenges and take advantage of opportunities dynamically, as they arise.
- The need for formal management institutions to focus on the creation of a common vision and/or common objectives to which all parties involved may aspire, yet work towards achieving in a number of different ways and,

- the need for discussion and clarity in the definition and understanding of the roles to be played by stakeholder groups on one hand and formal governance institutions on the other hand, across the various spheres of development (situational, institutional and social).

What remains abundantly clear, however, is that there is a long way to go in terms of refining and implementing such an approach in reality. On a positive note, though, the first step to solving a problem is realising the issue(s) in the first place and a number of authors, many of whom have contributed to this book, are outlining the fundamental challenges facing the pursuit of resilient development. The actuality, however, is that existing discourses on resilience as a concept and its pragmatic applicability to tourism and destination management are highly disjointed and often focus on one or two particular elements, which may limit general applicability. What is required are more collaborative research approaches that seek out diversity in using the theoretical and empirical resources available beyond the boundaries of specifically tourism-focused research. If we agree that resilience is a useful construct for sustainable tourism destination development and management, then we need to more proactively foster an interdisciplinary approach to assessing how resilience as a theoretical premise may be most effectively empirically applied. Without a coordinated interdisciplinary approach, the pragmatic implementation and implications of the requirements for progress, as suggested by the kind of model presented here, will be severely confined. For a start, significant bodies of literature exploring social and organisational complexity exist across the fields of urban and regional planning, business management sciences and social development fields, which provide an excellent point of departure from which to begin developing more tourism-applicable methods for resilient destination development in a more integrated manner, holistically viewing and connecting the situational or spatial context with the institutional and social levels of development. From this perspective, the real potential of resilience, as a guiding beacon for more sustainable destination development, is in re-framing our understanding of a much-discussed term and recognising it as a never-ending process of evolutionary improvement as opposed to a mere system of recovery.

References

Ahern, J. (2011). From fail-safe to safe-to-fail: Sustainability and resilience in the new urban world. *Landscape and Urban Planning, 100*(4), 341–343. doi:10.1016/j. landurbplan.2011.02.021

Anderies, J.M., Folke, C., Walker, B., & Ostrom, E. (2013). Aligning key concepts for global change policy: Robustness, resilience and sustainability. *Ecology and Society, 18*(2), 8–24. doi:10.5751/es-05178-180208

Ashton, A.S. (2014). Tourist destination brand image development – An analysis based on stakeholders' perception. *Journal of Vacation Marketing, 20*(3), 279–292. doi:10.1177/1356766713518061

Baggio, R., Scott, N., & Cooper, C. (2010). Improving tourism destination governance: A complexity science approach. *Tourism Review, 65*(4), 51–60. doi:10.1108/16605371011093863

Boschma, R. (2015). Towards an evolutionary perspective on regional resilience. *Regional Studies, 49*(5), 733–751. doi:10.1080/00343404.2014.959481

Chesbrough, H. (2003). *Open innovation: The new imperative for creating and profiting from technology.* Boston, MA: Harvard Business School Press.

Comfort, L.K. (1999). *Shared risk: Complex systems in seismic response.* Bingley, UK: Emerald Group Publishing Limited.

Davoudi, S. (2012). Resilience: "A bridging concept or a dead end?". *Planning Theory and Practice, 13*(2), 299–333.

Duit, A., Galaz, V., Eckerberg, K., & Ebbesson, J. (2010). Governance, complexity, and resilience. *Global Environmental Change, 20*(3), 363–368. doi:10.1016/j.gloenvcha.2010.04.006

Espiner, S., Orchiston, C., & Higham, J. (2017). Resilience and sustainability: A complementary relationship? Towards a practical conceptual model for the sustainability resilience nexus in tourism. *Journal of Sustainable Tourism,* 1–23. doi:10.1080/09669582.2017.1281929

Fodness, D. (2016). The problematic nature of sustainable tourism: Some implications for planners and managers. *Current Issues in Tourism,* 1–13. doi:10.1080/13683500.2016.1209162

Gassmann, O., Enkel, E., & Chesbrough, H. (2010). The future of open innovation. *R&D Management, 40*(3), 213–221. doi:10.1111/j.1467-9310.2010.00605.x

Hanna, S., & Rowley, J. (2011). Towards a strategic place brand-management model. *Journal of Marketing Management, 27*(5–6), 458–476. doi:10.1080/02672571003683797

Hartman, S. (2016). Towards adaptive tourism areas? A complexity perspective to examine the conditions for adaptive capacity. *Journal of Sustainable Tourism, 24*(2). doi:10.1080/09669582.2015.1062017

Holling, C.S. (1973). Resilience and stability of ecological systems. *Annual Review of Ecological Systems, 4,* 1–23. doi:10.1146/annurev.es.04.110173.000245

Holling, C.S. (1996). Engineering resilience versus ecological resilience. In P.C. Schulze (Ed.), *Engineering within ecological constraints* (pp. 31–44). Washington, DC: National Academy Press. doi:10.17226/4919.

Kavaratzis, M., & Ashworth, G. (2008). Place marketing: How did we get here and where are we going? *Journal of Place Management and Development, 1*(2), 150–165. doi:10.1108/17538330810889989

Line, N.D., & Wang, Y. (2017). A multi-stakeholder market oriented approach to destination marketing. *Journal of Destination Marketing and Management, 6*(1), 84–93. doi:10.1016/j.jdmm.2016.03.003

Loorbach, D. (2010). Transition management for sustainable development: A prescriptive, complexity-based governance framework. *Governance, 23*(1), 161–183. doi:10.1111/j.1468-0491.2009.01471.x

Luthe, T., & Wyss, R. (2014). Assessing and planning resilience in tourism. *Tourism Management, 44,* 161–163. doi:10.1016/j.tourman.2014.03.011

Mehaffy, M. (2013). *Beyond resilience: Toward 'antifragile' urbanism, better cities and towns.* Retrieved from http://bettercities.net

Ruiz-Ballesteros, E. (2011). Social-ecological resilience and community-based tourism. An approach from Agua Blanca, Ecuador. *Tourism Management, 32*(3), 655–666. doi:10.1016/j.tourman.2010.05.021

Sheppard, V.A., & Williams, P.W. (2016). Factors that strengthen tourism resort resilience. *Journal of Hospitality and Tourism Management, 28*(September), 20–30. doi:10.1016/j.jhtm.2016.04.006

Taleb, N.N. (2007). *The Black Swan: The impact of the highly improbable*. New York: Random House Inc.

Taleb, N.N. (2012). *Antifragile: How to live in a world we don't understand*. UK: Penguin Books.

Uğur, L. (2014). *Beyond the pilot project: Towards broad-based integrated violence prevention in South Africa*. Technische Universitaet Darmstadt.

Uğur, L. (2016a, December 3). Managing complexity. A case for adaptive management in tackling urban violence in South Africa. *Emergence: Complexity and Organization*. doi:10.emerg/10.17357.83b679e69ba1e0ab7e49964b8883ea2c

Uğur, L. (2016b). Mind the gap: Reconceptualising inclusive development in support of integrated urban planning and tourism development. In C. Pasquinelli & N. Bellini (Eds.), *Tourism in the city: Towards an integrative agenda on urban tourism* (pp. 51–66). Springer International. doi:10.1007/978-3-319-26877-4.

Ungar, M. (2003). Qualitative contributions to resilience research. *Qualitative Social Work*, *2*(1), 85–102.

8 Qualities and fields of action of destination resilience

An indicator analysis process

Andreas Koler, Stefan Ortner & Mike Peters

1. Introduction

Resilience is a very broad phenomenon which can include a social, ecological or even an economic dimension (Adger, 2000; Folke, 2006; Hassink, 2010). It is of special interest for tourism communities and destinations to understand attributes of resilience (e.g. analyzing the way people express resilience), the reasons (e.g. underlying causes such as man-made disasters) but also the receivers of resilience (e.g. authorities, society). When understanding these three dimensions, a destination manager is able to detect resilience and to react accordingly. However, it needs indicators which help to assess the degree of resilience, e.g. a resilience score. Such a score would be helpful for decision-makers in the destination.

This paper presents a cross-section examinational project – a survey of decision makers within public authorities and regional disaster management experts of 27 destinations in five countries (Austria, Greece, Italy, Spain and the UK). The answers contribute to an indicator and quality of resilience, and therefore we can form a resilience score for each destination. In addition, four main fields of action ('preparedness & response', 'risk & vulnerability reduction', 'risk assessment', and 'governance') have been identified and analyzed to be able to provide comprehensive feedback to the participating destinations that now form the basis for further improvement and strengthening of local resilience.

Finally, the authors were able to develop a score-net showing the quality of resilience in each of destinations with the help of the seven qualities of robustness, flexibility, resourcefulness redundancy, reflection and integration. The project highlights different indicators and the qualities of resilience derived from the empirical data. The results show strengths in all destinations in the indictor categories of partnerships, hazard and risk assessment and coordination. Weaknesses are financing, lack of early warning systems, response of education and training, maintenance and legal systems.

Lienz (Austria) serves as an exemplary case to show the resilience assessment process and its results and demonstrates the advantages of such an indicator development process.

2. Theoretical background

Scientific literature offers a wide range of the term "resilience". For instance, resilience can be defined as "the ability of a system to maintain and adapt its essential structure and function in the face of disturbance while maintaining its identity" (Biggs, Hall, & Stoeckl, 2012, p. 640; Cumming et al., 2005; Holling, 1973). Public institutions and governments have derived other working definitions of resilience. The Australian Department of Human Services defined it as "the ability to bounce back" (Australian Government, 2010), the UK Cabinet office as "the ability of the community, services, area or infrastructure to detect, prevent and, if necessary, to withstand, handle and recover from disruptive challenges" (UK Cabinet Office, 2010). The US department of Homeland-Security uses different terms to describe resilience: It is "the ability to reset, absorb, recover from as well as to successfully adapt to adversity or a change in conditions" (US Homeland Security, 2015). Resilience can also be defined as the 'capacity of a system, community or society potentially exposed to hazards to adapt by resisting or changing in order to reach and maintain an acceptable level of functioning and structure' (Public Safety Canada, 2009). All these definitions have some aspects in common and define a certain number of attributes of resilience, the reasons for including resilience into civil or community protection approaches and the potential stakeholders that are important for the successful implementation of resilience concepts. Verbs used to describe resilience are for instance bouncing back, recover, withstand, prevent, analyze, absorb, adapt, detect, handle or resist. Reasons for resilience are disruptive challenges, natural hazards, changing conditions, manmade disasters and new development. And receivers or stakeholders of resilience are areas, systems, infrastructures, communities, authorities, societies and individuals.

A major characteristic of each resilience system is the scale: while engineering scales describe smaller-scale systems that are required to completely return to their original states in the short and medium term, city or community scales refer to larger systems (cities, regions) that do not necessarily have to return to their original states after a shock or stress event.

Originally, resilience theory was developed by Holling (1973), an ecologist who provided the basis for an ongoing adaptation and usage of this concept in the understanding and exploration of social-economic systems (SES) (Cochrane, 2010). Overall, resilience tries to explain how (e.g. social or ecological or economic) systems respond or react to certain changes or impacts. Bec, McLennan, and Moyle (2015) describe in their review paper that the resilience concept was applied in various disciplines, e.g. social sciences (Adger, 2000), or engineering (Bergen, Bolton, & Fridley, 2001) – wherever systems' reaction on change deserved deeper understanding. Cochrane (2010) applied the resilience concept to industries, Krasny and Roth (2010) or Sriskandarajah, Bawden, Blackmore, Tidball, and Wals (2010) to organizations, Maguire and Hagan (2007), Maguire and Cartwright (2008) and Skerratt (2013) to communities and Gunderson (2000) to environments. Furthermore, the resilience concept was used to understand certain types of changes (for an in-depth review see Bec et al., 2015).

In tourism, this concept helped to understand regions' or destinations' reactions to short-term changes, such as crises or catastrophes (e.g. disasters or economic crises) (Eakin, Benessaiah, Barrera, Cruz-Bello, & Morales, 2011), but also for long-term impacts (e.g. from climate change or migration) (Adger et al., 2011; Biggs et al., 2012; Luthe, Wyss, & Schuckert, 2012). One model, the sphere of tourism resilience model, was developed to identify the "principal elements of a resilient tourism system" (Cochrane, 2010, p. 182). This path-breaking work first indicates the importance of learning from previous resilience cycles in order to develop managerial and policy-oriented implications or actions. Cochrane (2010) underlined that "in SES, learning from previous cycles can be used to plan interventions which facilitate the desired state of equilibrium" (p. 12). This holds true for community planning where planners need to deal with social support systems, well-being or quality of life, resource planning and budgeting. These areas need to be designed and managed sustainably – however, the focus of action mainly lies in maintaining (e.g. resources), preserving or conserving (e.g. culture), and protecting (e.g. nature). Community resilience indicators deal with the creation of change capacity, the improvement of environmental knowledge and the improvement of living conditions as well as social networking and collaboration (Lew, Ng, Ni, & Wu, 2015, p. 24). Therefore, resilience is looking at the adaptation or transformation of existing resources into new resources or resource combinations. Lew et al. (2015) strongly call for destination management's analysis and understanding of sustainability and resilience in order to create effective destination planning and development systems (p. 25).

From studying cases in city resilience, The Rockefeller Foundation derived seven major characteristics of resilient systems. These dimensions are able to describe the qualities of a resilient system (The Rockefeller Foundation, 2015a, p. 5, 2015b, p. 11):

- Reflective systems have mechanisms to evolve and are able to modify their standards and norms which are based on emerging evidence, not on a permanent situation.
- Robust system were well-constructed and managed physical assets.
- Redundancy refers to spare capacities. It includes diversity and a presence of many multiple ways to achieve a certain need or goal.
- Flexibility implies the possibility of change and adaption in response to a changing environment.
- Resourcefulness means that individuals and institutions can find different ways to achieve their goals.
- Inclusion targets the need for broad consultation and the engagement of many stakeholders in the communities.
- Integration and alignment address the exchange within and between resilient systems and across different scales of their operations.

The empirical part of the paper will illustrate a resilience analysis process in order to derive implications for further community resilience management.

3. Empirical analysis

3.1 Method

The following empirical results are an extract of findings developed in the EU-funded CP-model project.[1] The project aimed at analyzing the resilience level of municipalities and identifying the most urgent fields of improvement. Therefore, a questionnaire has been designed that allows municipalities to analyze their strength, weaknesses, opportunities and threats in the field of disaster resilience. It also enables municipalities to compare their results with other municipalities of the same characteristics or the average results of their country. The results of the survey will form the basis for the development of a Resilience MOOC (Massive Open Online Course) for civil protection stakeholders.

To create a single value that describes the degree of resilience, the concept of the "Resilience Score" has been developed and introduced. A diagram sums up all questions to one single value and allows showing the overall degree of the community's resilience. The result has been derived on the basis of the CP (civil protection) -model (see www.cpmodel.eu) resilience questionnaire which the municipalities of the participating countries have filled out together with their CP-model country coordinators. The results are an important input for the development of a MOOC for public authorities with the aim to promote the concept of resilience in the field of civil protection.

3.2 Questionnaire development

The main tool to achieve the goals mentioned above is the "Resilience Questionnaire". First, main measurements were derived from literature and second, questions have been derived and further developed during several project workshops in each city. In each city experts from the tourism industry, infrastructure and mobility, security and politics discussed these measurements. Finally, the questionnaire contains 112 questions that are assigned to 54 sub-indicators and 19 indicators in 4 fields of action. In addition, the questionnaire assigns each question to one of the seven qualities of resilience for an alternative, cross-section-analysis of the results by following internationally accepted standards (The Rockefeller Foundation, 2015b). Each question can be evaluated by choosing a value between 1 (completely disagree) to 100 (completely agree) on a scroll bar.

The following table shows the main structure of the questionnaire ranging from the fields of action to the sub-indicators. The specific questions measuring the sub-indicators or constructs, as well as the correlations, can be found on the project website, www.cpmodel.eu:

Table 8.1 Field of actions, indicator and sub-indicators – measurement constructs (*DRR = disaster risk reduction)

Field of action	Indicator	Sub indicator
Governance	Policy planning	Awareness of community members of the risk situation
		Political consensus on the importance of DRR*
		Up-to-date local DRR* policies
	Legal systems	Land-use regulations, building codes and other laws and regulations relating to DRR* are enforced locally
		Community understands the relevant legislation, regulations and procedures and their importance for a safe community
	Partnerships	Long-term partnerships between civil society, NGOs and private sector are established
		Stakeholders can adopt other tasks in case of capacity shortages of others
	Institutional mechanisms	Clearly defined mandates and responsibilities
		Resources for effective DRR* are in place
	Accountability	Effective quality control and audit mechanisms
		Regular reporting to higher-level authorities
	Financing DRR*	Access to internal financial resources
		Funding of external DRR* activities
Risk assessment	Hazard assessment	Hazard knowledge
		Hazard documentation
		Quality of hazard assessment
	Risk assessment	Up-to-date multi-risk assessment
		Community-based risk assessments
		Findings are publicly available
		Monitoring of identified risks
		Link to neighboring risk assessments
	Vulnerability assessment	Up-to-date vulnerability assessment
		Community-based vulnerability assessments
		Findings are publicly available
		Monitoring of identified vulnerabilities
		Link to neighboring vulnerability assessments
Risks & vulnerability reduction	Regulations and structures	Implementation of regulations
		Organizational structures
	Protection	Technical protection measures
		Organizational protection measures
	Maintenance	Regular maintenance
		Monitoring maintenance systems
	Role of local population	Self-protection
		Voluntary work
	Education and training	Professionals
		Local population

Field of action	Indicator	Sub indicator
Risks & vulnerability reduction	Coordination	Local responsibility for preparedness and response
		Structured coordination
	Early warning maintenance	Community and people centered EWS
		Communication of early warning messages
		Quality of EWS
		Awareness and trust of contingency plans
	Contingency planning	Existence of contingency plans
		Quality of contingency plans
		Testing of contingency plans
		Awareness and acceptance of contingency plans
	Recovery	Commitment of national level
		Coordination of recovery activities
		Role of local population in recovery
		Trust in recovery capability
	Response and education	Professionals
		Local Population

Each sub-indicator (see table 8.1) contributes to one of the seven qualities of resilience. If a sub-indicator can be assigned to more than one quality, the most dominating quality has been taken into account. The qualities represent a cross-cutting perspective on resilience without keeping the distinction into the four fields of action of DRR. The final questionnaire was developed in five languages and has been returned by 27 municipalities from five countries during the project.

3.3 Data analysis and presentation

For a quick and standardized analysis of the results, an Excel tool has been developed that allows to import the raw data and automatically produces a report for each participating municipality. In addition, it collects all data sets and therefore enables the project team to derive, e.g., region-specific analysis or a size-dependent identification of strength and weaknesses.

The consortium also developed a simplified and easy-to-use version of the analysis-tool that allows interested municipalities to analyze their level of resilience in a quick and easy way. The self-evaluation framework follows the structure and idea of the printed/pdf questionnaire, but is online-based and automatically develops the resilience-score as well as all graphs and diagrams. In addition, it also includes the aggregated results of other municipalities to allow for a benchmarking.

First of all, a resilience score shows how far an organization has progressed in the field of disaster resilience. This score is calculated by deriving the average evaluation value of the complete set of questions.

Second and third, each community received a fields-of-action Analysis and a Key-Indicator-Analysis. The first is an action diagram showing how far the community progressed in the main four fields of action of resilience (preparedness and response, risk and vulnerability reduction, risk assessment and governance). The key-indicator analysis shows the 19 key indicators which have been rated through the survey.

Fourth, a sub-indicator analysis was derived (based on the 112 specific questions) and as a fifth and final result the seven qualities defining resilience for each partner could be derived.

3.4 Results

The results are available for 27 municipalities. Exemplary, the findings are presented for the municipality of Lienz (Austria), which is a small town with about 12,000 inhabitants and is located in the state of Tyrol. It is the administrative center of the district of Lienz in East Tyrol. Lienz is located in the Eastern Alps and offers a wide range of tourism offers.

In Lienz several 4-hour workshops were held in 2016, each with 4 to 6 experts. Workshop one was conducted with tourism experts, the second one with experts from the area of infrastructure and mobility, the third and fourth one with experts from city safety and security and politics. Each workshop included an introductory part and a long session where the individuals evaluated all 122 measurement items, which finally constitute the sub-indicators and indicators. With the help of the online tool, the workshop moderators could immediately derive the overall result. This allowed a feedback and in-depth discussion of results during the workshop.

The overall resilience score for the municipality of Lienz is 48 out of 100. It can be interpreted as the overall level of resilience and aims to allow for a quick and easy benchmark with other municipalities as well as to communicate the results to a broader public.

The fields of action diagram shows how far Lienz progressed in the four main fields of action of resilience. Values below 40 can be considered as negative and represent an urgent demand for improvement. Values above 70 are generally considered as "very good".

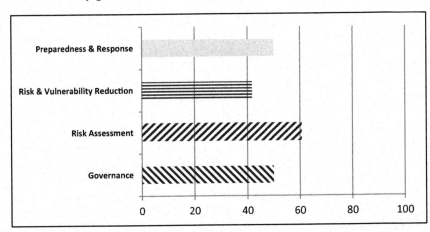

Figure 8.1 Field-of-Action Analysis for the municipality of Lienz, Austria (1 = completely disagree to 100 = completely agree)

Source: Own illustration

The FoA consist of 19 key-indicators that have been rated through the survey. The following graph shows the indicator-results and give some deeper insights into Lienz's resilience status.

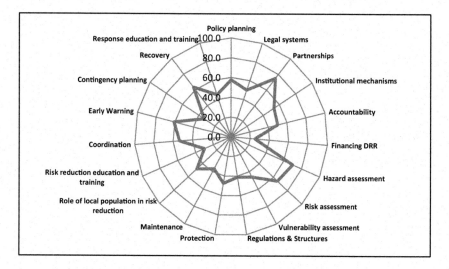

Figure 8.2 Key-Indicator-Analysis for the municipality of Lienz, Austria (1 = completely disagree to 100 = completely agree)

Source: Own illustration

The 19 indicators shown above have been derived, based on 53 sub-indicators and 112 specific questions. The following four graphs show Lienz's results on a sub-indicator level. The colors correspond to the relevant FoA.

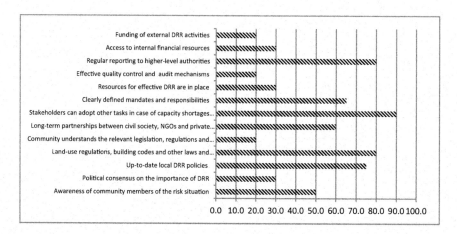

Figure 8.3 Sub-Indicators that correspond to the FoA Governance (1 = completely disagree to 100 = completely agree)

Source: Own illustration

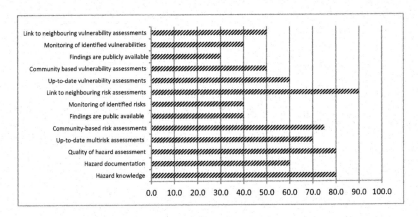

Figure 8.4 Sub-Indicators that correspond to the Field-of-Action "Risk Assessment" (1 = completely disagree to 100 = completely agree)

Source: Own illustration

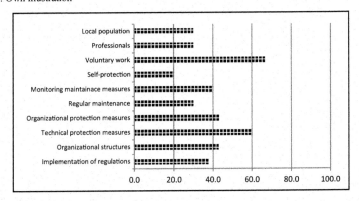

Figure 8.5 Sub-Indicators that correspond to the Field-of-Action "Risk & Vulnerability Reduction" (1 = completely disagree to 100 = completely agree)

Source: Own illustration

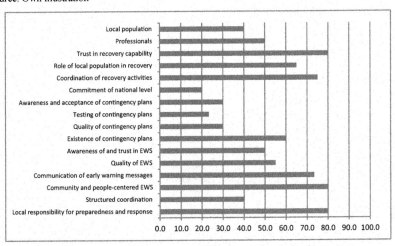

Figure 8.6 Sub-Indicators that correspond to the Field-of-Action "Preparedness and Response" (1 = completely disagree to 100 = completely agree)

Source: Own illustration

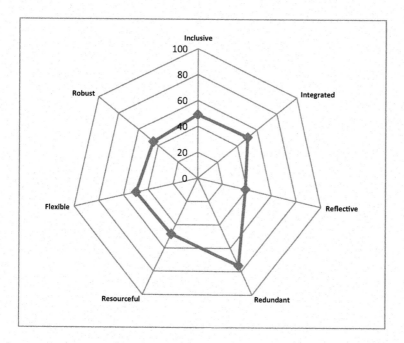

Figure 8.7 Seven qualities of Lienz's resilience (1 = completely disagree to 100 = completely agree)

Source: Author illustration

The final graph shows the resilience status with respect to the seven qualities of resilience described above. Similar to all other graphs in this report, one can easily identify the status quo of the city's resilience quality.

3.5 Discussion and implications

The objective of these above-presented tools is to create a learning space but above all to provide practical guidelines containing indications and suggestions about how to stimulate the debate and how to find solutions in the application of strategies towards resilience.

The ability of a municipality or a community to be resilient can positively be influenced by learning from initiatives of other communities. The circularity of information, the practice of open learning and the dissemination of positive experiences is important especially for those municipalities that don't have the opportunity to be connected daily with the centers of knowledge. The objective of the CP model is the realization of its products, and the contribution to the diffusion of resilience practices in order to implement cooperation among people.

By looking at the overall results, Lienz and other participating municipalities and their strength and weaknesses with regard to resilience can be clearly identified – especially when looking at the indicator level, as indicators are more detailed and profound than the four fields of action and at the same time still more clear and holistic than the sub-indicators.

As in the case of Lienz, all countries perceive "Financing of DRR" as the weakest aspect.

This holds true for "Vulnerability Assessment": Whereas "Hazard Assessment" and "Risk Assessment" are on a high, the assessment and analysis of vulnerabilities is still on a low level. This fact may arise from a lack of understanding and differentiating the terms "hazard", "risk" and "vulnerability" but also from the more complex approaches and corresponding high costs of vulnerability assessments.

Furthermore, it is obvious that financial aspects also influence other maintenance systems: Maintaining existing protection measures or organizational structures is expensive. A clear correlation between the lack of financing and the troubles in maintaining investments can be seen and should be considered in the long-term planning of municipalities on their way towards resilience.

Another critical aspect of Lienz's resilience status is the "Early Warning" system. An analysis of the underlying indicators and questions shows that the reason for this perception can be found in the communication of early warning systems to the local population. The systems themselves are on a high level and work reliably. But the impact of early warning systems is highly dependent on the acceptance, understanding and importance among the local population. Therefore, this might be a starting point for improvement for all countries.

Finally, "Response Training and Education" needs further improvement. It can be assumed that this indicator might have massive impacts on many others: Early warning systems, hazard, risk and vulnerability assessments, contingency planning, etc., demand a high level of education among civil protection professionals as well as volunteers and general public.

The analysis of the seven qualities of resilience is an alternative cross-section analysis of the results. The diagram indicates that Lienz meets the seven qualities on a very constant mediocre level – only "redundancy" was rated higher than the other six qualities, indicating that Lienz evaluates its distributed infrastructure networks and resource reserves quite positively.

4. Conclusion

The instrument and processes used in the project just presented supported communities to both critically discuss and evaluate their strengths and weaknesses regarding resilience and strategically re-think existing practices and measures. The process, for example, showed that Lienz needs to find solutions and strategies to raise financial resources in their community. This will be a future challenge for public authorities, especially because many other important aspects of resilience somehow are dependent on a strong financial commitment.

The process supports a self-reflection process amongst stakeholders in communities and is therefore a first step to redesign or implement resilience strategies. Certainly, the results depend on the communities' commitment and the composition of workshop participants and in some cases, are dependent on business and political life cycles.

However, the outcomes of the survey are a solid basis for the development of a MOOC that is specifically addressed to the needs and prerequisites of municipalities. It is accompanied by several guidelines and an online game that aims to increase the acceptance of resilience among decision makers on a municipality level. In addition, the project consortium aims to further increase the data basis and therefore developed an online version of the above-described survey tool (called RESAT – Resilience Self-Assessment Tool) that enables interested municipalities to easily derive their own resilience score, compare it to scores of other municipalities and contribute to the dataset. The MOOC, the online game and the RESAT are available on www.cpmodel.eu.

Note

1 The project "The Resilience Score: Analysis of the current level of resilience in Austria, Greece, Italy, Spain and UK" was co-financed by the EU-Civil Protection Financial Investment.

References

Adger, W.N. (2000). Social and ecological resilience: Are they related? *Progess in Human Geographies, 24*(3), 347–364.

Adger, W.N., Brown, K., Nelson, D.R., Berkes, F., Eakin, H., Folke, C., Galvin, K., Gunderson, L., Goulden, M., O'Brien, K., Ruitenbeek, J., & Tompkins, E.L. (2011). Resilience implications of policy responses to climate change. *Wiley Interdisciplinary Reviews: Climate Change, 2*(5), 757–766. doi:10.1002/wcc.133

Australian Government. (2010). *Critical infrastructure resilience strategy.* Canberra: Australian Goverment (AU).

Bec, A., McLennan, C.-L., & Moyle, B.D. (2015). Community resilience to long-term tourism decline and rejuvenation: A literature review and conceptual model. *Current Issues in Tourism, 19*(5), 431–457. doi:10.1080/13683500.2015.1083538

Bergen, S.D., Bolton, S.M., & Fridley, J.L. (2001). Design principles for ecological enineering. *Ecological Engineering, 18*(2), 201–210.

Biggs, D., Hall, C.M., & Stoeckl, N. (2012). The resilience of formal and informal tourism enterprises to disasters: Reef tourism in Phuket, Thailand. *Journal of Sustainable Tourism, 20*(5), 645–665. doi:10.1080/09669582.2011.630080

Cochrane, J. (2010). The sphere of tourism resilience. *Tourism Recreation Research, 35*(2), 173–185. doi:10.1080/02508281.2010.11081632

Cumming, G.S., Barnes, G., Perz, S., Schnmik, M., Sieving, K.E., Southworth, J., Binford, M., Holt, R.D., Stickler, C., & Van Holt, T. (2005). An exploratory framework for the empirical measurement of resilience. *Ecosystems, 8*(8), 975–987.

Eakin, H., Benessaiah, K., Barrera, J.F., Cruz-Bello, G.M., & Morales, H. (2011). Livelihoods and landscapes at the threshold of change: Disaster and resilience in a Chiapas coffee community. *Regional Environmental Change, 12*(3), 475–488. doi:10.1007/s10113-011-0263-4

Folke, C. (2006). Resilience: The emergence of a perspective for social – Ecological systems analyses. *Global Environmental Changes, 16*(3), 253–267.

Gunderson, L.H. (2000). Ecological resilience – In theory and application. *Annual Review of Ecology and Systematics, 31*, 425–439.

Hassink, R. (2010). Regional resilience: A promising concept to explain differences in regional economic adaptability? *Cambridge Journal of Regional Economic Society, 3*(1), 45–58.

Holling, C.S. (1973). Resilience and stability of ecological systems. *Annual Review of Ecology and Systematics, 4,* 1–23.

Krasny, M.E., & Roth, W.M. (2010). Environmental education for social – Ecological system resilience: A perspective from activity theory. *Environmental Education Research, 16*(5–6), 545–558. doi:10.1080/13504622.2010.505431

Lew, A.A., Ng, P.T., Ni, C.-C., & Wu, T.-C. (2015). Community sustainability and resilience: Similarities, differences and indicators. *Tourism Geographies, 18*(1), 18–27. doi: 10.1080/14616688.2015.1122664

Luthe, T., Wyss, R., & Schuckert, M. (2012). Network governance and regional resilience to climate change: Empirical evidence from mountain tourism communities in the Swiss Gotthard region. *Regional Enviromental Change, 12*(4), 839–854. doi:10.1007/s10113-012-0294-5

Maguire, B., & Cartwright, S. (2008). *Assessing a community's capacity to manage change: A resilience approach to social assessment.* Canberra, Australia. Retrieved from https://search.informit.com.au/documentSummary;dn=839750155412061;res=IELHSS

Maguire, B., & Hagan, P. (2007). Disasters and communities: Understanding social resilience. *The Australian Journal of Emergency Management, 22*(2), 1324–1540.

Public Safety Canada. (2009). *The regional resilience assessment program.* Public Safety Canada. Retrieved from www.publicsafety.gc.ca/cnt/ntnl-scrt/crtcl-nfrstrctr/crtcl-nfr-strtr-rrap-en.aspx (Accessed 5 September 2017).

The Rockefeller Foundation. (2015a). *City resilience framework 2015.* London, UK. Retrieved from https://assets.rockefellerfoundation.org/app/uploads/20140410162455/City-Resilience-Framework-2015.pdf

The Rockefeller Foundation. (2015b). *City resilience index.* London, UK. Retrieved from https://assets.rockefellerfoundation.org/app/uploads/20140410162455/City-Resilience-Framework-2015.pdf

Skerratt, S. (2013). Enhancing the analysis of rural community resilience: Evidence from community land ownership. *Journal of Rural Studies, 31,* 36–46. doi:10.1016/j.jrurstud.2013.02.003

Sriskandarajah, N., Bawden, R., Blackmore, C., Tidball, K.G., & Wals, A.E.J. (2010). Resilience in learning systems: Case studies in university education. *Environmental Education Research, 16*(5–6), 559–573. doi:10.1080/13504622.2010.505434

UK Cabinet_Office. (2010). *Sector resilience plan for critical infrastructure.* London, UK. Retrieved from www.gov.uk/government/collections/sector-resilience-plans

US Homeland_Security. (2015). *Resilience.* Retrieved from www.dhs.gov/topic/resilience

9 Business continuity management in the destination – proactive recognition, assessment and managing of disruptions

Germann Jossé & Knut Scherhag

1. Introduction

Catastrophes, accidents, the failure of management in times of crisis but also deficiencies in everyday operations lead to established processes in touristic destinations being disrupted. This can have major impacts on the customers, the company and the organization within the destination and often even past the destination's borders. There are various examples for this: flooding in Texas/ USA 2017, the fire in the glacier train in Kaprun in the year 2000 with 155 people dead, kidnapped tourists in Yemen or on the island of Bali, suicide attacks in luxury hotels in Jakarta in 2009, terrorists using vehicles for killing people (Nice 2016, Berlin 2016 Christmas Market . . .). These kinds of catastrophes are hardly foreseeable. However, it is possible to create respective scenarios and a catalogue of contingency measures prior to the incidents. Also, less-spectacular incidents and disruptions have to be handled proactively. This means that the planning process should not start when the disruption is already taking place. Instead, different scenarios of reaction and continuity plans should be prepared, so that the company can react to an incident without extensive forward planning. For example, the renovation of a water park in a holiday resort requires extensive planning, so that the company can, at least partly, continue its operating business. It is also crucial that the customers are being informed early. Furthermore, destinations are very diverse and are permanently in danger, because the trigger off the next crisis might be just around the corner (Pforr, 2006, p. 1). Nobody knows exactly when, where and how the next emergency is going to happen. However, it is going to happen for sure (similar to Faulkner, 2001, p. 135). For a few years, there has been a debate in the Anglo-American region concerning a proactive crisis management, which is already put into practice nationwide and is accepted by a large majority in order to handle disruptions: Business Continuity Management (BCM) is meant to identify and analyze significantly threatening disruptions as well as the development of basic defense and overcoming strategies and explicit measures. This article shows that it is inevitable to implement BCM to build up resilience and safeguard the complex system "destination".

2. Destination management

2.1 The term "destination"

Touristic destinations are composed of a connected geographical region, which forms – at least by its natural borders – a unity and is usually perceived as such. In this geographical region, there are various independent companies, which provide goods and services the customer can use during the stay. The main players in this region (with its natural components) form the competition unit destination. In order to represent this competition unit in the market, a coordinated organization – a destination management organization (DMO) – is necessary to match and coordinate the different interests of the companies. By this, a united representation of the destination in the market is made possible (Scherhag, 2011, p. 187; Scherhag, 2013). The addressees of the different activities of a DMO can be basically divided into two areas (figure 9.1): focused on internal players on one hand (main players, companies in the destination) and on external customers on the other hand (business partners such as airlines, tour operators as well as the customers in the destination). The activities of a DMO are quite general within the destination, e.g., political or administrative tasks, but it is also essential to coordinate the touristic-economical activities and the political objectives of the stakeholder in the destination. Furthermore, there is the cooperation with paramount organizations (e.g. regional marketing organizations or marketing cooperation like Magic Cities) to increase the range in external communication.

2.2 Disruptions in the destination

Destinations are complex, fragile formations with a variety of elements, which (partly) cooperate on different levels of effect. The cooperation can be based on a contract or on a practical basis. Numerous general disruptions or disruptions in

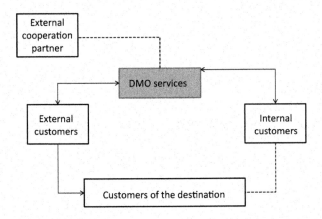

Figure 9.1 Addressees of activities in a DMO
Source: Own illustration

everyday processes can harm the performance sustainably. Possible reasons can be (similar to Jossé, 2004, p. 200; Kreilkamp, 2005, p. 36):

- Natural disasters (flooding, avalanches, volcanic eruption, tsunami, climate warming)
- Epidemics and pandemics (e.g. SARS)
- Terroristic or criminal acts (e.g. kidnapping tourists)
- Disagreement and lack of coordination of the main players in a destination (e.g. controversial advertisement, controversial appeal of target groups, overbooking)
- Old infrastructure or a disproportion between existing touristic offers and the needs of the attracted target group
- Restrictions to the offer (closure of natural areas, renovation of hotels)
- Failure of relevant infrastructure or important performance factors (e.g. health resort, swimming pool, ski lift – Theuerkorn, 2005, p. 243)
- Damaged performance processes (e.g. lack in quality, lack in coordination of linked performances)
- Change in legal form of a DMO

The examples stated above are partly cause and partly effect – in the sense of complex causal connections often even both. The causes can arise *within* the DMO (e.g. lack of assertiveness of the management, unclear positioning, suboptimal communication processes) or *outside* the responsibility of the destination management (e.g. natural disaster). They can be long-term and of strategic nature, but also considering operative processes (similar to Pikkemaat & Peters, 2005, p. 329ff.). Often the disruptions are experienced as sudden critical incidents in terms; however, many of them are based on long-term developments (or oversights) such as missing avalanche protections, postponed urgent invests, not-realizing of changing customers' demands.

Reasons for growing disruptions or enhanced vulnerability of the system "destination" are:

- Savings through cost-cutting programs, such as cutbacks in primary capacities (e.g. closure of public swimming pools, cutbacks in staff resources)
- Increased vulnerability through connection of system elements in e.g. electronic data bases and reservation systems. They summarize the potentials and products of the main players and build up (internal) logics and dependencies of booking processes (e.g. when accommodation A → than leisure facility B → for price X possible). The interdependency of the subsystems of a destination or the subsystems of the overall system increases.
- "Insidious" developments, where the effects are known latently, but do not require immediate action or the action is required on a higher level; those effects are usually experienced later, but are not reversible in most cases (e.g. climate warming).
- The general tendency towards centralization and the establishment of larger units (few big accommodations or leisure facilities instead of many small

ones) increase their vulnerability due to a higher dependency in a zero-mistake-promise.

- By stress the particular performance factors increases the overall vulnerability in case of a failure (e.g. failure of the mountain train, closure of the skiing area); this can also be applied if the damage is only suspected or communicated in a forum.
- Faster information processes
- Experienced and better-informed visitors
- Increasing number of nature-related impacts (e.g. hurricanes)
- Extensive reporting in the media in cases of disruption increase the pressure on the companies and the DMO

(Jossé & Scherhag, 2013, p. 39)

Equally various as the probable causes of a disruption in a destination are the effects of disruptions:

- Damage in general (e.g. damaged infrastructure)
- Costs of rescue
- Costs of tidying up
- Reduction or loss of capacity
- Compensatory payments or services
- Reduced usage until complete restoration (e.g. street closure, construction noise)
- Reduced attractiveness of DMO/drop in image
- Drop in revenues and profitability
- Compensatory costs for lost customer segments

(Jossé & Scherhag, 2013, p. 39)

The stated damages are causally connected. This can and has to be the starting point for any incident management: An earthquake itself cannot be prevented, but at least in case of a settlement decision, another location could be chosen or the building could be built up earthquake-proof. Using networks, e.g., a loss of capacity can be balanced on short-term or extensive and reliable information can help to avoid a drop in image.

3. Business Continuity Management (BCM)

3.1 History of business continuity management

Trouble-shooting has always been part of the everyday operation process. Another root of BCM is the military (especially concerning logistic problems), from business studies the contingency planning is a precursor – and ever since an essential part (UNISDR Africa, 2012, p. 16ff.). The alleged Y2K problem and "9/11" helped that BCM was focused on a disruption-free usage of hardware and software. The next level of development recognized companies in general as entities that are liable to break down.

Due to flooding, hurricanes and terror attacks as well as possible consequential effects (mass panic, economic disruption after an earthquake etc.) the government organizations developed resilient plans and instructions for BCM. In Great Britain, for example, local and regional forums about development, implementation and improvement of BCM exist (Greater London Authority, w.Y.). Since the Contingency Act in 2004 BC plans are used for maintenance of potentials and processes in cities and other regional authorities – and as well for touristic destinations (Faulkner, 2001, p. 136).

Since the ISO 22301 and various initiatives by the UN to secure the functionality of communities (e.g. UNISDR, 2011) the concept of continuity and its required instruments became a worldwide discussion topic that furthermore gains importance by contributing to build up resilience.

Being originally reactive and connected to emergency planning (e.g. BSI, 2009), BCM has evolved. According to current understanding there is a strategic dimension in a sense of an integral proactively designed guarantee of a continued existence (e.g. Elliott, Swartz, & Herbane, 2010, p. 3ff. and 23ff.). In fact, an operative view is not enough: the stoppage of a single supplier or a onetime lack in quality control can reach strategic importance in a short time period, in case the customers are unsatisfied due to respective infection potential, there is negative feedback in blogs and the image of the product and/or the company drops. Besides short-term measures, recovery measures have to be implemented on a strategic level, too (Brauner, 2001, p. 12ff.).

3.2 BCM approach in the destination management

Disruptions are the mission of BCM. Those can usually be removed, balanced or at least overcome by own means. However, the thereby created damages can be enormous: Apart from the *primary damages* (e.g. destruction of a hotel by avalanche), *secondary damages*, such as tidying up, special transportation, additional costs of compensating solutions, have to be recognized. Sometimes also *tertiary damages* are possible: maybe the disruptions involve an infection risk and consequences for other destination elements or functions (e.g. panic because of a single incident of robbery). A lack in crisis plans and unclear information policies can increase them and finally lead to a long-term drop in bookings and revenues.

This is how cause-and-effect chains arise in which individual objects or phenomena can have both cause and effect characteristics: the bad image of a destination can have an effect on its performance offer (which actually is not subject for complaint), and vice versa insufficient offers can have an effect on the image. Nature, extent and length of those consequences is basically dependent on the importance for the customer and the substitution possibilities (other equal or compensating offers).

Figure 9.2 shows which effects disruptions can have on the demand lines in destinations. Some offer parts are added for this example, while the erased offer parts are crossed out. The effects are highly dependent on the respective offer. This

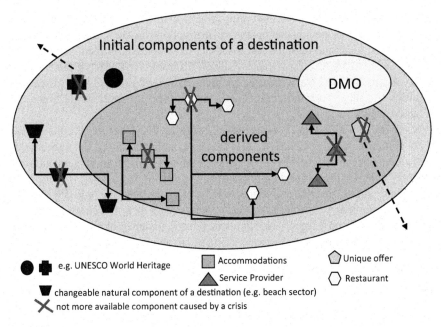

Figure 9.2 Streams of demand in case of disruptions in the destination
Source: Jossé & Scherhag (2013, p. 41)

means that in case of a disruption in the initial components/offer of a destination the demand can be diverted if there is a comparable substitute offer. For example, this is possible for the beach sector: If one beach sector is not usable, guests can usually use another one. This is equally applicable for a majority of derived components/offer, such as hotels, leisure services or gastronomy businesses. If main parts of the offer are affected, e.g., the theme park "Europapark" in Rust, the German Museum in Munich or the Oktoberfest in Munich, the major demand of the destination will shift towards another destination. The risk of this consequence is even higher concerning disruptions in the initial components, as could be seen with the oil contamination in the Gulf of Mexico after the disaster of the Oil platform Deepwater Horizon.

Furthermore, it has to be differentiated who or which organization is affected by the crisis. In case of a fire in a hotel this would be:

- The hotel, which is destroyed by fire (loss of existence basis) → during the renovation there are no earning; in worst case: insolvency
- The customers who booked the hotel have no accommodation for their stay → demand might be diverted to other hotels
- The hotel staff has no workplace → possibility to divert to other hotels as well

- The other hotels in the destination may profit from the extra demand, in case they are not already fully booked, and so the destination can profit as a whole, because there is no loss of customers for the destination itself
- The DMO as an organization is affected; it needs to provide the demanding customers with information

The scenario looks a bit different in the case of a disruption in main parts of the offer, because it is often a part of the offer which depicts a unique selling point for the destination. Being without a USP can lead to a decline in demand for the whole destination, which affects most of the main players in the destination. In this case, a corrected offer has to be communicated until the disruption is eliminated (e.g. cleaning up the beach after an oil catastrophe). In the extreme case, a new strategic orientation has to be developed for the destination, e.g., in case of the destruction of a world heritage object (e.g. destruction of temple in Timbuktu by Islamists).

Disruptions, their causes and risk potential with *primary and follow-up damages* have to be proactively identified. The next step is to develop compensation measures and alternative plans as well as to strengthen the overall resilience. It is not only about the handling of a perceived crisis but also about the avoidance and early development of alternative handling options, before the disruption is actually taking place.

Objects of BCM from the point of view of a destination (Jossé & Scherhag, 2013, p. 39):

- **Processes:** e.g. supply chain with consideration of involved main players, production and availability of flat rates and allocation of quotas of individual parts, target group definition, communication of offers as well as reservations/bookings – from the consumer's point of view one of the most important process steps.
- **Potentials:** e.g. parks, hotels, special equipment, transport infrastructure, natural offers
- **Products and programmes:** type of offer (e.g. transportation, health treatment) as well as the quality on the level of the main players as a direct provider of the service towards the customer
- **People (SPOF):** e.g. mayor, representatives, coordinators, testimonials
- **Structures:** e.g. structure of the DMO and the network of the different players in a destination as well as the responsibility for individual tasks; flexible provision of alternative capacities (by the DMO only restricted possibility, in case of failure of main players), but also – regarding the level of main players – successor arrangement for the family hotel businesses in a destination, as this could be a cause for less offers
- **Systems:** e.g. destinations in total, individual performance areas such as theme park, ski lifts, health resort, reservation systems, care of data bases by the main player (high potential for mistakes by the principle of "many hands")

Disruptions of those factors not only concern spectacular incidents well-covered by the media, but also insidious, less clearly perceived developments and problems (e.g. as mentioned the successor arrangement for the family hotel business, competitive behavior of the main player, slowdown in investment in a destination). The latter includes especially change market conditions and a changed consumer behavior, whereas both factors are mutually dependent; delayed investments lead to the offer not being appropriate for the customer expectations anymore so that they shift to "new" destinations.

3.3 The process of BCM

The heart of BCM is the identification of critical performance processes and potentials, the assessment of those (e.g. regarding extent of damage, vulnerability, risk of infecting other performance elements) conducted in the context of a business impact analysis (BIA) with the objective to secure the perception of the destination and its economic and ecological maintenance as well as to minimize the extent of damage to the DMO and the main players at the same time. In order to do that the business model of the destination has to be understood first and dependencies, interfaces and susceptibilities have to be examined (figure 9.3).

The first step ("**Understanding the business**") is about the basic structure, the players and the elements of a destination as well as the mutual interdependencies and external factors. This means the focus lies on the dependency of main players and activities of the DMO (e.g. marketing, outdoor advertising) but also on the measures of the individual companies. For example, an increase in prices in individual areas of the destination product's value chain can affect the other levels or

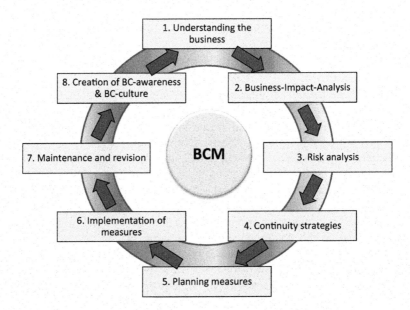

Figure 9.3 Detailed Process of BCM

Source: Jossé & Scherhag (2013, p. 43)

the established main players of those other areas (e.g. a significant increase in entry fees for the theme park in the destination as an important part of the derived offer). Furthermore, all endangered potentials and critical performance processes as well as their connections have to be captured. Afterwards, those will be evaluated in the (2) *business impact analysis* (BIA) with *focus on the effects* (e.g. the effect increased entry fees have on the number of days/nights booked). After this a (3) *risk analysis* will be carried out *focusing on the causes* (assessment of the probability of the occurrence of various scenarios and their evaluation regarding defined ratios and key figures such as revenue, pax, etc.). This assessment is followed by the basic decision of the (4) *continuity strategy* (e.g. build up own alternative capacities, secure a failure by cooperating with neighboring destinations, counteract proactive disruption causes, focus on strong image and quick communication), which has to be in line with the basic principle of the destination. Then, explicit *measures are planned* (5) and *implemented* (6), while providing the required infrastructure. Using regular *testing* strategies, plans and measures are proofed and adapted if necessary (7). These steps are accompanied by the creation of *BCM awareness* and a *BC culture* (8) – both a challenge for the domestic marketing of the DMO.

One of the main elements of the BC process is the BIA. For the assessment, the classical risk calculation (impact multiplied by the probability) should not be used: if there is even the slightest probability, there has to be preparation against any huge damage (e.g. tiny risk of an airplane crashing into a nuclear reactor). In comparison to risk management, the BIA examines major damages concerning a possible sustained disruption to a threat to existence (BCI, 2010, p. 12). In order to evaluate, different scenarios of failure should be created for all relevant business processes of vital importance; existing and possible measures for the reduction of effects should be taken into consideration (Engel, 2005, p. 44).

As an approach of evaluation, the following instruments can be applied (Jossé, 2015, p. 36):

- Bath-tub model
- Disruption-matrix
- Network analysis
- Cross-impact analysis
- Methods of error analysis, such as FMEA, Ishikawa diagram etc.

In the following, the first two and less-known instruments are presented. The bath-tub model (figure 9.4) will be explained first.

The y-axis shows for example the capacity (e.g. # of guests), the revenues or the profit; depending on the chosen figure, the curves in the diagram will differ! The x-axis shows the time. In phase I the company performs normally. In phase II the level of performance drops. Phase III shows the reduced performance (extreme case = 0). A change to emergency stage (in the picture illustrated as higher level) should at least secure the economically justifiable minimum of the service/production. At the same time, measures are taken in order to re-increase

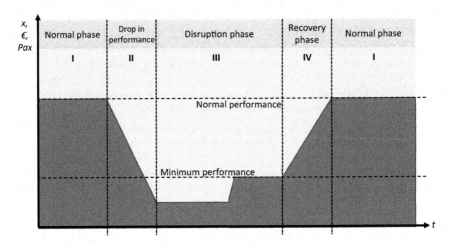

Figure 9.4 Bath-tub-model introduced by Jossé
Source: Jossé (2011, p. 19f.) and Jossé (2015, p. 36)

production as quickly as possible: this recovery curve in phase IV is a mirror-image of the curve in phase II, but it is also possible that the recovery curve looks different.

This depiction is only a basic model. In fact, there are infinite possibilities of what the curves especially in the phases II and IV can look like, e.g.:

- A vertical line as disruption or recovery: e.g. complete loss of power, closure of an airport, closure of a cable railway, closure of the only access road, health treatment card lacks in functionality because of a failure in the databank
- Linear: e.g. in phase II, traffic jam because of congestion
- S-curve: at first slow, then large drop or rise (compare with life cycle concept), e.g. mass evacuation
- In steps (like a staircase): e.g. in phase IV, new customer groups are won little by little
- Mix of the variations above

The failure is despicable as a surface area, which is meant to be reduced. In order to do so, there are three (combined) options to choose from, which will be explained using short examples (Jossé & Scherhag, 2013, p. 44).

First, delay the failure: controlled avalanche explosions, improve dyke protection, install flooding polder, secure neuralgic streets against weather (tunnel).

Second, earlier recovery: quick procurement of alternative capacities, diversion to disruption-free offers, proofed emergency and BC plans, crisis committees running smoothly, persuading crisis communication (within the DMO as well as towards external).

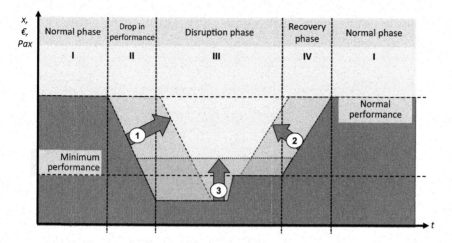

Figure 9.5 Options for minimization of damage
Source: Jossé (2011, p. 22f.) and Jossé (2016, p. 79)

Third, minimize the failure: directly usable free capacities, disruption-free diversions (e.g. hotel as well as all other local offers), disruption or restricted offer range compensated by attractive alternative offers, maintain the customer satisfaction despite the lack in offer.

Theoretically, the range of compensation possibilities is unlimited; however, there are geographic, physical and financial boundaries in a destination. One example should show that measures should be implemented combined, because as a bundle of measures an immense minimization of the overall damage might be possible.

For example, essential parts of the offer of a destination fail (e.g. parking space close to the Valley Station in a winter sport area). To balance the failure, the following coordinated options are put into practice (Figure 9.6): (A) balance by usage of free areas in direct proximity (crucial to signpost), (B) offer a shuttle service from parking spaces farther away, (C) communication of alternative entries to the winter sport area, (D) creation of alternative offers in the region (without the need to use the lift), etc.

The BIA examines disruptions *focusing on the effects*. In the next step, *the focus* has to be *on the origin*. Therefore, the relevant disruptions are checked for possible causes; in the following *risk analysis* those will be assessed and possible dealings with those causes are recommended. In fact, the risk as a negative divergence can occur at three points in the causal chain.

In all three starting points, measures can be taken. Basically, the options known from dealing with risks can be used here (risk avoidance, risk minimization, risk transfer, risk carrying).

The bath-tub model as well as the disruption matrix (Table 9.1) allows the integration of all essential BC process-steps by not only analyzing the disruptions

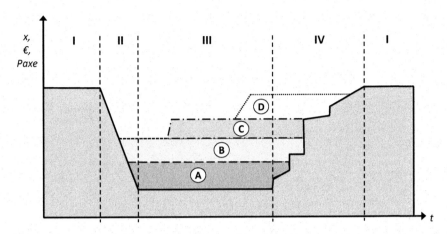

Figure 9.6 Compensation bundle to reduce effects
Source: Jossé & Scherhag (2013, p. 44) and Jossé (2016, p. 78)

Table 9.1 Disruption matrix

#	Disruption	Primary damage	Follow-up damages	Threat of infection for image?	Existing substitute?	Measures suffice?	Further measures	Required resources
1	Failure ski lift	x	x	**X**	partly	yes	. . .	. . .
2	Failure hotel	x		0	yes	yes		
3	Buried road	**X**	**X**	X	barely	no		
4	Target groups not compatible	x	**X**	**X**	partly	partly		

Source: Jossé & Scherhag (2013, p. 44)

but taking existing compensation possibilities, taken measures or measures to be taken in the future, into account. This makes sense as existing measures or measures which are easy to be taken can minimize, in deed, the examined damages during their creation and/or in their consequence. For example, a buffer of one week (considering other following processes) can be established for a procurement process; in case of a stoppage of the supplier, a substitute delivery can take place within three days. This existing option suffices; the disruption does not have to be pursued.

A table like this gives an overview and combines and discussed all relevant elements of the analysis and the derived measures in the context (similar Jossé, 2015,

p. 36f.). In the example, disruption #2 is well prepared, while the consequences of disruption #3 are immense as the existing measures do not suffice. Effective plans and measures have to be developed and prepared so that they can be taken directly into action in case of a crisis. Immense damage of image is possible in disruption #4, in case of a clash of target groups which differ in their behavior a lot. The available measures suffice only partly, e.g. the individual decisive behavior of the customers can hardly be influenced; customer streams have to be managed by the target group adequately by the respective offers of the main player or the tour operators.

While developing adequate BC plans compensation possibilities plays a decisive role (e.g. other means of transportation in case of a closed road), the substitute can be within the entity (change booking to other offers), provided that the main players are able to cooperate. In comparison to a tour operator, who probably has contracts with multiple hotels and therefore can quickly react in case of an emergency, individual arrangements are necessary within a destination: A DMO rarely contains such contractual connections or rather the main players compete with each other and are therefore only conditionally available for compensation of individual providers. This shows that for a fundamental BCM, it is crucial to establish a network of cooperation partners or rather a network of the main players within a destination and strengthen the team spirit. On the other hand, it is barely possible to prepare alternative capacities in a SME structure (family businesses are very common). In case of a closed ski area, the establishment of a shuttle to the next ski area or the usage of alternative capacities in other hotels leads to additional costs; however, the customer satisfaction and the image of the destination remain intact. The individual player might have to expect a reduction in his own economic success.

Following the mitigation by existing or built-up compensation solutions, appropriate measures for the remaining disruptions have to be taken. Adapted risk strategies, known from risk management, can be applied here, also in combination with each other (Jossé & Scherhag, 2013, p. 45):

- *Avoid the disruption or the consequences* (e.g. seaweed is removed from the beach before the guests wake up → a device made of sound-absorbing material is necessary), avoiding a stone avalanche by securing the mountain with concrete, nets, etc., or by over tunneling the street itself (counteracting many disruptions)
- *Reduce* the disruption or the consequences (optimized and confidence-building communication with the main players, the customers, the partners; extreme weather warning, clear signposting, control systems, controlled explosion of snow floors)
- *Transfer* the disruption or the consequences *internally* (within the destination from one player to another, e.g. substitution of means of transport or overnight options; within the DMO, e.g. competent staff who can replace each other)
- *Shift* the disruption or the consequences *externally* (e.g. disaster control, insurances)
- *Carry* the disruption or the consequences (in case of huge damages referring to a remaining risk after a damage reduction has been achieved by other measures)

All stated cases aim for *preventive* (e.g. increase overall robustness and flexibility of the DMO) as well as *reactive* options (e.g. vouchers as compensation for noise pollution) (Engel, 2005, p. 40).

4. Conclusion

Disruptions in a destination can develop into substantial crisis, whereas the crisis does not start with an emergency situation but long before by wrong decision making or by no disruption prevention. A particular problem is that the susceptibility for disruptions increases due to a multitude of connected subsystems and processes as well as the general dependence on the environmental impact. BCM aims to recognize and overall reduce causes, courses and consequences of operative and strategic disruptions, in order to continue the processes as quickly and smoothly as possible, while protecting the destination, the DMO and its main players from larger restrictions and existential damages.

The DMO is the main leader supporting the process of awareness, kicking off the analysis of critical potentials and processes, as well as escorting the development of appropriate strategies and measures (Ghaderi, Som, & Henderson, 2012, p. 83). The costs of BCM should not be decisive. The question rather should be "what would it cost us not having BCM?" Therefore, a change in awareness has to take place in destinations – willingness of the players in the tourism industry to cooperate is a basic requirement to avoid and overcome crisis anticipatively. BCM is an indispensable approach.

References

BCI – Business Continuity Institute. (2010). *Good practice guidelines 2010*. Ein Leitfaden zur Umsetzung. Retrieved from www.bcmnet.ch/downloads/Publikationen/2012-03-08-gpg2010de.pdf (Accessed 24 February 2013).

Brauner, C. (2001). *Präventive Schadensbewältigung. Mehr gewinnen als verlieren*. Zürich: Swiss Re.

BSI – Bundesamt für Sicherheit in der Informationstechnik. (BSI 2009). *Notfallmanagement. BSI-Standard 100–4 zur Business Continuity*. Köln.

Elliott, D., Swartz, E., & Herbane, B. (2010). *Business continuity management* (2nd ed.). New York and Abingdon: Routledge.

Engel, H. (2005). Gesprengte Ketten. *Risknews*, 05/2005, 39–45.

Faulkner, B. (2001). Towards a framework for tourism disaster management. *Tourism Management, 22*, 135–147.

Ghaderi, Z., Som, A.P.M., & Henderson, J.C. (2012). Tourism crises and island destinations: Experiences in Penang, Malaysia. *Tourism Management Perspectives, 2–3*, 79–84.

Greater London Authority. Retrieved from www.london.gov.uk/priorities/london-prepared/preparing-emergencies (Accessed 23 February 2013).

Jossé, G. (2004). *Strategische Frühaufklärung in der Touristik*. Wiesbaden: Springer.

Jossé, G. (2011). *Business continuity management, lecture at the DMU Leicester*. Leicester (Lecture sheets).

Jossé, G. (2015, September/Oktober). Business Continuity Management – Identifizierung und Analyse von Großstörungen als Kernaufgabe. *Controller Magazin*, S. 32–38.

Jossé, G. (2016, Juli/August). Business Continuity Management – Entwickeln von Kontinuitätsstrategien, Ableiten und Umsetzen von Maßnahmen und Absicherung der BCM-Prozesse. *Controller Magazin*, S. 77–84.

Jossé, G., & Scherhag, K. (2013). Business Continuity Management in der Destination. Störungen proaktiv erkennen, bewerten und handhaben. *Update 17*, WS 2013/14, S. 38–47.

Kreilkamp, E. (2005). Strategische Frühaufklärung im Rahmen des Krisenmanagements im Tourismusmarkt. In H. Pechlaner & D. Glaeßer (Eds.), *Risiko und Gefahr im Tourismus. Erfolgreicher Umgang mit Krisen und Strukturbrüchen* (pp. 29–61). Berlin: Erich Schmidt Verlag.

Pforr, C. (2006). *Tourism in post-crisis is tourism in pre-crisis: A review of the literature on crisis management in tourism*. Curtin University of Technology, School of Management. Working Paper Series, No. 2006:1. Retrieved from https://espace.curtin.edu.au/handle/20.500.11937/36215 (Accessed on 20 February 2017).

Pikkemaat, B., & Peters, M. (2005). Alpine Katastrophen als Impuls für Innovationen im Tourismus. In H. Pechlaner & D. Glaeßer (Eds.), *Risiko und Gefahr im Tourismus. Erfolgreicher Umgang mit Krisen und Strukturbrüchen* (pp. 323–336). Berlin: Erich Schmidt Verlag.

Scherhag, K. (2011). Das Destinationsimage als Basis eines Wettbewerbsvorteils im Destinationsmanagement. In W. Gronau (Ed.), *Zukunftsfähiger Tourismus – Innovation und Kooperation* (pp. 187–194). Mannheim: MetaGIS Systems.

Scherhag, K. (2013). Destinationsmanagement als komplexe Aufgabe in der Touristik. *Update 16*, 26–31.

Theuerkorn, S. (2005). Krisenmanagement in touristischen Destinationen – Dargestellt am Beispiel Sachsen nach dem Hochwasser im August 2002. In H. Pechlaner & D. Glaeßer (Eds.), *Risiko und Gefahr im Tourismus. Erfolgreicher Umgang mit Krisen und Strukturbrüchen* (pp. 241–254). Berlin: Erich Schmidt Verlag.

UNISDR. (2011). *Disaster through a different lens*. Retrieved from www.unisdr.org/files/20108_mediabook.pdf (Accessed 10 May 2013).

UNISDR Africa. (2012). *Drought contingency plans and planning in the greater Horn of Africa*. Nairobi, Kenya. Retrieved from www.unisdr.org/africa (Accessed 10 May 2013).

Part III
Business aspects and strategies to increase resilience

10 Regional resilience – the special case of "money"

Georg Hechenberger

1. Introduction

Resilience is *"in"*, just like regionality – also understood as tourism-related destination management. Taken one at a time, both fields are experiencing a veritable boom. Combined, that is to say as a regional resilience, research is only starting out, none more so than regional resilience in the context of money and finance. One reason for this is that right there the dominating, yet related concept of *risk management* already covers large areas like, e.g., the recognition, appraisal, governance, surveillance, and communication of risks which are relevant for resilience. Moreover, it has hitherto not been possible to define resilience in a coherent way (Hechenberger, 2017, p. 249). Searching the countless definitions for commonalities, one again and again ends up with terms like resistivity, robustness, self-help, and autonomy. Contrary to risk management, here the crisis as such is, thus, focused on. In other words: resilience designates those properties (and their appropriation) which are essential to survive crises unscathed if possible, or even come off crises in a strengthened way. Resilience does not have a passive connotation, but it is closely connected with self-reliance, autonomy, and self-help. It is necessary to overcome crises by one's own efforts as far as possible. This is exactly where the "special case of money" already becomes apparent. Hardly any other system is more complex and more interconnected than the modern system of money and finance; even regional structures are integrated, after all. Insofar, there is no *beyond the system*. The resulting proverbial *systemic risk* is ever-present. Plus, the last crisis which is basically still enduring has revealed that, if indeed something of the kind is to be solved, it can only be done together with united forces.

Why is that? Is it even possible to achieve regional resilience in the money and finance sector under such conditions? If so, how? Plus, does this apply to tourism as well? These are the questions which are to be considered subsequently.

2. The optimal currency zone

Behind the questions asked are the complex and controversial issues of the optimal currency zone which is both complex and debated vigorously, along with the corresponding institutional framework (banks) – a large issue, which can only be introduced briefly in this context:

To the extent that a binding aspect to the various currency zone theories can be emphasized at all, it is that of a socio-economic homogeneity, or the existence of mechanisms for the creation of such homogeneity, which is as comprehensive as possible (which can also be described as "dependencies"). Mundell focused on the latter, when he defined regions as "areas within which there is factor mobility, but between which there is factor immobility" (Mundell, 1961, p. 658). Mundell's model of 2 countries displayed the insufficient balancing mechanism through exchange rates with asymmetric shocks, as opposed to internal devaluation. An effective balance thus rather takes place through factor mobility (migration flows of employees and capital). Likewise J. C. Ingram (1969) who focuses his analyses on capital flows. He confirms the mobility criterion by emphasizing the importance of integrating capital markets as fully as possible; the prerequisite for this is that capital flows can quickly and sensitively react to changes in interest rates. McKinnon (1963, 2001) finally focused on trade and concluded that the intensity of trade relations between two countries was crucial to their suitability for a common currency zone. The higher this *degree of openness*, the more damaging are exchange rate changes. Peter Kenen (1969) did not analyze Mundell's shocks in a country-specific way, but in a sector-specific way and arrived at the obvious conclusion that both sectoral structures and foreign trade structures which are strongly diversified can spare exchange rates. Hence, they are apt for a currency zone. Anyway, if stable exchange rates and similar preferential structures are prevailing over a long time, then a currency union likewise makes sense – as is stated by Vaubel (1978). De Grauwe (2012) has finally analyzed the most general political and institutional parameters (political context, economic-ideological basic orientation, financing of government expenses, similarities on the capital market and labor market, and the like) and, hence, brings a very comprehensive and much earlier represented understanding of the financial system full circle. As according to J. A. Schumpeter this reflects everything that a "people wants, does, suffers from, and . . . at the same time an essential influence on economic activities and the destiny of a people altogether springs from the financial system of a people" (Schumpeter, 1970, p. 1). In short: "The state of a financial system of a people is a symptom of all of its states" (Schumpeter, 1992, p. 12). Even here, money has already been more than just an economic factor, namely a social and, hence, particularly political factor. Insofar it does not surprise that the aptitude for participating in the Euro-currency union was indeed determined according to OCA-indices on the basis of regression and accompanied by empirical data. However, it has eventually to be classified much more a political than an economic decision (Korniichuk & Sorokina, 2007, pp. 20–21).[1]

Money zones and currency zones, hence, do not seem to be subject to *fundamental* limitations on size. If one thinks this through to the end, it does, however, lead to developing oligopolies or even monopolistic traits.[2] Opposite to this stands the idea of a pluralism of currencies, primarily represented by the Austrian school of political economy. Particularly Friedrich A. v. Hayek postulates the competition of currencies and even goes as far as to promote the privatization of the banking system and, thus, the creation of money (Hayek, 1978). Even more notable, though, is that J. M. Keynes, a classical economist who otherwise takes contrary positions to Hayek in many aspects, argues similarly on this point; he thinks:

> I sympathize . . . to those, who rather want to minimize than maximize the economic interconnections between nations. Ideas, knowledge, arts, hospitality, voyage – these are fields which should be international due to their nature. Yet, let us draw on domestic products whenever this seems prudent and is feasible in a reasonable way; and most of all, keep the finances primarily in a national context.
>
> (Keynes, 1933, p. 236)[3]

This brief outline shall particularly show one thing: discussions on an optimal currency zone have always been controversial and are by no means over. Behind this are just as many political-ideological positions as there are economic positions, which quite often leads to the fact that optimal currency zones are not brought about by appropriate homogeneity and balancing mechanisms of mobility, but – quasi the other way around – unified currency zones (shall) create (geo) politically strong unions – one of the main reasons for the tendency towards *size*.

Reinforcing this direction, general management principles like, e.g., principles for rationalization, cost-cutting, economies of scale (at best also "economies of scope")[4] and the like, apply for the institutional-organizational level (banks and other financial institutions) which accompany or precede such developments. This comes together with accumulation constraints and agglomeration constraints which are, after all, reinforced through *safety rules* required by law (particularly concerning equity and liability capital defined by, i.e., Basel I, II, III and IV). These, in turn, create bigger ownership structures, liability networks, and mutual investments.[5] So what does this mean for money and finance in the context of regional resilience?

One can support large currency unions or advocate national or even private currency competition, but a region or destination neither way is regarded an optimal currency zone.[6] Particularly with the monetary system and the finance system, small-scale design seems to be anachronistic, dysfunctional, economically inefficient, in any case socio-economical and politically suboptimal at the most. This does particularly apply to tourism. Not by chance it is most notably the export-oriented fraction of economy and, thus, tourism which welcome a preferably unified system for money and finance. Globalized, liberalized and standardized money and financial systems simplify the touristic core business. *Convenience* is rising. More trivially expressed: money transactions and, thus, money expenditure in general and travel as a rule become more low-threshold (keywords: price comparisons, conversions, payment transactions, etc.). Personal freedom to travel is therefore typically often accompanied by a comprehensive freedom of money and capital (see the 4 fundamental freedoms of the EU: freedom to travel and freedom of capital; plus freedom of goods and services[7]). On the other hand, however, there is an almost equally strong principle of the EU: that of *regionalism*, that of a Europe of *regions*. One can say *almost* because this principle is used in almost all areas of life and economy, except for money and finance. Regional food production, regional energy supply, regional infrastructure, even regional identity as such in its various forms (e. g., culturally) are not only well received, but also massively promoted – and, thus, regional resilience in these fields.

Regionality in the sense of a proper currency (including the corresponding, largely autonomous institutional and organizational framework) therefore does not seem desirable. But what if the globally interconnected and large monetary and financial system, which seemingly is without alternative,[8] no longer works? What about resilience in the sense of self-help of a region or destination? To do that, it is necessary to ask what it actually means that something is working in this context. In accordance with the classical-economic monetary functions, this means that money can no longer fulfil and especially can no longer adequately fulfil its exchange or payment function, its value retention and calculation function. As has already been suggested, however, money is much more than that; it is also a social and political factor. If you try to specify this factor, you will very quickly come up against the central concept of *trust*.[9]

Regarding the relationship between resilience, small-scale design in the form of regions or destinations, and trust as the core of money and finance, there is only so much to be said in advance: if *trust* is the central element in money and finance, then especially in times of crisis a small-scale, well-known, familiar socio-economic unit, e.g. the region or destinations, has a quasi-natural *competitive advantage*. Then, in times of crisis, the region can become an optimal currency area.[10]

In order to understand why and how money could become a *social construct* in the form of a *trust product*, however, a brief excursion into the history of money is necessary.

3. Excursion: the abstraction of money[11]

Up to now, only the classic-economic monetary *functions* have been mentioned: exchange or payment function, value retention and calculation function, i. e. what money does or can do, but not what it *is*. Money can only do all this if it has value and, thus, purchasing power. Tracing back to the origin of this value shows a continuous *process of abstraction*. Ludwig von Mises was the first to suggest this process in that he identified the value and purchasing power of money as traditional (and thus learned).[12] The origin of this *tradition* lies in the fact that money was not yet a means of exchange but a commodity itself – a commodity which was particularly well suited as an indirect means of exchange. Precious metals in general and gold in particular had this special suitability, proven in world history (especially gold repeatedly proved to be a particularly valuable and durable commodity).[13] The ratio of gold to other commodities, thus, determines the purchasing power of this *gold money*. In other words: at the beginning of the monetary economy, money still embodied real value itself. The rise of modern banking (in upper Italy at the times of Renaissance) began what can be called the *process of dissolution* or *abstraction*. From here on, money economy and the real economy, money and the real world as such, separated more and more.

Historically, the introduction of promissory notes and bills of exchange is regarded as a milestone in this development, which "uses money in a targeted manner and in a new "aggregate form" to overcome spatial and temporal distances" (Musil, 2005, p. 42) (Here, too, the tendency to large systems is already swinging with). Coins (first as curative or commodity money with corresponding material or minting value, later on with successively decreasing material value), banknotes, deposit money, various forms of promissory notes, credit cards, and finally digital money in its currently most extreme form, the bitcoins, mark the way of these *aggregate forms*. Values and symbols representing these values have been visibly separated. Ongoing standardization and generalization flanked this development.

The separation of money symbol and value was a prerequisite for an even more profound abstraction. This was the only way to gradually reduce or dissolve these (background or coverage) values. In particular, the *gold standard*, i.e. the tried and tested (original) coverage by gold stocks (even until the 19th century, silver cover was often valid) was noticeably weakened. (Bretton-Woods, for example, stands for a far-reaching abandonment of gold cover by tying it to a partially gold-covered dollar, flanked by floating exchange rates within the IMF. Although exchange rate systems are again more heterogeneous today – a mixture of fixed and variable ratios – this further decoupling of real values remained. Current gold stocks can only be described as *emergency funds*.) The (preliminary) *high-end product* of this development is *digital fiat money*. Digital stands – as already mentioned above – for the ultimate detachment of symbolism (coins, notes, bills, and the like). Fiat money (fiat derived from Latin *"it will"*) is money drawn *from nothing* and is without real cover.

As an insubstantial digital code, detached from any symbolism (Kalthoff & Vormbusch, 2012, p. 20), the prerequisites for maximum size and speed of the system were now optimized. The abolition of the *old* system's remnants (especially cash) is currently under discussion, following this trend. The validity (money = derived from *valid* or *to be valid*) did not cancel this; on the contrary. Ultimately, money achieves *cipher status*, a status usually attributed only to religions.[14] Because ciphers construct "forms of meaning" without "relation to something else, but they are themselves" (Luhmann, 1992, p. 33). Since then, money has stood for itself. With other words: as a *cipher*, there is no longer any need for real references – and it still works.

Money can, thus, practically at the touch of a button, be created directly via central banks and indirectly – through the credit system – also by commercial banks in a theoretically unlimited way. As the current monetary policy of the European Central Bank (ECB) shows, this is increasingly becoming practice. And to the extent that this development took place and is still taking place, the validity and acceptance of money has been growing and continues to grow from a question of real value to a question of pure faith and trust.[15]

In summary, and based on the concepts of the new institutional economy: the development of money marks the way from an asset of search via an asset of experience to an asset of trust.[16] As a social convention based on trust, money has achieved a degree of freedom that was and is ultimately fundamental for all liberal and neo-liberal developments. Its extraordinary performance and its great dangers are based on this fact.[17]

Trust is always accompanied by communication. In this respect, it is helpful to refer to a concept of money based on sociological system theory, where money is regarded as a *symbolically generalized communication medium*. Once again, the high degree of abstraction is *symbolically* underlined. *Generalized* indicates high standardization. And *communication* points to a constitutive element of society that goes beyond mere economic effects (similar to what Schumpeter already sees as being reflected in the currency, as mentioned above), especially since in systems theory society consists of communication.[18] Going beyond the already discussed question of the optimal currency zone, this communicative conception of money helps to better understand the *ambivalence of its system size* and, thus, the "special case of money".

The economic-technical interpretation of a communication medium leads to the question of *mass suitability*. In contrast, the social interpretation supports small, manageable and *familiar* units. The conceptual similarity (communication medium) already points to analogies to (technical) communication media (e.g. mobile phone) with the characteristics of network goods; that is to say goods whose (functional) value[19] increases with the number of users (which in turn requires a high degree of generalization and standardization). Success mainly results from the number of participants and the size of the network. Technical media often reach capacity limits (network congestion). Pure network assets are correspondingly rare. Money, especially in view of the almost unlimited creation mentioned above, combined with the most efficient (technical) networks (keyword: high-frequency trading; *real-time money transfer* is in preparation) is close to it. Once again, this shows the way to size and standardization in the monetary and financial system.

On the other hand, there is the social interpretation. With a medium whose substance is trust, communication can stabilize and strengthen that trust, but also the opposite. In small, manageable, well-known (i.e. highly traditional), and thus, *familiar* social unities, where social mechanisms (also sanctions) still have a direct effect, e.g., in a region or destination, confidence-building measures can be more easily set and verified than, for example, in global structures.[20] In other words: Trust in large structures is system trust (Luhmann, 1989, p. 23). Confidence in small structures is personal or at least more personal trust. Accordingly, any communication of those who are in charge of politics in general and of the heads of central banks in particular serves only one purpose: to strengthen (system) trust! (No wonder that every syllable that is pronounced or not pronounced[21] at an ECB or FED press conference is put on the gold scale.[22])

(System) confidence[23] is influenced by any kind of communication – including omitted ones – due to the communicative function of money (which is reflected in prices at product level). For this reason, the mere idea of (system) alternatives at regional level – e.g., in the form of regio funds – can, reinforced by network characteristics, have a negative impact on the system confidence of the existing system. Put in an exaggerated way: confidence in a small, regional system can be interpreted as distrust of the large system. Consistently thought through to the end, proper decoupled regional monetary and financial systems may, thus, promote the occurrence of the case for which they are designed to cope. Trust is not divisible in this sense. Overly autonomous (regional) developments in the monetary and financial system therefore always run the risk of being interpreted as system-threatening, lacking in solidarity or even separatist. (Central bank privileges are therefore well protected. As a rule, they are thus tolerated by the appropriate authorities only as long as they remain marginal in economic terms.[24]

Nevertheless, the number and diversity of alternative initiatives – above all complementary currencies and regio funds – is considerable (regarding Germany: http://community-currency.info/de/).

4. Complementary currencies resp. regio funds[25]

The name says it all. Such systems are complementary to the existing monetary system[26]; a rough distinction of complementary currencies is made between those which are oriented towards a reserve currency and those which are performance-based. For the former, an exchange ratio to a reserve currency (usually euro or dollar) is defined. The latter are based on defined performance units (e.g., units of time), thus, getting close to natural exchange systems. The classic economic monetary functions are then restricted to varying degrees. For example, the means of payment function due to regionally restricted validity, the value retention function due to *"compulsory use"* for other negative interest rates in order to increase the circulation rate (but due to the crisis the euro zone, too, is now already working with negative interest rates), and the calculation function through conversion ratios (discounts are often used for social purposes in the region).

Money and, thus, value creation remain increasingly concentrated in the region – this is the core of the argumentation. However, while regional economic effects are discussed critically (Rösl, 2008), the social and trust-building effects are largely without controversy. There is also no dispute about the resilience effect, i.e. regio money as a tried and tested self-help instrument in the event that "domestic money fulfils its function as a means of exchange, as a computing unit or as a means of preserving value only to a very limited extent" (Rösl, 2005, p. 243), especially since the origin of regio money lies in the crisis.[27] Thus, for example, the introduction of a parallel currency to deal with the current crisis in Greece is proposed (Mayer, 2012).

However, a boom of regio money spurred on for years by the financial crisis seems to have passed its zenith.[28] The oldest still existing system, the Swiss *WIR system*, shows how complementary currency systems can be successful beyond any crisis for decades. A secret of its long existence since 1934 lies in its *flexibility* and *adaptability*. Today, WIR is both a fully-fledged commercial bank and a proper currency system linked to the CHF. (The WIR-Frank is certified according to ISO 4217 with a letter code, corresponding to the CHF.) WIR itself refers to its function of creating money by means of loans, similar to the Swiss National Bank. This means that there are no costs for credit and refinancing – a cost advantage that is reflected in lower interest rates. With WIR money, payments can be made to all appropriately identified actors within Switzerland. WIR sees itself as *complementary*, namely as a "meaningful supplement to the established cash cycle and makes a valuable contribution to a healthy domestic economy" (www.wir.ch). The system is organized in a cooperative manner, as is the case with almost all complementary currencies. (Cooperatives form an ideal framework under company law, because they were also created as self-help instruments in times of crisis. Membership promotion and regionalism are fundamental principles.). However, critics say that although organized in the form of a co-operative society, WIR, as a full-fledged commercial bank today, is by now too far removed from its original idea (see Creutz, 2005, p. 30). In the author's opinion, however, this is precisely the *recipe for sustainability* in the form of the necessary flexibility and adaptability. In its beginnings as an instrument for self-help and crisis management, WIR, too, was demarcated and delimited in a stricter way, i.e. "protectionist". In *normal*, prosperous times, however, as long as the established monetary and banking system continues to function satisfactorily, it is closely linked to this. Similar to Kennedy (Kennedy, 2005, p. 22), it even has an anti-cyclical effect and can thus contribute to an overall stabilizing effect. If the economy is booming, it will grow more moderately or even more strongly during periods of stagnation or recession.

Many regional currency systems (see Becker, 2006, pp. 32–37, Creutz, 2005, p. 31) find themselves in such a field of tension between functionality and idealism. Only in times of crisis can complementary or regional currency systems exploit their full potential. The rule of thumb for the degree of resilience efficiency can be: The stronger the crisis, the greater the decoupling from the central currency system and its institutions (banks); or in short: from systemic risk. The transitions from reserve currency to performance-covered systems, possibly mixed forms, should be adapted to the situation and handled flexibly. (Flexibility, adaptation and situational orientation are regarded as basic resilience qualities.[29])

5. Résumé

As long as the established monetary and banking systems continue to function, the author believes that the expectations in regional-economic effects of complementary money systems and regio money systems should not be exaggerated; such effects should play a secondary role. Conversely, he says, too little reference is made to the roots and, thus, to the crisis effects or resilience effects of such concepts. Moderate regional economic success outside of crises should play a secondary role. According to the findings of the *learning region* (see Brückner, 2002), action should nevertheless not be taken too late, i.e. only in the event of a crisis. In variation of a well-known proverb the following rather holds true: "*practice in time, and then you can do in distress*" (not by chance one of the most successful regio money systems, the Chiemgauer, has started as a school project).

Last but not least, it is also the timely learned strengthening of social cohesion that can represent the "decisive difference for regions in times of crisis" (Volkmann, 2009, p. 254).

Although there is a lack of research, it can be assumed that there is little or no incentive for tourists to participate in regional monetary systems.[30] To this end, there would need to be an extraordinarily strong connection with the region. At best, it must even be assumed that from an external, i.e. also from a tourist point of view, a region money principle that is too consistently applied encourages the accusations of protectionism that are repeatedly raised anyhow (see Rösl, 2006, p. 12). In any case, however, there are positive effects for tourists indirectly. This is the case, for example, when regions rely on regional products and producers are, thus, supported, which in turn helps to ensure that tourist businesses are supplied with high-grade, regional quality. (However, all of this has to be relativized in that similar effects can also be achieved by (other) voluntary self-binding; for example, simply through the commitment – at best marketing-supported – to buy or commission only regionally.) Therefore, the relatively neglected crisis context seems to be more important here, too: namely, as regional currencies can contribute to stabilizing a region or destination in times of crisis, especially since the region can then exploit its *social potential*, its *confidence potential* and, thus, its *self-help potential* – aspects which in turn are a prerequisite for any economic and therefore also tourist (further) development.

Notes

1 Right when this article is written, Jean Claude Juncker demands the "wholesale" introduction of the Euro into all EU-member states on the occasion of the annual fall address of the European Commission President – after all as a proof of a political decision. (The circle is closed where political decisions are brought about by respective economic interest groups and their lobbying.)

2 J. Stiglitz event talks – beside other examples – about the exploitation of the monopoly power in such an everyday business as the payment system (Stiglitz 2017, p. 306f.).

3 While Keynes views the currency zone linked to a nation, Hayek even talks about a "Denationalization of Money" (Hayek 1978); insofar Hayek's terminology is closer to the one of a region, which can be seen as a currency-compliant and homogeneous unity beyond any national statehood. After all, value-related questions play a more important role than nationalities (the current EU-discussions on the most different "questions of solidarity" are an example for this).

4 Therefore compound effects; a lot of products offered and traded by investments banks can be interpreted as such (derivatives, leverage products and the like). The shown interest in a rather blurred distinction between commercial banks and investment banks can as well be explained by size effects and compound effects.

5 On the one hand, this makes the system more stable, but on the other hand, it also makes it more interconnected and therefore more virulent. (The system participants are more resistant, but if the disease does break out, it spreads faster.) This is particularly worrying in that at the head of the generally 2-layered bank hierarchy (especially in the case of cooperative banks also with 3-layer structures) the distinction between commercial and investment banks is too blurred. (Or better: *again* to blurred, because this was already in the 1920s one of the main reasons for a world financial crisis and led to the Glass-Steagall-Act.) And although regional banks – particularly in times of crisis – like

to emphasize their regional orientation as a particular strength, they are ultimately inseparably linked to the global financial market via precisely such structures, which is why the author believes that payments are more likely to be made from the bottom up, if systemic risks (particularly liabilities) become significant (not seldom argued by systemic relevance.)

6 Of course, the accuracy of this statement depends on how the region is ultimately defined (see Hechenberger, 2016, pp. 54). This is not being pursued any further here, as tourist regions in particular are defined as smaller in any case than the usually smallest currency zone, the nation or the nation state. Economically definable currency zones are usually politically overshaped!

7 More complex interrelationships ceteris paribus, especially since opportunities and risks are usually equalized; e.g., currency parity changes: devaluations are boosting exports and, thus, tourism (Greece could well use such devaluation at the moment); conversely, exports and tourism are suffering from a currency that is too strong (current example: Switzerland).

8 *No alternative* is to be put into perspective insofar as there are, of course, approaches to such alternatives; e.g., ethical banking or public-interest banks.

9 It's not surprising if J. Stiglitz points out that "more than money trust rules the world" (Stiglitz, 2017, p. 272).

10 However, in times of crisis the above-mentioned classic-economic currency zone factors are likely to remain more stable in small-scale structures than in large-scale economies.

11 Also see Hechenberger (2016, particularly 42)

12 L. v. Mises followed Carl Menger: According to Menger, the value of money simply results from supply and demand. However, demand presupposes its value (purchasing power). Menger's circular conclusion is: money demand arises because money has purchasing power, and it has purchasing power because it is in demand. This circle can only be resolved along the time axis. Current purchasing power is derived from previous purchasing power by the market participants; today's purchasing power is derived from yesterday's, yesterday's purchasing power is derived from yesterday's purchasing power, etc. Incidentally, abstraction of money has many names with Mises: commodity money (with cover), token money, credit money, money substitutes, certificates, etc. (Mises, 1924, particularly part 2: on monetary value; other monetary theorists argued even earlier in a similar vein; for example, Simmel's pioneering work "Philosophy of Money" is a representative example.; Simmel, 1989).

13 Even though the value of gold in large parts of the equation is only *attributed* and *conventional*. (In this respect, all money has always been a matter of trust, which is also reflected in traditional vocabulary: Credit, for example, is derived from the Latin *creditum* and means trust. And a creditor believes in the repayment of the borrowed money.) The true cover value can only be defined as a benefit, namely the benefit to be provided in the future.

14 Particularly Deutschmann refers to countless parallels between religions and modern money and finance (see Deutschmann, 2001).

15 Apart from that, trust is socially regarded as a "mechanism of reducing social complexity" (Luhmann, 1989). From this point of view, with increasing complexity and decreasing connection to reality, only trust could guarantee the "mass suitability" of the system. You don't need to understand money to use it. All you need is sufficient faith and trust (see Reifner, 2010, p. 410).

16 The quality of search goods can already be determined before the purchase (e.g., gold content), those of experience goods only after the purchase (begin of passing on) and those of trust goods only in a very difficult way or not at all (money is used, it has always worked, but one does not know why it actually works, and above all it can't work tomorrow).

17 Institutionally, the peak of this development is reflected in the investment banking system with its innumerable derivatives, leverage products and high-frequency trading.

18 In this context, it is negligible that the system-theoretical view of communication (Luhmann, 2010, p. 193) differs from that of everyday language use.

19 And, thus, most of all the economic value: but in terms of quantity and, more rarely, price (not to be confused with inferior goods, whose demand decreases with rising incomes).

20 One reason for this is that in small structures, cause-and-effect relationships are generally less diffused than in large systems, which are often even suspected of being some kind of "structured irresponsibility" (Honegger et al., 2010) and, thus, provide the ideal framework conditions for socializing losses and privatizing profits. Significantly some authors, including Joseph Stiglitz, calls this "American style socialism" (Stiglitz, 2017, p. 239).

21 *Omission,* insofar as we know, at the latest since Watzlawick, is impossible not to communicate (Watzlawick et al., 2000).

22 *Gold scale* is to be understood insofar as in a not unintentional double meaning the cover value of currencies is essentially no longer gold (or another tangible asset) but trust. A justified trust is backed by a corresponding economic performance, yes, social performance (see the explanations on the optimal currency zone) – more and more often also those that are only to be provided in the future (debt of future generations). Here, the concept of trust is transferred to the concept of expectations, which is more frequently used in economic terms. The concepts are no longer clearly defined when we speak of confidence in the fulfilment of expectations. Yet, because trust leads to expectations, it must also be "feared" that trust will be strengthened most when circumstances justify this least – insofar as a communicative dilemma, as omission at best contributes to the fact that what is to be prevented happens even more quickly (self-fulfilling effects).

23 On system trust or personal trust (Luhmann, 1989, p. 23, 1964, p. 72).

24 Increasingly, however, the problem of lack of controllability and auditability arises; e.g., for digital cryptocurrencies, such as bitcoins.

25 Regio funds are a special form of complementary currencies. On the one hand, the synonymous use of the terms used here allows highlighting the supplementary redundancy of a complementary currency and, thus, the special resilience quality, and on the other hand, it highlights the small-scale regional aspect of the regio money. For example, an overview of complementary currencies is provided by Volkmann (2009, pp. 19).

26 In view of the above explanations on the indivisible core quality of trust, however, the term *complementary* is misleading; from this point of view, *subtractive* would at best be more suitable.

27 The "Wörgl miracle" is probably the most-cited historical example. The small town of Wörgl in Tyrol created an internationally acclaimed economic upswing during the crisis in the 1930s with the use of a regional monetary system, the "Wörgler Notgeld". Even at that time, the central bank ultimately banned a continuation. (www.unterguggenberger.org).

28 The disadvantages compared to a functioning reserve currency system quickly emerge outside the crisis (https://regionetzwerk.blogspot.co.at/2014/09/regiogelder-auf-basis-nimmt-ab.html).

29 Flowing and situationally adapted transitions or mixed forms can also be constructed economically in the sense of the term. Based on Keynes' 3-currency-model (Keynes, 1933/1982, 236): Internationally available goods that are not necessary for the region in the event of a crisis could therefore be paid for in internationally accepted currency, while regional goods that are essential for survival would have to be settled in a regional currency. Walter pursues a similar logic, which "continues to see the primary currency (credit money) as 'investment money' in the' yield portion' of the economy and circulating for value preservation, while the complementary currency is seen in the low yielding secondary part of the economy as an "additional means of exchange" (Walter, 2008, p. 29), which would correspond to a kind of "monetary division of labour" (Walter, 2008, p. 29). The interplay of (such, annotation of the author) a "near money" and a

"long-distance money" results in a healthy mix of regional orientation and global exchange" (Gellerie, 2005, p. 12).

30 In countries with a weak local currency, it is not uncommon for a strong foreign currency (usually US dollar or euro) to be used as a parallel currency (systematically comparable to regio funds) especially for tourists, whether its use is either obligatory or de facto.

References

Becker, R. (2006). Entwicklungstand und Perspektiven der Regionalgeldbewegungen. *ZfSÖ*, *149*, 32–37.

Brückner, H.-J. (2002). Lernende Regionen – wer oder was lernt denn da eigentlich? Anmerkungen zu einem politiknahen regionalwissenschaftlichen Diskurs. In J. Becker, C. Felgentreff & W. Aschauer (Eds.), *Reden über Räume: Region – Transformation – Migration. Festsymposium zum 60* (pp. 51–69). Potsdam: Geburtstag von Wilfried Heller.

Community Currency Knowledge Gateway. Retrieved from http://community-currency. info/de/ (Accessed 4 October 2017).

Creutz, H. (2005). Möglichkeiten und Grenzen praktischer Geldexperimente. *ZfSÖ*, *144*, 29–32.

De Grauwe, P. (2012). *Economics of monetary union*. Oxford: Oxford University Press.

Deutschmann, C. (2001). *Die Verheißung des absoluten Reichtums. Zur religiösen Natur des Kapitalismus*. Frankfurt am Main: NY. Campus.

Gellerie, C. (2005). Regiogeld und Spieltheorie. *ZfSÖ*, *144*, 12–19.

Hayek, F.A. v. (1978). *Denationalisation of money* (2nd ed.). London: The Institute of Economic Affairs.

Hechenberger, G. (2016). Einseitig Alternativ. Zur Frage des *Alternativen* im Geld- und Finanzsystem. In DIW, Deutsches Institut für Wirtschaftsforschung, *Vierteljahresheft zur Wirtschaftsforschung, 85*(2), 35–48.

Hechenberger, G. (2017). *Regionale Resilien – der Sonderfall "Geld"*. PhD Dissertation, am Institut für Soziologie der Universität Innsbruck.

Honegger, C., Neckel, S., Magnin C. et al. (2010). *Strukturierte Verantwortungslosigkeit. Berichte aus der Bankenwelt*. Berlin: Suhrkamp, pp. 302–316.

Ingram, J. (1969). Comment: The currency area problem. In R. Mundell & A. Swoboda (Eds.), *Monetary problems of the international economy* (pp. 41–60). Chicago and London: University of Chicago Press.

Kalthoff, H., & Vormbusch, U. (2012). Einleitung: Perspektiven der Wirtschafts- und Finanzsoziologie. In H. Kalthoff & U. Vormbusch (Eds.), *Soziologie der Finanzmärkte* (pp. 9–28). Bielefeld: Transkript Verlag.

Kenen, P.B. (1969). The theory of optimum currency areas: An eclectic view. In R. Mundell & A. Swoboda (Eds.), *Monetary problems of the international economy* (pp. 41–60). Chicago and London: University of Chicago Press.

Kennedy, M. (2005). Komplementärwährungen zur wirtschaftlichen Lösung sozialer Probleme. *ZfSÖ*, *144*, 20–28.

Keynes, J.M. (1933, 1982, 2006). *Allgemeine Theorie der Beschäftigung, des Zinses und des Geldes*. Berlin: Duncker & Humblot 1966.

Korniichuk, O., & Sorokina, A. (2007). *Eine Region als optimaler Währungsraum*. Studienarbeit Universtität Trier, Volkswirtschaft: Grin-Verlag.

Luhmann, N. (1964). *Funktionen und Folgen formaler Organisation*. Berlin: Duncker & Humblot.

Luhmann, N. (1989). *Vertrauen: Ein Mechanismus der Reduktion sozialer Komplexität*. Stuttgart: Enke.

Luhmann, N. (1992). *Funktion der Religion. 3. Aufl.* Frankfurt am Main: Suhrkamp.

Luhmann, N. (2010). *Soziale Systeme. Grundriß einer allgemeinen Theorie (= Suhrkamp-Taschenbuch Wissenschaft 666). Nachdruck.* Frankfurt am Main: Suhrkamp, pp. 193ff.

Mayer, T. (2012). *Der Geuro: Eine Parallelwährung für Griechenland? Research Briefing Europäische Integration: Deutsche Bank.* Retrieved from www.dbresearch.de/PROD/DBR_INTERNETDE-PROD/PROD0000000000288868/Der+Geuro%3A+Eine+Paral lelw%C3%A4hrung+f%C3%BCr+Griechenland%3F.PDF bzw. ZfSÖ 172–173, S. 57–60, Report: Vom Regiogeld zum nationalen Parallelgeld – Ein Beispiel: die griechische Drachme, (Accessed 25 September 2017).

McKinnon, R. (1963). Optimum currency areas. *American Economic Review, 53,* 717–725.

McKinnon, R. (2001). *Optimum currency areas and the european experience.* Stanford University, mimeo.

Mises, L. v. (1924). *Theorie des Geldes und der Umlaufmittel. 2. Auflage.* Berlin: Dunker & Humblot.

Mundell, R. (1961). A theory of optimum currency areas. *American Econoc Review, 51,* 657–665.

Musil, R. (2005). *Geld. Raum. Nachhaltigkeit. Alternative Geldmodelle als neuer Weg der endogenen Regionalentwicklung?* Lütjenburg: Verlag für Sozialökonomie.

Regiogeld e.V., Magdeburg. Retrieved from https://regionetzwerk.blogspot.co.at/2014/09/regiogelder-auf-basis-nimmt-ab.html (Accessed 25 September 2017).

Reifner, U. (2010). *Die Geldgesellschaft. Aus der Finanzkrise lernen.* Wiesbaden: Verlag für Sozialwissenschaften.

Rösl, G. (2005). Schwachpunkte der Freigeldlehre und der Regionalgeldmodelle. In Mathias Weis & Heiko Spitzeck (Eds.), *Der Geldkomplex: Kritische Reflexionen unseres Geldsystems und mögliche Zukunftsszenarien, Bd. 41: St. Galler Beiträge zur Wirtschafsethik* (pp. 242–257). Bern: Haupt.

Rösl, G. (2006). *Regionalwährungen in Deutschland – Lokale Konkurrenz für den Euro? Diskussionspapier.* Reihe 1: Volkswirtschaftliche Studien Nr. 43, Deutsche Bundesbank.

Rösl, G. (2008). Regionalgeldausgabe in Deutschland – Eine kritische Betrachtung. *ZfSÖ* (Zeitschrift für Sozialökonomie), *45,* Jahrgang Nr. 158/159.

Schumpeter, J.A. (1970/2008). *Das Wesen des Geldes. Aus dem Nachlaß hrsg. und mit einer Einführung versehen von Fritz Karl Mann.* Göttingen: Vandenhoeck & Ruprecht.

Schumpeter, J.A. (1992/2005). *Kapitalismus, Sozialismus und Demokratie.* Stuttgart: UTB.

Simmel, G. (1989). *Philosophie des Geldes. Gesamtausgabe, Band 6.* Frankfurt am Main: Suhrkamp.

Stiglitz, J. (2017). *Reich und Arm. Die wachsende Ungleichheit in unserer Gesellschaft* (Erste Auflage). München: Siedler Verlag München in der Verlagsgruppe Random House GmbH.

Unterguggenberger Institut Wörgl e.V. Retrieved from www.unterguggenberger.org (Accessed 25 September 2017).

Vaubel, R. (1978). Strategies for currency unification. the economics of currency competition and the case for a European parallel currency (Kieler Studien. 156). Mohr, Tübingen 1978.

Volkmann, K. (2009). *Regional und trotzdem Global. Solidarische Ökonomie im Spannungsfeld zwischen Regionalität und Globalität. Eine explorative Studie zu Regionalwährungen.* Münster, Hamburg, and London: LIT Verlag.

Walter, J. (2008). Staatliche Komplementärwährungen: "dritter Weg" zwischen Geldreform und dezentraler Regionalwährungen? *ZfSÖ, 158–159,* 26–37.

Watzlawick, P., Beavin, J.H., & Jackson, D.D. (2000). *Menschliche Kommunikation – Formen, Störungen, Paradoxien.* Bern: Huber Hans.

WIR Bank Genossenschaft, Basel. Retrieved from www.wir.ch (Accessed 25 September 2017).

11 Destination resilience and the sharing economy

An exploration of the case of Airbnb

Michael Volgger, Christof Pforr & Dirk Reiser

1. Introduction

Many destinations around the world are confronted with a wide range of challenges triggered by natural and/or human-induced crises and disasters in form of major shocks (e.g. cyclones, earthquakes, flooding, bush fires) or stressors (for instance changing economic circumstances). These economic, social or environmental shocks (rapid onset) and stressors (cumulative effects) pose an unprecedented challenge for tourism and often place increased pressures on destinations over time (Carlsen & Hughes, 2007; Farrell & Twining-Ward, 2005; Pforr & Hosie, 2009; Walker, Holling, Carpenter, & Kinzig, 2004). The way these disruptions are depicted by modern mass media creates a perception of omnipresence, as events that confront the tourism and hospitality industries on a regular basis. As the tourism sector is susceptible to these internal and external forces, tourism destinations appear to take a unique position, being faced with both actual and perceived consequences (Mair, Ritchie, & Walters, 2016; Pforr & Hosie, 2009).

According to Walters and Mair (2012) shocks have led to significant academic activities in recent years while the effects of stressors that influence tourism have received considerably less attention. This is all the more astonishing as the long-term co-presence of stressors and adaptive response strategies will impact the reactivity to shocks. The relationship appears analogous to the one between continuous preparatory training and sporadic matches against competitors. Furthermore, there has been little research focusing on tourism destinations' capacity to react and to remain operational in the context of multiple and unpredictable disruptions. Hartman and Sijtsma (2017) highlight that destination governance and resilience building remain under-researched in tourism.

This study focuses on the cumulative stress factors of the sharing economy, which have affected traditional economies in many countries around the globe in various ways, and challenged tourism destinations' response and adaptation capabilities. It is likely that in the medium term, the sharing economy stress will impact a destination shock response and absorbance capability. In our analysis of these impacts of the sharing economy on a tourism destination's resilience, we will specifically focus on one of the most prominent peer-to-peer companies, Airbnb, a platform which facilitates accommodation bookings online. We first introduce and discuss the concept of destination resilience and then empirically analyse selected potential impacts of the sharing economy stress to a destination's resilience. We conclude by arguing that the interplay between the sharing economy and a destination's resilience will highly depend on the adaptive responses moderated through destination governance.

2. Theory: destination resilience

There is no doubt that Airbnb has transformed many aspects of the traditional tourism and hospitality sectors. The internet and new technologies, which act as intermediary between demand and supply, play a central role (Belk, 2014; Cheng, 2016; Ert, Fleischer, & Magen, 2016; Heo, 2016; Karlsson & Dolnicar, 2016; Richardson, 2015). It is widely agreed that Airbnb has been amongst the most disruptive developments in tourism over the last ten years. Changes triggered in a destination due to the rise of Airbnb and the response to this disruption has implications for the entire destination system, including its resilience and adaptive capacities. In this context, Hall, Prayag, and Amore (2017, p. 106) point out that "the resilience of tourist destinations emerges from the many features of the tourist supply as well as from its demand. Moreover, it manifests itself at different scales and dimensions."

However, interest in resilience thinking is not new. The concept of resilience can be traced back to Holling (1973) who departed from focusing on achieving stability and a state of equilibrium in ecological systems. Instead, Holling (1973, p. 19) introduced the concept of resilience which "determines the persistence of relationships within a system and is a measure of the ability of these systems to absorb changes of state variables, driving variables, and parameters". This understanding of resilience by differentiating between stability and change has advanced our understanding of managing complex socio-ecological systems in different contexts (Bhamra, Dani, & Burnard, 2011; Cochrane, 2010; Luthe & Wyss, 2014).

Translated into the tourism system, where it has led over the past decade to a growing number of both conceptual and empirical studies (e.g. Bec, McLennan, & Moyle, 2016; Becken, 2013; Biggs, Hall, & Stoeckl, 2012; Butler, 2017; Cochrane, 2010; Espiner, Orchiston, & Higham, 2017; Farrell & Twining-Ward, 2004, 2005; Tyrrell & Johnston, 2008; Larsen, Calgaro, & Thomalla, 2011; Lew, 2014; Mair, Hughes, Pforr, & Griggs, 2014; Orchiston, Prayag, & Brown, 2016; Ruiz-Ballesteros, 2011), Luthe and Wyss (2014, p. 161) define resilience as "the capacity of these systems to deal with stresses by maintaining the stability of the tourism-related regional economy while ensuring the flexibility and diversity necessary for innovation and further development."

According to Walker et al. (2004), resilience is closely linked to the concepts of adaptability and transformation, which in the face of disruptions allow the tourism system not only to cope, but to react and to innovate (Hall et al., 2017). Luthe & Wyss (2014, p. 161) argue that this process requires "initiatives by various tourism actors with different functions in the tourism supply chain, and on different scales of governance, to be able to assess, plan and manage resilience over time."

Thus, destination resilience-building capacities depend on the existence and strength of social connections or ties between destination actors.

Existing literature mentions a number of factors that impact a territory's (e.g. a destination's) resilience, i.e. its capability to adapt to changing conditions. We reproduce the basic capabilities and characteristics suggested by Christopherson, Michie, and Tyler (2010) and Hassink (2010):

- Learning and innovation
- Infrastructure
- Both flexible and collaborative relationships (internally and externally) as well as trust
- Entrepreneurship and skilled as well as committed workforce
- Supportive and adaptive governance, government and financial systems
- Diversity and a diversified economic basis (in various senses)

This overview of generic factors shall guide the following discussion of potential impacts of the Airbnb phenomenon on a destination's resilience.

3. Empirical research: the Airbnb phenomenon and destination resilience

In the following we discuss two exploratory empirical studies to support our investigation of the interplay between destination resilience and the so-called "sharing economy" (which should probably be better conceived as "access-economy", see e.g. Bardhi & Eckhardt, 2012), with particular attention paid to one of the most prominent examples of this phenomenon, i.e. the accommodation platform Airbnb. In the following we will simply speak of "the Airbnb phenomenon" to denote the empirically observable comprehensive whole of developments around the appearance of the Airbnb platform without implying prejudgement of responsibilities for certain developments.

We present selected results of two recent studies: first, a number of tourism stakeholder interviews conducted to understand opinions about Airbnb in Western Australia (2015–2016); second, a number of assessments gathered in the context of an online survey among Airbnb users, hosts and guests, in Germany (2017). Results will be organized around three questions that are of interest here:

- What can be detrimental impacts of the Airbnb phenomenon on a tourism destination's resilience?
- What can be the Airbnb phenomenon's perceived positive contributions to a tourism destination's resilience?
- (How) Can the Airbnb phenomenon contribute to strengthen social capital in tourism?

The third question has multi-faceted links with the resilience discussion. We treat it specifically and separately from the other two questions, because the sharing economy and Airbnb tend to self-portrait themselves as community-based or community-oriented phenomena (see e.g. Airbnb, 2017a, b). Therefore, this part will investigate claims regarding a generalized increase in social capital around tourism through the appearance of the Airbnb phenomenon, which, if confirmed, could be regarded as a contribution to overall resilience.

3.1 What can be detrimental impacts of the Airbnb phenomenon on a tourism destination's resilience?

Between 2015 and 2016, we interviewed 12 tourism stakeholders in Western Australia about their opinions regarding risks and opportunities related to the Airbnb phenomenon. Interviewed stakeholders included representatives of peak industry bodies, tourism organizations and destination management organisations both at regional and state level, single tourism service providers, short-term rental associations, trade associations and representatives of government bodies at various levels.

Amongst others, these stakeholders reported on several potential negative effects that the Airbnb phenomenon may generate with respect to Western Australia's tourism destination resilience. An aspect that received repeated sceptical commentaries were negative impacts on residents and "neighbours". One interviewee argued that "[it] comes down to residents becoming aware of that they don't know if the person next door is a resident or not. Rubbish gets left out etc.". It should be noted that Western Australia is relatively far from experiencing situations of some (European) destinations in terms of tourism density and intensity. Thus, the Airbnb phenomenon does not seem to be perceived as contributing to severely jeopardizing liveability for residents in general. However, as noted by the cited respondent, there are concerns of adverse impacts within the neighbourhood context.

Next to impacting on amenity and immediate quality of life of residents, more tangible risks involved in providing unregulated accommodation may arise in terms of safety and security, and relate to both the customers and the general public. If viewed from the perspective of competition, this may translate into unlevel playing fields. An interviewee made exactly this point:

> It is about state and local government missing out on proportional charges and taxes. There is also the cost burden of building like a normal hotel or apartment establishment, they could be 30–40% higher because of building standards. Through the doorways, fire escape, fire protection systems etc. That are all requirements and that is different in residential buildings.

Interviewees were worried that the Airbnb phenomenon could enable some providers to engage in unfair competition. If this were to coincide with reality, this could hardly promote a destination's resilience, because it would rather provide disincentives on obeying rules and regulations and thus punish those who made efforts to comply with the general public's expectations. An interviewee asked with respect to the latter: "How are they going to compete with someone who isn't paying for garbage, GST, etc.?"

As mentioned by interviewees, one might foresee varied impacts on investment calculations as well. For instance, building apartment blocks might gain in relative benefit compared to straightforward tourism accommodations such as hotels, because of the availability of both a long-term and a short-term accommodation option. Moreover, the lack of clear regulation might lead to sunk cost and wrong investment decisions – in case of a sudden regulation that overturns expectations. As one interviewee argued:

> [I]f someone is going to invest in an apartment, that is off the plan now and opens up in 18 months' time and they are assuming that they are going to put it into the short-term accommodation market and then all of a sudden we get the regulation of the government that it is not allowed, it is going to be a problem.

3.2   *What can be the Airbnb phenomenon's perceived positive contributions to a tourism destination's resilience?*

The interviewed stakeholder in Western Australia also referred to potential positive aspects of the Airbnb phenomenon for destination resilience (see Table 11.1 for an overall summary). Amongst others, they mentioned "flexibility benefits", which means that the Airbnb phenomenon can contribute to create or strengthen a relatively flexible part of the accommodation supply to better absorb peak demand. For instance, one interviewee argued: "If you have a flexible inventory of additional short stay licensed and regulated legal accommodations, it can assist in peaks in the market, particularly when there are major events."

In addition, according to interviewees, the Airbnb phenomenon can contribute to lower market entry barriers and thus inject additional competition into sometimes rigid accommodation sectors. One interviewee claimed that "[e]verything changes. You have got to embrace it and use it to your advantage. Every business needs to get better and innovation calls for quality. Competition is a good thing". As has been argued above, competition and dynamism are often regarded to be features supporting resilience.

In addition, the interviews brought to the fore a thought that the Airbnb phenomenon can contribute to distribute guests differently within regions and across destinations. According to one interviewee, "[A]irbnb has a capacity to go into areas or regions or suburbs that don't have any host accommodation". In other words, there is a palpable hope that the Airbnb phenomenon can contribute to visitor dispersal into otherwise less-visited areas. In addition, we encountered another belief that the Airbnb phenomenon might also contribute to a diversification in markets, thus potentially reducing the reliance of a destination on a particular set of markets or customer segments.

Last but not least, interviewed Western Australian tourism stakeholders voiced hope that Airbnb (and similar accommodation platforms) users will show a more dispersive spending behaviour. Whereas some hotel and accommodation concepts are based on the idea to capture the biggest share of visitor

Table 11.1 Selected perceived impacts of the "Airbnb phenomenon" on destination resilience in Western Australia

Perceived positive impacts on destination resilience	*Perceived negative impacts on destination resilience*
Increased competition (micro businesses)	Elements of unfair competition
Increased level of innovation and dynamism	Reduction of neighbourhood amenity and residents' quality of life
Flexible inventory	Reduced level of safety and security (consumers, public)
Visitor dispersal	Impact on relative return of tourism investment
Diversification in markets and visitor segments	
Increased dispersal of spending	
Updating of regulatory frameworks	

Note: Negative effects that might be perceived in other places (such as gentrification, or "over-tourism") have not been mentioned by interviewees in the Western Australian context.

expenditure (see Freitag, 1994), the Airbnb phenomenon is sometimes thought to promote a visitor and spending behaviour that more directly benefits other tourism service providers outside the accommodation sector such as grocery stores, restaurants, bars and eventually tourism attraction points. For instance, one interviewee was sure: "[I]t brings a spin to the economy in terms of shopping, restaurants, etc."

3.3 (How) can the Airbnb phenomenon contribute to strengthen social capital in tourism?

By looking at motivations to participate in the sharing economy, Sänger (2017) has analysed how the sharing economy in general and the Airbnb phenomenon in particular can strengthen the social sustainability aspect of tourism. At the core of her work is the hypothesis that the sharing economy may lead to higher degrees of "social capital" (Bourdieu, 1972, 1983) due to an eventually intensified interpersonal interaction. Sänger (2017) justifies this hypothesis by alluding to "sharing" behaviour as being underpinned by values such as "community", "empathy", "generosity" and "hospitality". Indeed, Benkler (2004) concisely defines sharing as "nonreciprocal pro-social behaviour". In a similar vein, Belk (2010, 2014) differentiates the practice of sharing from gift giving and marketplace exchange by emphasizing that features of non-reciprocity and non-transfer of ownership uniquely differentiate the act of sharing. Therefore, "no debt incurs when partaking of sharing as would be the case with gifts and market transactions" (Belk, 2014, p. 1596).

To explore the hypothesized link between the Airbnb phenomenon and levels of social capital, Sänger distributed her questionnaire to both Airbnb hosts and

Airbnb guests in Germany (n = 176). In their responses, the German participants only partly agreed

- that they felt they were part of a wider Airbnb community (3.4% full agreement);
- that partaking in the Airbnb phenomenon contributed to increasing their inter-cultural competencies (5.1% full agreement);
- that it contributed to heightened generalised trust towards other people (5.7% full agreement);
- that it amplified their openness with respect to strangers (4.5% full agreement);
- that it increased their general readiness to help (1.1% full agreement).

Only 5.1 percent (full agreement) declared that they used Airbnb to get to know different people and just 2.8 percent (full agreement) stated that participating in the Airbnb phenomenon helped to build long-term relationships.

As these figures unambiguously indicate, full agreement with most of the above statements was rare. Considering the whole distribution of answers along the applied five-point Likert scale, the ideas that the Airbnb phenomenon can help to build long-term relationships or that it increased the overall readiness to help received the weakest support overall. In contrast, the contribution of the Airbnb phenomenon to supporting openness to strangers and in fostering more generalized trust towards others was acknowledged more consistently on average. Similarly, respondents mentioned "making contact with new people/locals" as the second-biggest advantage of Airbnb compared to more traditional tourism accommodation.

In trying to make sense of these exploratory results among Airbnb users in Germany, we might be tempted to argue that the overall impact of the Airbnb phenomenon on social capital seems to lag behind more optimistic hopes. Long-term relationships and altruistic behaviour do not appear to receive significant boosts solely by engaging with the Airbnb phenomenon. However, what the exploratory analysis *does* seem to support is that Airbnb aids in learning to deal with strangers and in increasing trust towards them in general. Following the wording of Granovetter (1973), we might therefore see a contribution to building (very) "weak ties", without immediate, functional long-term impacts. From a theoretical point of view, one could conceive a vague and generalized contribution to resilience by promoting variance in ideas through an increase in weak ties. However, tangible contributions of the Airbnb phenomenon to resilience from a social capital perspective are less evident.

4. Outlook: co-evolution and destination governance as an adaptive response mechanism

The above exploratory analysis highlights that the Airbnb phenomenon may challenge and affect a destination's resilience in various and, in particular, in mixed ways. Theoretically and in the view of tourism stakeholders, the phenomenon exhibits some features that are likely to strengthen a tourism destination's resilience and others that are more likely to weaken or hamper it. However, it is our firm belief that the specific impact of the Airbnb phenomenon on a tourism destination's resilience will be substantially moderated by destination governance responses. Beyond that, it could even contribute to make destination governance itself more resilient in the medium term. We will conclude this article by outlining and justifying this "belief" in more detail.

One of the challenges destinations face in a context of destination vulnerability and resilience is that tourism experiences are delivered by a highly fragmented and diverse sector. Tourist destinations represent a complex system of actors and clusters of interrelated stakeholders. Crouch (2011), for example, points out that in general the tourism experience is delivered by the cooperation of a number of stakeholders which include typical tourism enterprises and allied industries, a range of destination management organisations, government entities and last but not least, the host community. This assessment reflects the current view of destinations as "loosely bounded networks of organisations" (Cooper, 2012, p. 32). Thus, a destination's response to shocks and stressors largely depends on a combination of individual and organisational resilience in a destination governance context. Generally speaking, the closer these actors work together and the more efficiently and effectively they are coordinated, the greater is the destination's resilience potential (Hall et al., 2017).

Destination governance therefore takes an important role in managing destination adaptation and resilience. It necessitates different forms of working together to foster partnerships, networks and collaborative arrangements between government, industry and community (Dredge & Pforr, 2008; Hall, 2011; Pechlaner, Volgger, & Herntrei, 2012; Pforr, 2006; Volgger & Pechlaner, 2015; Wesley & Pforr, 2010). It is this interaction, engagement and deliberation, which entails shared decision making and collaboration among stakeholders, that is seen to enhance the adaptive capacity of a destination. Thus, the success of adaptation and resilience strategies relies on the expertise of a diverse range of stakeholders within a destination and their willingness to collaborate (Hall et al., 2017).

However, Dredge and Gyimóthy (2017) point out that the traditional tourism policy and planning approach has led to a strengthening of selective interests within and between governments and industry networks. Consequently, the political process too often has ignored stakeholders who represent broader interests of society, outside of these exclusive policy circles (Pforr, 2006). This narrow focus of tourism policy and planning has been challenged by the advent of the sharing economy, which increasingly disturbs traditional alliances of power. As Dredge and Gyimóthy (2017, pp. 83–84) emphasize, "the entrance of platform companies are disrupting the marketplace, challenging the sustainability of traditional business models and supply chains, and the landscape of power relations."

In the context of Airbnb, for instance, which sees new micro-scale actors aligned with a globally operating online platform with more than 3 million listings in more than 190 countries and challenges existing business models, governments are forced to reassess their traditional policy networks, being caught between innovation and regulation. Around the world, governments have therefore started to respond to the Airbnb phenomenon in a variety of ways. Some are deliberately refraining from proactive agency entirely, or at least until a regulatory and governance framework has been established or public consultation has concluded. Others have banned short-term leasing of residential accommodation, or restricted the number of days allowed, with and without registration requirements. It can be assumed that the decision for governments to initiate policy or regulatory responses may be influenced by the magnitude of the impact of increased short-term rentals in different communities (Pforr, Volgger, & Coulson, 2017). It can also be assumed that the specific impact of the sharing economy and the Airbnb phenomenon on destination resilience will highly depend on these policy and governance responses.

Through stressors like Airbnb, the inherent equilibrium in long-standing destination governance models has been profoundly disrupted, challenging and altering the resilience of destinations to respond to and to adapt to a changing marketplace. However, it has become obvious that resilience is destination specific and that there is no one-size-fits-all approach that will provide the right mix between regulation and innovation for all contexts (Dredge & Gyimóthy, 2017; Hall et al., 2017). Therefore, no conclusive and generic analysis of the impact of the sharing economy and the Airbnb phenomenon on destination resilience seems possible at least at this stage. The co-evolution of the phenomenon and the destination governance responses are still causing high levels of uncertainty in conclusions and of dynamism in development. Therefore, whilst impacts on destination resilience are more than likely and we aimed to provide a snapshot of such, the particular shape of these impacts will be affected by adaptive destination governance responses. All is possible, but there is the excuse that there is no room left for local manoeuvre when confronted with a phenomenon that seems to be too big to be dealt with.

References

Airbnb. (2017a). *A global community of hosts like you.* Retrieved from https://community.withairbnb.com/t5/Community-Center/ct-p/community-center (Accessed 20 September 2017).
Airbnb. (2017b). *Airbnb citizen.* Retrieved from www.airbnbcitizen.com/ (Accessed 20 September 2017).
Bardhi, F., & Eckhardt, G. (2012). Access based consumption: The case of car sharing. *Journal of Consumer Research, 39*, 881–898.
Bec, A., McLennan, C.L., & Moyle, B.D. (2016). Community resilience to long-term tourism decline and rejuvenation: A literature review and conceptual model. *Current Issues in Tourism, 19*(5), 431–457.
Becken, S. (2013). Developing a framework for assessing resilience of tourism sub-systems to climatic factors. *Annals of Tourism Research, 43*, 506–528.
Belk, R. (2010). Sharing. *Journal of Consumer Research, 36*, 715–734.
Belk, R. (2014). You are what you can access: Sharing and collaborative consumption online. *Journal of Business Research, 67*(8), 1595–1600.
Benkler, Y. (2004). Sharing nicely: On shareable goods and the emergence of sharing as a modality of economic production. *Yale Law Journal, 114*, 273–358.
Bhamra, R., Dani, S., & Burnard, K. (2011). Resilience: The concept, a literature review and future directions. *International Journal of Production Research, 49*(18), 5375–5393.

Biggs, D., Hall, C.M., & Stoeckl, N. (2012). The resilience of formal and informal tourism enterprises to disasters: Reef tourism in Phuket, Thailand. *Journal of Sustainable Tourism, 20*(5), 645–665.

Bourdieu, P. (1972). *Esquisse d'une théorie de la pratique.* Geneva: Librairie Droz.

Bourdieu, P. (1983). Ökonomisches Kapital, kulturelles Kapital, soziales Kapital. In R. Kreckel (Ed.), *Soziale Ungleichheiten* (pp. 183–198). Göttingen: O. Schwartz & Company.

Butler, R. (Ed.). (2017). *Tourism and Resilience.* CABI.

Carlsen, J., & Hughes, M. (2007). Tourism market recovery in the Maldives after the 2004 Indian Ocean tsunami. *Journal of Travel and Tourism Marketing, 23*(2/3/4), 139–149.

Cheng, M. (2016). Sharing economy: A review and agenda for future research. *International Journal of Hospitality Management, 57,* 60–70.

Christopherson, S., Michie, J., & Tyler, P. (2010). Regional resilience: Theoretical and empirical perspectives. *Cambridge Journal of Regions, Economy and Society, 3*(1), 3–10.

Cochrane, J. (2010). The sphere of tourism resilience. *Tourism Recreation Research, 35*(2), 173–185.

Cooper, C. (2012). *Essentials of tourism.* Harlow: Prentice Hall-Pearson Education.

Crouch, G.I. (2011). Destination competitiveness: An analysis of determinant attributes. *Journal of Travel Research, 50,* 27–45.

Dredge, D., & Gyimóthy, S. (Eds.). (2017). *Collaborative economy and tourism.* Berlin: Springer.

Dredge, D., & Pforr, C. (2008). Policy networks and tourism governance. In C. Cooper, N. Scott & R. Baggio (Eds.), *Network analysis and tourism: From theory to practice* (pp. 58–76). Clevedon: Channelview.

Ert, E., Fleischer, A., & Magen, N. (2016). Trust and reputation in the sharing economy: The role of personal photos in Airbnb. *Tourism Management, 55,* 62–73.

Espiner, S., Orchiston, C., & Higham, J. (2017). Resilience and sustainability: A complementary relationship? Towards a practical conceptual model for the sustainability – Resilience nexus in tourism. *Journal of Sustainable Tourism, 25*(10), 1385–1400.

Farrell, B.H., & Twining-Ward, L. (2004). Reconceptualizing tourism. *Annals of Tourism Research, 31*(2), 274–295.

Farrell, B.H., & Twining-Ward, L. (2005). Seven steps towards sustainability: Tourism in the context of new knowledge. *Journal of Sustainable Tourism, 13*(2), 109–122.

Freitag, T.G. (1994). Enclave tourism development: For whom the benefits roll? *Annals of Tourism Research, 21*(3), 538–554.

Granovetter, M.S. (1973). The strength of weak ties. *American Journal of Sociology, 78*(6), 1360–1380.

Hall, C.M. (2011). A typology of governance and its implications for tourism policy analysis. *Journal of Sustainable Tourism, 19*(4–5), 437–457.

Hall, C.M., Prayag, G., & Amore, A. (2017). *Tourism and resilience: Individual, organisational and destination perspectives.* Channel View Publications.

Hartman, S., & Sijtsma, F.J. (2017). *Resilient tourism destinations? Governance implications of bringing theories of resilience and adaptive capacity to tourism practice.* Paper presented at the Social Progress for Resilient Regions Conference. Retrieved from https://ersa.eventsair.com/QuickEventWebsitePortal/2017-ersa-congress/official-website/Agenda/AgendaItemDetail?id=5ffe8c51-4ded-43c3-a080-8e828c3f5544)\ (Accessed 1 September 2017).

Hassink, R. (2010). Regional resilience: A promising concept to explain differences in regional economic adaptability? *Cambridge Journal of Regions, Economy and Society, 3*(1), 45–58.

Heo, C.Y. (2016). Sharing economy and prospects in tourism research. *Annals of Tourism Research, 58,* 156–170.

Holling, C.S. (1973). Resilience and stability of ecological systems. *Annual Review of Ecology and Systematics, 4,* 1–23.

Karlsson, L., & Dolnicar, S. (2016). Someone's been sleeping in my bed. *Annals of Tourism Research, 58,* 159–162.

Larsen, R.K., Calgaro, E., & Thomalla, F. (2011). Governing resilience building in Thailand's tourism-dependent coastal communities: Conceptualising stakeholder agency in social – ecological systems. *Global Environmental Change, 21*(2), 481–491.

Lew, A.A. (2014). Scale, change and resilience in community tourism planning. *Tourism Geographies, 16*(1), 14–22.

Luthe, T., & Wyss, R. (2014). Assessing and planning resilience in tourism. *Tourism Management, 44,* 161–163.

Mair, J., Hughes, M., Pforr, C., & Griggs, D. (2014). *Creating and building resilient tourist destinations.* Paper presented at the 2014 Council for Australasian University Tourism and Hospitality Education Conference. Brisbane, Australia. February 10–13, 2014.

Mair, J., Ritchie, B.W., & Walters, G. (2016). Towards a research agenda for post-disaster and post-crisis recovery strategies for tourist destinations: A narrative review. *Current Issues in Tourism, 19*(1), 1–26.

Orchiston, C., Prayag, G., & Brown, C. (2016). Organizational resilience in the tourism sector. *Annals of Tourism Research, 56,* 145–148.

Pechlaner, H., Volgger, M., & Herntrei, M. (2012). Destination management organizations as interface between destination governance and corporate governance. *Anatolia, 23*(2), 151–168.

Pforr, C. (2006). Tourism policy in the making: A network perspective from Australia. *Annals of Tourism Research, 33*(1), 87–102.

Pforr, C., & Hosie, P. (Eds.). (2009). *Beating the odds: Crisis management in the tourism industry.* Aldershot: Ashgate.

Pforr, C., Volgger, M., & Coulson, K. (2017). *The impact of Airbnb on WA's tourism sector.* Perth: Bankwest Curtin Economics Centre.

Richardson, L. (2015). Performing the sharing economy. *Geoforum, 67,* 121–129.

Ruiz-Ballesteros, E. (2011). Social-ecological resilience and community-based tourism: An approach from Agua Blanca, Ecuador. *Tourism Management, 32*(3), 655–666.

Sänger, S. (2017). *Soziale Nachhaltigkeit des Reisens in der Sharing Economy: Am Beispiel von Airbnb.* Bachelorarbeit, Hochschule Rhein-Waal.

Tyrrell, T.J., & Johnston, R.J. (2008). Tourism sustainability, resiliency and dynamics: Towards a more comprehensive perspective. *Tourism & Hospitality Research, 8*(1), 14–24.

Volgger, M., & Pechlaner, H. (2015). Governing networks in tourism: What have we achieved, what is still to be done and learned? *Tourism Review, 70*(4), 298–312.

Walker, B., Holling, C.S., Carpenter, S.R., & Kinzig, A.P. (2004). Resilience, adaptability and transformability in social-ecological systems. *Ecology and Society, 9*(2).

Walters, G., & Mair, J. (2012). The effectiveness of post-disaster recovery marketing messages – The case of the Australian 2009 bushfires. *Journal of Travel and Tourism Marketing, 29*(1), 87–103.

Wesley, A., & Pforr, C. (2010). The governance of coastal tourism: Unravelling the layers of complexity at Smiths Beach, Western Australia. *Journal of Sustainable Tourism, 18,* 773–792.

12 Hotel resilient – plan ahead, stay ahead. Promoting the business case for disaster and climate resilience in the tourism sector

Mareike Bentfeld, Stephan Huppertz, Bijan Khazai & Trevor Girard

1. Introduction

The United Nations Global Assessment Report 2013 (GAR 13) has identified tourism as one of the fastest-growing business sectors with a profound impact on global GDP and the labor market (UNISDR, 2013). Recognizing the strong linkage between tourism and economic development, the Sendai Framework for Disaster Risk Reduction (SFDRR) explicitly stresses the importance of promoting and integrating disaster risk management approaches throughout the tourism industry under Priority 3: Investing in disaster risk reduction for resilience (2015). However, tourism destinations are mostly located in hazard-prone areas such as mountain areas, rivers and coastlines. As stated by Mahon, Becken, & Rennie (2013), investors are also using increasingly higher-risk locations for hotel development due to an increased demand for limited coastal regions.

In the last years, the tourism sector has been increasingly affected by large-scale hazards. The Indian Ocean Tsunami in 2004 and the Nepal Earthquake in 2015 are just examples of large-scale events that had or will have a long-term effect on the tourism sector in the affected countries. Even a single disaster event has the potential to cause widespread damage and economic disruption, affecting private and public investments in tourism destinations and the country's image and reputation, while posing a threat to the lives of tourists, workers and surrounding communities. The immediate impact of a disaster event includes a decreased influx of tourists, the closing of hotels and other tourist facilities, the destruction of cultural attractions and a loss of jobs and revenue (Tuladhar, 2016). Furthermore, the impacts of large-scale disaster events are often not limited to a single destination but will also affect neighboring regions or countries (Cavlek, 2002). The impact of such events can last for months or years as recovery is often slow. In the case of the 1999 Taiwan earthquake, it took over a year until international tourist arrivals recovered to previous levels (Huang & Min, 2002).

Hotels and resorts play a particular role with regard to tourism and disasters. While hotels can be severely affected by disaster events, they also play an important role in the aftermath of a disaster for their surrounding community. Being equipped with lifesaving equipment, food and water and communication channels with various stakeholders, hotels can be "islands of resilience" in the aftermath of a disaster (Becken & Hughey, 2013). Hotels can function as a key agent in response and recovery, providing immediate support to the surrounding communities as well as supporting the recovery of economic activity in the affected area. Especially in cases of tsunamis, hotels can also be used for vertical evacuation, not only for the guests, but also for the surrounding communities (FEMA, 2009). However, research suggests that hotels tend to be poorly prepared (Faulkner, 2001; Ritchie, 2008). Reasons for the limited investment in disaster preparedness have been identified as lack of money, lack of knowledge, low risk perception, lack of responsibility and the small size of the business (Wang & Ritchie, 2012; Hystad & Keller, 2007).

A study by Hystad and Keller (2007) found out that the majority of hotels feel that the public disaster and emergency management agencies in their region are responsible for the safety of tourists, and that hotels should be merely focusing on the recovery efforts after a disaster event. In addition, AlBattat and Som (2014) found that most hotel managers think that it is unlikely to be affected by a crisis and that preparing for a disaster event would be a waste of resources. Therefore, hotel managers prefer to deal with a crisis on an ad-hoc basis. Another study found that hotels that have been previously affected by a disaster were more likely to invest in emergency plans (AlBattat & Som, 2013). However, even when hotels do prepare an emergency plan, there is an emphasis on disaster response and recovery and a lack of holistic and integrated approaches that focus on reducing both disaster and increasingly common climate risks (Ritchie, 2008).

2. Hotel resilient initiative

The findings presented in the previous section stress the fact that while hotels play a very important role in disaster risk reduction and resilience building of tourism destinations, so far there have not been any programs or initiatives to engage hotels in building resilience using risk-based and multi-hazard approaches. In order to improve disaster risk management capacities and to strengthen resilience in hotels and at tourist destinations, the Deutsche Gesellschaft für Internationale Zusammenarbeit (GIZ) GmbH within the framework of the Global Initiative on Disaster Risk Management (GIDRM) in collaboration with the United Nations Office for Disaster Risk Reduction Asia and Pacific (UNISDR) and the Pacific Asia Travel Association (PATA) has developed the Hotel Resilient Initiative.

The Hotel Resilient Initiative is based on the understanding that hotels serve an important role with regard to strengthening the resilience of destinations in addition to official disaster risk management and emergency response operators. The assumption is that building the resilience of hotels and resorts in a specific tourism destination will have spill-over effects on the surrounding communities. This will be done through knowledge transfer from the trained hotel staff to their families and other community members. At the same time, an increase in resilient hotels in one destination will lead to overall risk reduction in the area, higher levels of preparedness, more efficient emergency response and quicker recovery processes which will benefit the surrounding communities.

The Hotel Resilient Initiative is a risk-based and multi-hazard approach to improve disaster risk management in the tourism sector focusing on hotels and thereby recognizing their critical role before and after disaster events. The Hotel Resilient Initiative is engaging hotels in the process of resilience building and provides them with the necessary tools and guidelines to proactively build their disaster resilience. At the core of the initiative are the following four components (1) engaging hotels, (2) setting standards, (3) providing support and (4) building a business case. Each of the components will be discussed separately in this article to provide an in-depth understanding of the Hotel Resilient Initiative and what it offers to the tourism sector.

3. Engaging hotels

3.1 Scoping study

Hotel Resilient is a stakeholder-driven response to the findings of the Global Assessment Report 2013, which stated that many hotels and resorts lack the know-how, resources and systems to reduce their risks and be prepared for disasters (UNISDR, 2013). In preparation of the initiative, a scoping study has been conducted in Bohol and Cebu in the Philippines; Lombok in Indonesia; Phuket in Thailand; and the Maldives. As part of the scoping study, semi-structured interviews were conducted with senior representatives of various organizations and businesses in the focus countries (e.g. hotels, tourism ministries, tourism associations, tour operators, insurance agencies). The interviews were conducted to get a better understanding of the opportunities and barriers to the Hotel Resilient Initiative as well as to understand the most important aspects that had to be included in the initiative. The study showed amongst others that there is an interest in the tourism sector to develop internationally recognized standards to strengthen disaster resilience in the tourism industry. The promotion of consistency and best practices through a standard was regarded as particularly useful according to this study (UNISDR & GIDRM, 2015).

3.2 Hotel resilient expert group

The tourism sector and especially the hotels have also been engaged through participation in the Hotel Resilient Expert Group. The objective of the Hotel Resilient Expert Group was to advise the Hotel Resilient Steering Committee (GIDRM/GIZ, PATA, UNISDR) in the development of a marketable multi-hazard risk management standard. The Hotel Resilient Expert Group consisted of senior representatives from the region including government and hotel representatives. Under the guidance of the Hotel Resilient Expert Group, a multi-disciplinary technical group in disaster risk management and tourism and the disaster risk management and tourism communities in the respective countries have been engaged and actively participated in the development of the Hotel Resilient Standards. The same hotels will be engaged again during the testing of the standards and the training package to ensure maximum participation throughout the whole process and a practice-oriented end product.

3.3 Hotel resilient alliance

The Hotel Resilience Alliance is a mechanism to engage relevant stakeholders in building resilience in the hotel sector after the development phase of the Hotel Resilient Initiative. Currently being formalized, the Hotel Resilient Alliance is providing a platform for hotels and other relevant stakeholders to receive support with regard to the implementation of the Hotel Resilient Standards, as well as third-party certification. Being set up on the national level with a regional umbrella structure, the Hotel Resilient Alliance connects hotels that are interested in implementing the Standards with like-minded hotels in the country, as well as national guarantors, certification bodies and technical partners that can support hotels in their endeavor.

Through the active engagement of hotels from the start of the initiative, it could be ensured that the developed product fits with the needs of the hotel industry and speaks their language. Throughout the whole process, the needs of hotels and other relevant stakeholders have remained in focus, ensuring relevance and ownership.

4. Setting standards

The Hotel Resilient Standards form the core of the Hotel Resilient Initiative. As stated earlier, the scoping study showed that standards related to disaster risk management were something missing in the industry and very much needed. The tourism industry is using standards in a wide range of areas (e.g. building standards, food safety standards), but no standard was specifically dedicated to disaster risk reduction or resilience building before the development of the Hotel Resilient Standards. To prevent duplication and ensure coherence with existing standards, the Hotel Resilient Standards are based on existing standards and frameworks from the hospitality sector such as TsunamiReady, HORTEC Hotel Fire Safety, HACCP, LEED as well as generic international standards such as disaster risk management ISO31000, business continuity management ISO22310 and emergency management ISO22320.

The Standards were developed through a participatory process with the support of the Hotel Resilient Steering Committee and the Hotel Resilient Expert Group composed of international experts in the field of tourism and disaster risk and emergency management advising the technical team. Since the focus was on producing an internationally recognized risk management standard, a multidisciplinary research team was engaged to develop draft guidelines. The Hotel Resilient Initiative therefore worked in close cooperation with the Karlsruhe

Institute of Technology and its partners (Bournemouth University, University of Queensland, Griffith University, Risklayer GmbH and TwoEco Inc.) to develop a Draft Multi-hazard Risk Management Standard Module for the tourism sector. The 'test case' has been the Philippines – a country highly exposed to a wide range of hazards, and at the same time with a growing tourism industry. The project has been advanced with the support of the Philippines' Department of Tourism and the Promotion of Green Economic Development (ProGED) Program and was implemented jointly by GIZ and the Philippines' Department of Trade and Industry.

Representatives from various hotels and other stakeholders from the tourism industry were engaged in the development and review of the Standards, ensuring relevance and applicability. To collect essential background information and get expert input, the initiative conducted several consultation workshops and 15 in-depth interviews with hotels, hotel and tourism associations, tour operators and governmental agencies in early 2016. From March to July 2017 the draft framework was developed, adjusted and revised and presented in several round-table workshops and further interviews, and site visits in Manila Cebu City, Bohol and Bantayan, the Philippines. A final survey in a feedback workshop with 33 main stakeholders in Cebu City and an international expert team provided input on which standards and requirements are: (i) doable or not in terms of implementation; (ii) relevant or not; and (iii) potentially confusing.

While the Standards have been developed based on a pilot study within three tourism destinations in the Philippines, the overall framework was designed for global application. Implementation of the Standards always need to be tailored to the type and nature of the individual hotel as well as adapted to the particular context (e.g. national legislation), geography and size of the hotel. The overall framework of the requirements, however, stays the same.

During the development of the Standards, multiple natural and man-made hazards were taken into account. The basic assumption is that hotels always need to prepare for multiple hazards. Therefore, the Hotel Resilient Standards encourages the use of multi-hazard risk assessment techniques to address all possible hazards in a region as a basis for crisis and disaster management planning. The tool also needs to allow for a rapid assessment of key features that affect the resilience of the particular hotel or resort. To this end, several modules are required that can quantify the risk associated with a given property (e.g. to natural hazards that can lead to catastrophic losses) and the resilience of the building system and the people that operate within it to resist, absorb, accommodate and recover from such an event.

The Hotel Resilient Standards reflect technical and managerial dimensions of hotel disaster resilience. The standards and guidelines have been written with large hotels in mind (20+ bedrooms and many staff) but are also applicable to smaller enterprises. The Hotel Resilient Standards are comprised of three main components – Buildings, Systems and Management – which can be easily understood and applied.

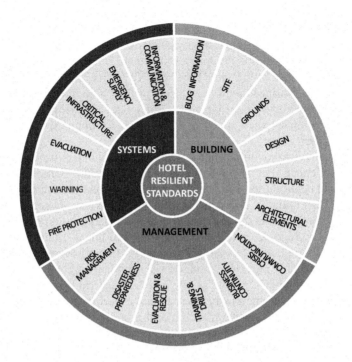

Figure 12.1 Components of the Hotel Resilient Standards
Source: GIDRM/GIZ

The "Buildings Component" of the Standards has specifically been designed to provide hotels with a tool for self-evaluation of the vulnerability of the hotel buildings and grounds. Facilitating the use of self-evaluation tools increases the likelihood of hotels to use these tools. While the self-assessment can only be regarded as an indicative measure of risk, it still provides hoteliers with important information on critical weaknesses with respect to different natural hazards.

The "Systems Component" deals with the physical design and implementation of hotel equipment, infrastructure and other systems to provide safety against natural hazards, fire and other crises. This component describes key requirements and "good practices" which a hotel needs to comply with to become a "Hotel Resilient".

The "Management Component" has been designed to cover various aspects of comprehensive disaster and crisis management. Good disaster and crisis management is regarded as a fundamental part of the resilience strategy for hotels. However well a hotel is designed and constructed, unless there is effective disaster and crisis management, there is a serious risk that the hotel could be compromised during a disaster event. Similar to the "Systems Component", the "Management Component" also describes key requirements for a resilient hotel.

5. Providing support

In order to support hotels in the implementation of disaster and crisis management, a web-based software tool and a comprehensive training package are being developed.

5.1 Hotel resilient software

The software serves two purposes: first, the calculation of risk profiles and second, the management of disasters and crises.

5.1.1 One-Step Risk Profiles

The software provides hotels the possibility to generate "one-step risk profiles". The software uses the information provided by the hotel and combines it with location specific hazard and vulnerability data to quickly generate a risk profile. The risk profile is in line with the Hotel Resilient Standards and includes a resilience score for specific hazard events. In addition, the risk profile contains information about the annual average losses due to specific hazards to guide hotels in their decision-making process.

5.1.2 Management Dashboard

In addition to the risk profiles, the software allows hotels to manage their disaster risk and crisis management procedures. It provides a central place for the storage of existing procedures and protocols, listing of ongoing risk management tasks and situation updates. Providing a central place for management ensures a more comprehensive approach to disaster risk and crisis management and facilitates knowledge sharing among the different departments and responsible staff members.

5.2 Hotel resilient training package

In addition to the software solution, hotels are supported in their process of becoming a Hotel Resilient through trainings that have been developed based on the Hotel Resilient Standards. In these trainings, the responsible staff members are introduced to the Standards as well as their roles and responsibilities with regard to disaster risk and crisis management.

6. Building a business case

The private sector is known to be reluctant to invest in disaster and climate resilience building as long as there are no obvious benefits and an indication on the return of investment for them. Therefore, the Hotel Resilient Initiative has been developed in order to provide a strong case for investment for hotels. There are four reasons why hotels should invest in the Hotel Resilient Initiative, which will be briefly presented in the following sections.

6.1 Systematic analysis of risk

As indicated earlier, the software solution that is part of the Hotel Resilient package allows hotels to systematically analyze their risks and receive tailored information about their current resilience status as well as their expected annual average losses due to specific hazards. Having this kind of information readily available allows hotels to make more risk-informed management and investment decisions, thereby strengthening their overall business resilience. As stated by AlBattat and Som (2014), most hotel managers think that it is unlikely that their hotel will be affected by a crisis and that preparing for a disaster event would be a waste of resources. It was also found that one of the reasons that hotels are poorly prepared for disaster events is their limited risk perception (Wang & Ritchie, 2012). Being able to showcase potential damage and losses to hotel managers therefore increases their willingness to invest in activities to build their disaster and climate resilience.

6.2 Guidance to prepare for crisis situations

As indicated in the introduction, hotels tend be poorly prepared for disaster events, and if they prepare, there is an emphasis on disaster response and recovery and not on integrated approaches to decrease disaster risk (Faulkner, 2001; Ritchie, 2008). The reasons for that are amongst others lack of knowledge and lack of responsibility (Wang & Ritchie, 2012; Hystad & Keller, 2007). The Hotel Resilient Standards provide hotels with guidance on how they should prepare themselves, receive early warnings and what they need to do in order to increase their resilience to various hazards. The knowledge of the hotel staff is also increased through the Hotel Resilient trainings that provide hotel staff not only additional guidance about the implementation of the Hotel Resilient Standards, but also about the general aspects of disaster and climate resilience, thereby supporting the engagement of the industry in this field. The perceived lack of responsibility is targeted by the Standards as well. Given the hospitality sector, a standard based on their inputs and needs gives a clear message to hotels that it is indeed their responsibility to get engaged and invest, and that they should not rely on the surrounding communities in the case of crisis.

Building the capacities of the hotel staff in preparing for disasters and dealing with crisis has a direct impact on the resilience of the communities as well. Most hotel staff live in the surrounding communities and are able to use the newly acquired skills in their communities.

6.3 Competitive advantage and marketing value

In times of increasing risks and interconnected markets, being able to showcase their resilience becomes more and more important for hotels. There are already certificates available to showcase environmental friendliness or sustainability of hotels to the partners and clients (e.g. Green Growth 2050); however, engagement in disaster and climate risk management could not be showcased until now.

Especially for tour operators and other travel businesses (e.g. TUI) it can be reassuring to know that a hotel has invested in its own disaster resilience. Hotels that can show that they implemented the Hotel Resilient Standards can therefore be favored as business partners as they are more trusted by their partners.

In addition, hotels may have a competitive advantage with regard to other hotels in their destination, especially in the aftermath of disaster events. Having decreased their disaster risk by implementing the Hotel Resilient Standards, these hotels have a higher chance of being in business after a disaster event while other hotels have to recover from the disaster impact.

6.4 Access to risk financing and transfer solutions

Being able to showcase the efforts in increasing the resilience of the hotel to disaster and climate risks allows hotels to access financing options that are not available to other hotels. A common approach is the offering of reduced premiums by insurances to hotels that are actively reducing their risks. According to the scoping study carried out by UNISDR and GIDRM (2015), a number of hotels were able to gain reduced insurance premiums by demonstrating proactive approaches to reducing risks. It is expected that it will be even easier for hotels to obtain these reduced premiums by implementing the Hotel Resilient Standards.

7. Conclusion

The Hotel Resilient Initiative is an innovative approach to increase disaster resilience in the tourism industry by targeting hotels as the key agents of change. By triggering individual private investments from hotels, the hotels are building and maintaining their own resilience and at the same time the resilience of the surrounding communities and the overall destination is increased. From the beginning, hotels have been engaged and have contributed to the development of the overall Hotel Resilient Initiative as well as to the creation of specific products, namely the Hotel Resilient Standards, the Hotel Resilient Software and the Hotel Resilient Training Package. Through the constant engagement of the key stakeholders, it could be ensured that the products developed fit with the hospitality sector and are not only needed but also applicable in this sector.

Taking into account existing frameworks and standards from the hospitality sector as well as internationally accepted ISO standards, the Hotel Resilient Initiative ensures that the Hotel Resilient Standards are in line with existing requirements and add specific indicators related to disaster risk and crisis management. In addition, the engagement of the hotels throughout the development process ensures that the Standards are accepted, implemented and sustained by the industry.

As indicated in the introduction, most tourism destinations are in risk prone areas, facing various hazards at the same time. The Hotel Resilient Initiative follows a multi-hazard approach to resilience building, by providing hotels with tools to deal with various hazards. As such, hotels can prepare for a wide range of hazards rather than being restricted to a single hazard type (e.g. fire). This allows for a broader application of the Hotel Resilient Standards and increases the likelihood of application in the industry.

The Hotel Resilient Initiative provides a number of support tools to the hotels to facilitate the implementation of the Hotel Resilient Standards. The software allows hotels to visualize their actual risks and provide them with loss scenarios, based on which hotels can invest in disaster and climate resilience. Furthermore, the software allows hotels to generate a comprehensive disaster risk and crisis management strategy by ensuring access to all relevant information and facilitating the implementation of various disaster risk and crisis management processes. The Hotel Resilient Standards are complemented by a comprehensive training package that builds the capacities of hotel staff and management with regard to the Standards as well as overall disaster and crisis management. Providing tailored support to the Hotel Resilient Standards facilitates the implementation of the Standards by hotels and increases the usefulness and applicability of the Standards in the sector.

Last but not least, the Hotel Resilient Initiative provides hotels with market benefits and investment opportunities. Better access to risk financing and risk transfer schemes and competitive advantages in the market can provide hotels with financial benefits while at the same time reducing their risks and building their resilience. As indicated in the introduction, hotels play an important role before and after disaster events, not only for themselves but also for the communities surrounding them. In addition, the tourism industry plays an important role in advancing development and makes a significant contribution to the local, national and global economy. The Hotel Resilient Initiative provides an innovative way to engage the private sector in disaster risk reduction and resilience building while providing them with clear advantages.

References

AlBattat, A.R., & Som, A.P.M. (2013). Emergency preparedness for disasters and crises in the hotel industry. *SAGE Open*, July-September, 1–10. Retrieved from http://journals.sagepub.com/doi/pdf/10.1177/2158244013505604 (Accessed on 22 January 2017).

AlBattat, A.R., & Som, A.P.M. (2014). *Disaster preparedness of hotel industry abroad: A comparative analysis*. Paper presented at the 4th International Conference on Tourism Research (4ICTR), Malaysia.

Becken, S., & Hughey, K. (2013). Linking tourism into emergency management structures to enhance disaster risk reduction. *Tourism Management, 36*, 77–85.

Cavlek, N. (2002). Tour operators and destination safety. *Annals of Tourism Research, 29*(2), 478–496.

Faulkner, B. (2001). Towards a framework for tourism disaster management. *Tourism Management, 22*(2), 135–147.

Federal Emergency Management Agency. (2009). *Vertical evacuation from tsunamis: A guide for community officials* (FEMA P646A). Retrieved from www.fema.gov/media-library-data/20130726-1719-25045-1822/fema_p646a.pdf

Huang, J.-H., & Min, J.C.H. (2002). Earthquake devastation and recovery in tourism: The Taiwan case. *Tourism Management, 23*, 145–154.

Hystad, P., & Keller, P. (2007). Towards a destination tourism disaster management framework: long-term. Lessons from a forest fire disaster. *Tourism Management, 29*(1), 151–162.

Mahon, R., Becken, S., & Rennie, H. (2013). *Evaluating the business case for investment in the resilience of the tourism sector of small Island developing states.* A Background Paper Contributing to the Global Assessment Report on Disaster Risk Reduction. Retrieved from www.preventionweb.net/english/hyogo/gar/2013/en/home/index.html

Ritchie, B. (2008). Tourism disaster planning and management: From response and recovery to reduction and readiness. *Current Issues in Tourism, 11*(4), 315–348.

Tuladhar, S. (2016). Impact of the Great Earthquake-2015 on hospitality industry of Nepal. *Journal of Tourism and Hospitality, 7,* 87–115.

UNISDR. (2013). *Global assessment report 2013.* Retrieved from www.preventionweb. net/english/hyogo/gar/2013/en/home/index.html

UNISDR & GIDRM. (2015). *Developing strategies to strengthen the resilience of hotels to disasters.* Retrieved from www.gidrm.net/site/assets/files/1121/20150728_hotel_resilient_scoping_study_final.pdf

Wang, J., & Ritchie, B.W. (2012). Understanding accommodation managers' crisis planning intention: An application of the theory of planned behaviour. *Tourism Management, 33,* 1057–1067.

13 How to make destinations resilient – from theory to practical application

Bernd Schabbing

1. Introduction: finding an adequate approach to resilience for tourism destinations

Thinking about resilience in tourism means on the one hand to understand, that it is – however – not only a "technical" (see Holling, 1996), but also a geographical and spatial topic (see Luthe & Wyss, 2014). Doing so, it becomes clear that increasing and ensuring resilience of tourism destinations is quite a more complex task than resilience of "normal" systems and even cities (in comparison to regions as destination) (see Duit, Galaz, Eckerberg, & Ebbesson, 2010). Only considering solution approaches at the planning level already leads one to regard simple ways to solve problems or prevent them in advance as difficult – due to the complexity of planning share- and stakeholders and the interrelationship to many other fields of interest connected to the planning process already at this level (see Uğur, 2016).

Talking about resilience is often done with a focus on infrastructure, energy, water or traffic services within a city, region or country. However, with respect to (tourism) destinations, it is on the other hand important to also take destination images and brands into consideration. They are crucial for the destination competitiveness, and they can influence the economic and social prosperity of a destination quite quick, strong and with a long-lasting impact (see Adjouri & Büttner, 2008; Ritchie & Crouch, 2005; Schabbing, 2015). Furthermore, an adequate brand concept also guides to the main success factors and unique selling propositions a destination has – which usually will be the most important factors for the destinations future as a tourism attractor – and due to that, might also be the most important factors to be secured in order to increase the resilience of the destination. Additional to that, the concept of identity-based brand development and management also often brings the main issues (and historical vulnerabilities and sensitivities of the inhabitants as well) of the people in power – and of all destination inhabitants – into mind and thus helps to understand the main issues and motives of the relevant persons and groups (see Burmann, Halaszovich, Schade, & Hemmann, 2015). So, this approach also brings the meaning of share- and stakeholders in mind, which means that focusing on systems, infrastructure and companies (e.g.) is only one part. It has to be completed by also taking the persons behind those structural approaches into consideration – and by doing so add intangible elements beyond infrastructure focus.

Finally, it must be considered that we, even if we would understand – and even might steer – all the factors we know, would never hold a total knowledge of all factors and their interrelationship and interactions (see Taleb, 2012; Aramberri & Butler, 2006).

Regarding all those findings could bear a big frustration for the issue of resilient destinations. However, on the other hand, looking for ways to strengthen destination resilience doesn't mean to necessarily understand all factors and interrelationships, but just to identify, analyze and strengthen the most important ones in a first step. So, this will be the focus of this paper, especially, as several papers in this book already address the theoretical and systematic approach to destination resilience.

2. Understanding and measurement of brand meaning and brand image as a mean to create a stakeholder assessing system for strengthening destination resilience

Brand image and brand meaning is an important and intensively researched field of economic studies. During the last years, city and destination brands become an attractive field of research. So, this area seemed to be well researched. However, the meaning of the internal stakeholders for a destinations brand is not that well researched in detail up to now and also a system of combining internal and external views, influences and players, is not yet fully described for destinations (see Schabbing, 2015). This seems to be the most outstanding task by developing a resilient destination system and destination image. As demonstrated above, the concept of brand image and brand management, however, might strengthen the approach to destination resilience in a good and concrete way.

Due to this, the suitability of the "identity-based" process of brand management as a means for a destination resilient system will be analyzed here, whether or not this process might help to solve this task. This process seems to be useful for the current question, as it combines the internal and the external view and focus. Doing so, it helps to integrate all aspects, decisions and activities which are influencing the brand management process (Burmann et al., 2015, p. 84). So, it helps to build a long-time, stable brand identity with substantial value with respect to all relevant target groups (see Meffert & Burmann, 1996, p. 15 and Meffert, 2003, p. 16f. as well as Kühne, 2008, p. 44). The model can be described as combining three elements:

1   a strategic analysis of the current situation and the definition of the aims of the brand. This forms the brand identity (see Esch, 2014, p. 15, Esch, Knörle, & Strödter, 2014, p. 15 and Burmann et al., 2015, p. 110).
2   Transfer of the brand identity into brand behaviour of the whole staff (internal) and into clear brand benefit promise for all relevant target groups (Meffert, Burmann, & Kirchgeorg, 2012, p. 376).

3   The result is a clear positioning of the brand, which creates a unique, purchase-behaviour-relevant image of the brand in the consumer's experience by usage of the strong and substantial brand identity (Burmann et al., 2015, p. 95). The aim of this step is to establish and strengthen the specific brand benefit promise by focusing the aspects of brand identity to the specific benefits (function as well as symbolic) of the brand for the respective target group(s) and its specific communication (Burmann et al., 2015, p. 14ff.)

The last step is a measurement of internal and external success of the brand – as well as then adapt the whole brand concept by using the results of the measurement (and establishing an optimization-cycle, see Burmann et al., 2015, p. 85 and Belz, 2006, p. 63)

After analyzing the requirements of destination resilience and the needs of such a system, the "identity-based" process of brand management seems to fulfill the requirements, but – however – has to be adopted to the specific tasks and framework of a destination (in comparison to a company). Doing so seems to ensure a clear analysis, strict development and focusing as well as identifying the core images, attractions and products of the respective destination as well as the respective main players.

The main success factors seem to be – in addition to focusing on main aspects and main players – the incorporation of the main influence(r)s into consideration without limitation to specific fields, areas or industry sectors. All relevant aspects of influence (and support) have to be considered, described and analyzed. Doing so, the system also becomes a booster for destination development by including the main target groups, shareholder, stakeholder and their specific approaches and views (Block, 2011, p. 24f.).

This means high complexity, but also usage of synergies and ability of big campaigns (Schabbing, 2015, p. 83). And it means to understand destination resilience as well as destination brand as a continuous process instead of a fix system. Fundament for all efforts is the clear view on the specific resources, abilities and competencies of the specific destination, which allow one to reach and ensure competitive advantages – and the focused brand management to embed, strengthen and protect the effect of those resources, abilities and competencies. And this means building up networks, keep them working and continuously deepening and strengthening binding of all main players in the network even (better: especially) if aspects of the main image/identity are changed.

3. Identifying, assessing, evaluating and connecting share- and stakeholders in destinations

3.1 Main areas of destination resilience

So, analyzing the meaning and implementation of share- and stakeholder with respect to strengthening resilience does not only mean considering e.g. infrastructure and supply, but also taking the influence on external image means and brand performance and brand experience into consideration. Taking all this into consideration, destination resilience needs a consideration of all share- and stakeholders, which are influencing or are important for:

- tourism-relevant "general" infrastructure (e.g. traffic access, energy, water, health care)
- supply chain in tourism (e.g. hospitality (hotels, resorts, leisure residences), attractions, tourism travel, restaurants)
- tourism-related information bases and information channels/content providers

Concerning the first, current literature on city/region resilience can be used (see Fontanari, 2017 for current state of affair in Germany); concerning the second, literature on supply chain management and operations in tourism is helpful; concerning the third point, literature on brand creation and brand management can be used. So, a useful and convenient literature base is accessible. Considering this, it becomes obvious that several influencing factors and share- and stakeholder might be relevant for a destination's resilience. So, to focus on the most relevant influencing factors or share- and stakeholders means to filter. This should help to clarify:

- which of the share- and stakeholders have the most meaning and/or impact on the destinations resilience
- whether the influence is over a short time (e.g. physical/basic supply) or long time (image and brand) related
- how they are connected/dependent
- how vulnerable they are (from which influence)

(For such a general destination/region analysis and a theoretical framework for development of a system of players re resilience see Fontanari, 2017.)

Here, in a first step, the general scanning of influencing factors with a relevant meaning for the destination means to do the first step from a general overview of all factors to a concrete selection of the relevant factors for the concrete destination case. To find a most complex but also clear model which combines destination infrastructure, planning, management and marketing quickly leads to the Model of a competitive destination from Ritchie and Crouch (2005). It mentioned and described all relevant aspects and fields which influence a destination's competitiveness – and, by doing so, also its resilience.

The next step would be to become more detailed in the analysis of the relevant fields of influence of the respective destination which should be analyzed. Considering the most relevant fields of influence, a long list of potential influencers/supporters then can be collected and addressed as exemplified in Table 13.1 (for more details on share- and stakeholders in destinations see e.g. Schabbing, 2015, Bieger & Beritelli, 2013, Ritchie & Crouch, 2005).

Qualifying and amplifying determinants					
Location	Safety / security	Cost / values	Interdependencies	Awareness / Image	Carrying Capacity

Destination policy, planning and development							
System definition	Philosophy / values	Vision	Positioning / branding	Develop-ment	Competitive / collaborative analysis	Monito-ring and evaluation	Audit

Destination management								
Organi-zation	Marke-ting	Quality of service / experience	Informa-tion / research	Human re-source de-velopment	Finance & venture capital	Visitor manage-ment	Resource steward-ship	Crisis manage-ment

Core resources and attractors						
Physiography and climate	Culture and history	Mix of activities	Special Events	Enter-tainment	Super-structure	Market ties

Supporting factors and resources					
Infrastructure	Accessibility	Facilitating Resources	Hospitality	Enterprise	Political Will

Figure 13.1 The model of a competitive destination from Ritchie and Crouch
Source: Ritchie & Crouch (2005, p. 233)

Table 13.1 Types and fields of influence of relevant destination share- and stakeholder

Share-/stakeholder	*Relevant field of influence of the share-/stakeholder*	
	Tourism-related "general" infrastructure	*Supply chain in tourism products/travel experience*
Food providers (e.g. supermarket)	X	
Train/railroad, airplane/airport, car & bus/streets	X	
Water supply (in Europe often municipal utilities)	X	
Energy supply (in European Cities often municipal utilities, in regions mostly private companies)	X	

Share-/stakeholder	Relevant field of influence of the share-/stakeholder	
	Tourism-related "general" infrastructure	*Supply chain in tourism products/travel experience*
Staff of local tourism companies (also if they are inhabitants)	X	X
Hotels		X
Restaurants		X
Local tourism travel (e.g. local public transport, mountain railway)		
Regional tourism travel		
Tourism attractions		X
Inhabitants of the destination		X
Destination Management Organisation (DMO)		X
Tour operators		X
Travel agencies		X
Local government		
Journalists		
Media		
Non-tourism industry		
NGOs		
Retail		
. . .		

Source: Own compilation, based on Schabbing (2015), Bieger & Beritelli (2013) and Ritchie & Crouch (2005)

3.2 Identifying and assessing the meaning and influence of share- and stakeholder

It can be helpful to also identify potential supporters for strengthening the destination's resilience (whether to strengthen the destination or to replace a content or a supporter in case of blackouts of parts of the system or of specific players).

Adding those considerations, a result would be a kind of measurement for relevance and vulnerability of destination payers regarding destination resilience – a type of "vulnerability list/map" with the following measures for each player. By adding the results of every player of a respective group and the weighting of the group's meaning for the destination (which can also be derived from adding the individual meaning of all group members!), it can also be clarified how important a group is for the whole destination (at all, but also following to the sum of the group members influence/vulnerability):

• Meaning for the destinations physical or image stability – which area and in which amount?

- Dependency from other players (who, how deep) – number of dependencies at all?
- Dependency from which other source (e.g. energy, water . . .) (who, how deep) – number of dependencies at all?
- Potential: Current amount of support to the destinations physical or image status – possible (future) amount of support?
- Group vulnerability

3.3 Application of the destinations share- and stakeholder analysis to a specific destination

Applying this concept on a specific destination would then mean to fill the list. Before doing so, an analytical view on the destination's main products and brand image aspects would help to clarify the focus and the specific meaning of every player. This can be done by e.g. usage of Ritchie & Crouchs Concept of a "competitive Destination" (see. Ritchie & Crouch, 2005) with a destination management focus (but also with relevant marketing aspects – see explanation above), or by using e.g. Biegers Approach (Bieger & Beritelli, 2013), which is more focused on the work and strategy of a destination management organization (DMO) and external brand and marketing activities.

However, measures of the brand image and meaning seem to be a specific task. Nevertheless, e.g. the "Brandmeyer Stadtmarken-Monitor" might be a useful way to reach clear measures (Brandmeyer Markenberatung, Konzept, & Markt GmbH, 2017). It takes factors into consideration as sympathy, external image, uniqueness, "liveability" for inhabitants, willingness to move to the city, willingness of giving a recommendation, attractiveness for visitors and guests, potential for future development, attractiveness of infrastructure (town/region picture, quality of life in the destination, safety . . .).

4. Apply the concept/approach of the "identity-based brand management" to destination resilience

Combining the several approaches and concepts mentioned before, a step-by-step development of a resilient destination and destination brand system might work like this:

Seeking/identifying/assessing the main character and services of the destination is done by:

How to embed all relevant share- and stakeholders into a system, how to clarify the aims of destination economy and sustainability, how to discuss and decide future aims, strategies and operations as well as current way of analyzing threats and the communication and interaction system is explained in general in different books e.g. Bieger and Beritelli (2013), Ritchie and Crouch (2005) and Fodness (2016).

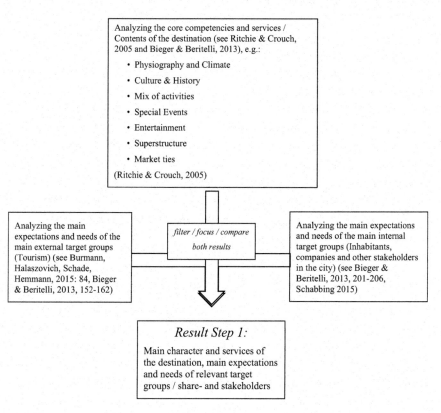

Figure 13.2 Step 1 to increase a destination's resilience
Source: Own illustration

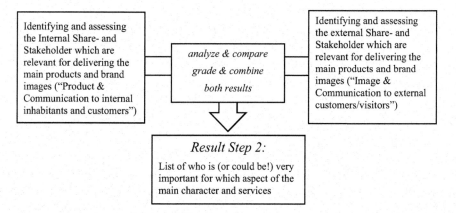

Figure 13.3 Step 2 to increase a destination's resilience
Source: Own illustration

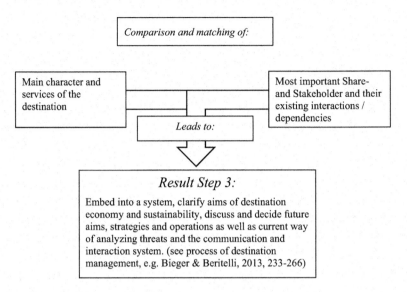

Figure 13.4 Step 3 to increase a destination's resilience
Source: Own illustration

5. Conclusion: why and how to establish and stabilize a resilience network in tourism destinations

To find a concrete and useful approach to increase destinations resilience, it is important to first scan *all* possible general relevant fields of influence, whether they are directly related to tourism and/or planning or not – and only *then* focus on the most relevant individual factors of influence in the specific destination.

This means to first use a quite broad interdisciplinary approach, where, for example, the fields of urban and regional planning and development are far more advanced in discourses of complexity and adaptive governance whereas tourism planning remains somewhat stagnated in the technical rational approaches (see the article of Lauren Uğur in this book).

Then, necessarily an agile and open-minded approach helps teams respond to unpredictability through a broad and open-minded systematic scanning, but also a strict and focused practical view on the individual main topics and influences of the respective destination.

To plan to increase the resilience of destinations requires a coordinated development and cooperative institutional structures to not only to coordinate areas or factors of influence, but also to coordinate, convince and bind people which are responsible for those areas or factors to the progress of increasing resilience.

Broad possible factors of influence, heightened uncertainty and limited predictability characterize the discussion and practical approach of destination resilience. And all this means to talk about focusing on the most influencing factors, regarding the task as an enduring and changing process and considering the task as a mix of structural, socio-cultural, economic and human-related approaches.

References

Adjouri, N., & Büttner, T. (2008). *Marken auf Reisen. Erfolgsstrategien für Marken im Tourismus*. Wiesbaden: Gabler.

Aramberri, J., & Butler, R. (2006). Tourism development: Vulnerability and Resilience. In J. Aramberri & R. Butler (Eds.), *Tourism development: Issues for a vulnerable industry* (pp. 293–308). New Delhi and Mumbai: Viva Books Private Limited.

Belz, C. (2006). *Spannung Marke. Markenführung für komplexe Unternehmen*. Wiesbaden: Gabler.

Bieger, T., & Beritelli, P. (2013). *Management von Destinationen* (8th ed.). Munich: Oldenbourg.

Block, J. (2011). Zum Verhältnis von Stadtmarketing & Kultur. In KM – Das Monatsmagazin von Kulturmanagement Network. *Kultur und Management im Dialog*, April, *54*, 24–26. Retrieved from https://www.kulturmanagement.net/downloads/magazin/km1104.pdf (22 January 2017).

Brandmeyer Markenberatung GmbH & Co. KG, Konzept & Markt GmbH. (2017). *Brandmeyer Stadtmarken-Monitor*. Hamburg: Brandmeyer Markenberatung GmbH & Co. KG, Konzept & Markt GmbH. Retrieved from www.brandmeyer-markenberatung.de/veroeffentlichungen/studien/brandmeyer-stadtmarken-monitor-deutschland-2015 (Accessed 4 July 2017).

Burmann, C., Halaszovich, T., Schade, M., & Hemmann, F. (2015). *Identitätsbasierte Markenführung. Grundlagen – Strategie – Umsetzung – Controlling* (2nd ed.). Wiesbaden: Gabler.

Duit, A., Galaz, V., Eckerberg, K., & Ebbesson, J. (2010). Governance, complexity, and resilience. *Global Environmental Change, 20*(3), 363–368. doi:10.1016/j.gloenvcha.2010.04.006

Esch, F.-R. (2014). Die Zukunft der Marke. Herausforderungen an erfolgreiche Markenführung, Transfer. *Werbeforschung & Praxis – Zeitschrift für Werbung, Kommunikation und Markenführung, 60*, 69–76, Hamburg: New-Business-Verlag.

Esch, F.-R., Knörle, C., & Strödter, K. (2014). *Internal Branding. Wie Sie mit Mitarbeitern Ihre Marke stark machen*. München: Vahlen.

Fodness, D. (2016). The problematic nature of sustainable tourism: Some implications for planners and managers. *Current Issues in Tourism*, 1–13. doi:10.1080/13683500.2016.1209162

Fontanari, M. (2017). *Risiko- und Resilienzbewusstsein der Versorgungs- und Nachfrageseite. Empirische Analysen und erste konzeptionelle Ansätze zur Steigerung der Resilienzfähigkeit von Regionen*. ISM Working Paper, No. 9, Dortmund and Münster: Readbox Publishing GmbH.

Holling, C.S. (1996). Engineering resilience versus ecological resilience. In P.C. Schulze (Ed.), *Engineering within ecological constraints* (pp. 31–44). Washington, DC: National Academy Press. doi:10.17226/4919

Kühne, M. (2008). *Die Stadt als Marke. Eine qualitativ-empirische Untersuchung zur identitätsorientierten Markenpolitik von Städten*. Aachen: Shaker.

Luthe, T., & Wyss, R. (2014). Assessing and planning resilience in tourism. *Tourism Management, 44*, 161–163. doi:10.1016/j.tourman.2014.03.011

Meffert, H. (2003). *Identitätsorientierter Ansatz der Markenführung. Eine entscheidungsorientierte Perspektive*. Münster: Wissenschaftliche Gesellschaft für Marketing und Unternehmensführung.

Meffert, H., & Burmann, C. (1996). *Identitätsorientierte Markenführung. Grundlagen für das Management von Markenportfolios*. Arbeitspapier Wissenschaftliche Gesellschaft für Marketing und Unternehmensführung, Bd. 100. Münster: Wissenschaftliche Gesellschaft für Marketing und Unternehmensführung.

Meffert, H., Burmann, C., & Kirchgeorg, M. (2012). *Marketing. Grundlagen marktorientierter Unternehmensführung: Konzepte – Instrumente – Praxisbeispiele* (11th ed.). Wiesbaden: Gabler.

Ritchie, J.R.B., & Crouch, G.I. (2005). *The competitive destination: A sustainable tourism perspective*. Cambridge: CABI Publishing.

Schabbing, B. (2015). Stadtmarketing 3.0: zielgruppenbezogene, konsistente und authentische Stadtmarken sind die Herausforderung des 21. Jahrhunderts. In I. Böckenholt (Ed.), *ISM-Research Journal 2* (pp. 81–98). Dortmund and Münster: MV-Verlag.

Taleb, N.N. (2012). *Antifragile: How to live in a world we don't understand*. UK: Penguin Books.

Uğur, L. (2016). Mind the gap: Reconceptualising inclusive development in support of integrated urban planning and tourism development. In C. Pasquinelli & N. Bellini (Eds.), *Tourism in the city: Towards an integrative agenda on urban tourism* (pp. 51–66). Springer International. doi:10.1007/978-3-319-26877-4

14 Agro-tourism in Belarus

Resilience in development as a success factor

Georgi Gribov & Veronika Rakitskaja

1. Introduction

The article analyzes the history of formation and development of the "agroecotourism" destination in Belarus. It proves that among the factors contributing to the success in this sphere, its resilience to existing internal and external changes plays a pivotal role. The research has discovered that the sustainability of the destination as well as its stability as a form of business is defined by liberal and flexible methods, and innovative approaches in the creation of new services and working practices. The article also provides the analysis of the existing agro- tourism estates in modern conditions.

In the article the author sets the following tasks: a) to provide a brief description of the history of agroecotourism development in Belarus, b) to reveal the dynamics of the development of this sphere in Brest region, c) to determine the factors of its success, including autonomy and resilience as the most important ones and d) to outline the main problems of the branch.

2. The origin of agroecotourism in Belarus and its main goals

Analyzing the given problem, it is necessary to pay attention to various terminology such as agrotourism, ecological tourism, agroecotourism, rural tourism, "green tourism", and recreation in the country. Having no intention to clearly define these concepts in this article, we would only like to note that while organizing a holiday in a rural agroestate, you can face diverse aspects of tourism, reflected in these terms.

Based on the experience of Belarus and other countries, it is possible to single out the following main goals and objectives of agroecotourism:

1 Sustainable development of rural settlements and their local communities;
2 Increase in employment of rural population and their incomes;
3 Development of tourism infrastructure in rural areas;
4 Organizing healthy and active recreation for tourists;
5 Preservation of cultural and historical heritage of the region;

6 Preservation of natural potential of the area;
7 Providing information and organizing educational events in order to raise the awareness of people about nature and cultural values of regions in belarus;
8 Introduction of cluster model in the sphere of agroecotourism;
9 Integration of belarus and its regions into the european economic environment;
10 Growth of inbound tourism and promotion of the positive image of the country abroad.

Agroecotourism in many countries appeared as an alternative activity for agricultural product producers, which was especially important in the crisis conditions when villagers were trying to find a way out of the difficult situation, searching for possibilities in other spheres of entrepreneurship. Agroecotourism as a kind of small family business in many countries has become a means of additional income for rural dwellers compensating for a decline in income from the sale of agricultural products. This trend is typical for those countries where the share of farmers is quite significant. The situation in Belarus is different and is determined by a long historical period when the collective way of farming dominated in the agrarian sector of the economy of Belarus as well as of other post-Soviet countries. Large agricultural enterprises like collective farms did not have economic freedom and were under the strict control of the government. Even nowadays the consequences of this governmental policy are still present. The private sector in this sphere of the economy is quite weak, and the number of farmers is small. According to the data from The National Statistics Committee of the Republic of Belarus of January 1, 2016, the share of private sector engaged in land processing was only 1,9 percent (The National Statistics Committee of the Republic of Belarus, 2016). In this regard, a significant part of the actors in agroecotourism in Belarus are professionals in various fields, often town dwellers who moved to the country and bought their houses in rural areas with the aim to start an agroecotourism business rather than rural residents engaged in agrarian business.

Rural tourism in its current form in Brest region as well as in Belarus in general began to emerge at the turn of 2002–2003. At that time, the information was published about the creation of the Belarusian public association "Agroecotourism", which set out its goals and raised the problem of the formation of this type of activity in our country (Tarasjonok, 2014).

The publication of these articles gave impetus to those who had already realized the potential opportunities of Belarus in this area, and many owners of houses in the village got in touch with this public association. The public association organized a series of educational seminars in Belarus, Ukraine, Lithuania, and Poland, where the owners of estates received the knowledge required. It should be noted that the start of agroecotourism was not the result of a decision or directive of governmental structures, it was also not envisaged by state programs or plans. Agroecotourism in Belarus was initiated by residents who had homes in rural areas and who could foresee that this small business had good prospects and that their country had good ecotourism potential. This fact is the evidence of the great power of civil society, which, in our opinion, is not always taken into account in our country (Klitsunova, 2016). Even at the very beginning of its formation, the sector of agro-ecotourism was autonomous and relatively independent from the government. Rural estates were developing and improving their infrastructure at their own expense, showing creativity and imagination, and expanded the package of services they provided. They proved to be self-sufficient units with internal potential for self-development, capable of maintaining stability even under the influence of external unfavorable factors. In this case, it is appropriate to recall the dialectical conception of the development of the German philosopher G. Hegel described in Part 1, "Science of Logic", of his fundamental work "The Encyclopaedia of the Philosophical Science" as well as the dialectical materialism of K. Marx in his work "Critique of Political Economy", who thought that the main source of progress and development must be searched for within the developing object, and not beyond it.

3. The development stages of the sector

At the first stage, rural tourism was developing almost spontaneously, with its main actors being the owners of the estates, farmers, and private entrepreneurs. Due to the work of the NGO "Agroecotourism" and the NGO "Recreation in the Village", it got more structured as well as more coordinated. It should be noted that a significant contribution to the improvement of the structure of agroecotourism was made by the United Nations Development Program, which in 2003 announced a competition of mini grants aimed at improving the estates adjacent to Belovezhskaya Pushcha (Kamenets, Svisloch, Volkovysk and Pruzhany districts) (Hursik, 2015). As a result of the competition, financial and information support was provided to ten agroestates of the above-mentioned regions.

The next stage is connected with the publication of the Decree of the President of the Republic of Belarus No. 372 of June 2, 2006 "On measures for the development of agroecotourism in the Republic of Belarus", which for the first time determined the legal basis for the reception and providing services to tourists in agroestates. This legal document, on one hand, streamlined the activities of rural tourism entities, and on the other hand, it did not become a hindrance or a barrier to the creative potential of agroecotourism. Progressive, simple, and understandable, as well as liberal in its content, the Decree has contributed and still contributes to the successful development of the sphere in question. After the publication of the Decree, the problem of agroecotourism in the country drew the attention of both governmental and local authorities, thus creating the mechanism of interaction between these structures and owners of estates (Kochurko, 2013).

The third milestone in the quantitative and qualitative development of the rural tourism sector was the adoption of the Participation Program of Belagroprombank OJSC in the development of agroecotourism in the Republic of Belarus, which was launched on July 25th (Shadrakova & Sharuho, 2015). According to the Program, agrotourism entities were able to get soft loans that resulted in a significant increase in the number of estates and in the improvement in the level of their services.

The fourth stage is connected with the publication of the new version of the Presidential Decree of November 23, 2010, which kept the existing privileges to the actors engaged in agroecotourism activity and also introduced the new ones. The current stage of the development of agroecotourism is characterized by the fact that there is a heated discussion about the new amendments to the presidential decree that are planned to be introduced in January 1, 2018, and which can significantly influence the further development of this sector of the economy in our country (Demyanchik, 2015; Poljakov & Kalitenja, 2007).

4. The dynamics of the development of the sector

The experience of agroecotourism development in the republic has shown that this sector includes three real participants:

1   The owners of rural estates registered with local authorities.
2   Farmers, combining the production of agricultural products with the reception of tourists in their estates.
3   Large agricultural enterprises (agricultural production complexes, regional unitary agricultural enterprises, etc.)

Analysis shows that the largest share in the volume of agroecotourism services is provided by the first of the above-mentioned groups, and the smallest by the third one. It should be noted that 80 to 85 percent of holidaymakers in agro-estates are domestic tourists, whereas the share of foreign customers is quite low. In addition, the largest share of those arriving from abroad is made up of visitors from Russia, mainly residents of mega-cities like Moscow and St. Petersburg (Tarasjonok, 2014).

As for large farms in rural areas, their opportunities are not yet practically employed, although some of the leaders of such enterprises have already taken steps in this direction. The potential of private farms has not been fully utilized too.

Throughout its existence, agroecotourism in the country analyzed maintains a stable, positive dynamic of its development. Here is some statistical data obtained in the research conducted in Brest region as a confirmation of this thesis.

Table 14.1 Development of agroecotourism sector in Brest region

Year	Number of rural estates	Number of tourists received
2010	151	13,758
2011	195	16,187
2012	218	20,259
2013	253	30,993
2014	296	38,640
2015	311	41,617
2016	343	48,154

Source: The National Statistics Committee of the Republic of Belarus(2016)

Table 14.2 The dynamics of the development of the agroecotourism sector

Year	Number of rural estates	Number of tourists received	Number of foreign tourists received	Income (in BYR)
2014	296	38640	5106	11 775 615 800
2015	311	41617	5409	14 125 100 000
2016	343 (+10,3 %)	48154 (+15,7 %)	6817 (+ 26,0 %)	20 113 358 000 (+ 42,4 %)

Source: The National Statistics Committee of the Republic of Belarus (2016)

Table 14.3 Leading regions (2016)

Regions	Number of rural estates	Number of tourists received	Income (in BYR)
Brest	53	13 337	634 641. 3
Kobrin	35	8 023	27 6 618. 0
Kamenets	60	5 789	28 0 330. 4
Pinsk	24	5 650	255 629. 5
Baranovichi	27	2 647	8 4 561. 8

Source: The National Statistics Committee of the Republic of Belarus (2016)

The dynamics of the last three years is quite impressive (see Table 14.2).

In 2016, 43 new agro estates were registered in Brest region, while 14 ceased their activity. Moreover, all the above indicators were achieved as a result of the activity of 249 estates from 343 registered ones. A significant number of businesses did not receive tourists in 2016 for various reasons.

From year to year, the leading regions in agroecotourism are rural areas located around the largest cities or natural reserves (see Table 14.3).

5. The factors contributing to the successful performance of the sector

What is the basis for the fairly successful development of agroecotourism in the country? Based on the study conducted by the authors, the reasons are the following.

First, it is liberal legislation. According to the aforementioned Decree of the President of the Republic of Belarus, the declarative principle of registration of rural estates is quite simple, and the amount of the annual tax on the activities of agroecotourism entities is quite low.

Second, it is the partnership of government bodies, public organizations and agro-business entities. Having relative freedom of action, not being directly subordinate to officials, the owners of estates with the active assistance of civil society institutions were able to establish mutually beneficial, constructive relations with local and regional government bodies. In all regions of the republic, regional and district public councils for agroecotourism have been established, which have assumed the function of coordinating efforts to develop this small business.

Third, these are creative and creative personalities working in this field, who, thanks to simple and understandable rules of agro-ecotourism, have an opportunity for self-realization.

Fourth, preferential loans of OJSC Belagroprombank can be applied for by any agroecotourism entity.

Fifth, these are investments received through different grant programs and international technical assistance projects. Participation in the projects allowed a significant number of owners of estates to gain the necessary knowledge, to study the best practices of this type of activity abroad, and eventually to improve the quality of the services they provide.

Special attention should be devoted to resilience and adaptability of the owners of estates to unfavorable external circumstances. In 2015, due to the economic crisis in Russia and Belarus, there was a sharp decline in the exchange rate of these countries' currencies, which led to significant decline in tourism activity and decrease in revenues. Agroecotourism in Belarus was the only kind of tourism that showed positive dynamics of its development in 2015 with all its indicators growing (Tarasjonok, 2014). It should be stated that many owners of rural estates managed to keep and even increase their incomes during the crisis period due to the introduction of such services as organization of weddings, anniversary celebrations, and corporate events that have become very popular among urban residents of Belarus. Parties and celebrations in rural estates, as an alternative to city cafes and restaurants, are very much in demand today, and the owners of the estates showed flexibility and initiative, thus making up the decline in revenues caused by a decrease in the flow of tourists.

Resilience and adaptability of the agroecotourism sector in Belarus is expressed not only in the ability to recover in times of crisis, but also in anticipating and capturing new trends of tourism industry thus reshaping its forms and context. In the 21st century, for instance, travellers need not only good service and the possibility to observe natural and cultural values. They feel the need for thrills and impressions, the need to be an active participant. Impressions become an important tourist product, and the economy of service and information is replaced by the economy of impressions. Owners of rural estates in Belarus are aware of this trend, and some of them have already learned how to create this new tourism product (Klitsunova, 2016).

The success of the sphere is quite apparent. But the study has also revealed that there is still the need to improve the quality of agroecotourism services. The conditions at some of estates and the services they provide require serious improvement. A certain amount of agroestates are still under reconstruction, and in addition, not all of them have the required sanitary and hygienic conditions. The owners who have recently joined this activity have little experience in the receiving of guests, foreigners in particular. They do not speak foreign languages, and they lack intercultural communications skills. There is also no differentiated approach to different categories of holidaymakers.

The experience of recent years has shown that the following target groups (categories) of clients of rural estates can be distinguished.

1   Domestic tourists mainly urban residents;
2   Foreign tourists;
3   Groups of colleagues united by common place of work;
4   Groups of friends or acquaintances;
5   Families;
6   Groups engaged in cycling tours or boat trips.

Basic types of the services provided have also been determined.

1   Organization of short-term recreation at weekends;
2   Long-term recreation in a rural estate;
3   Organization of family celebrations or corporate parties;
4   Reception and maintenance of touring tourist groups.

The list of services includes the following types: accommodation, catering, fishing, swimming, sauna, collecting mushroom, berries, and herbs, doing sports, entertainment activities, hiking trips, boat trips, cycling routes, visiting nearby historical and cultural sites, concerts of local folklore groups, meetings new people, engagement in the handicrafts of local craftsmen, and others.

6. What are the priorities for further development of agroecotourism in the country?

As a witness and as an active participant of all positive achievements of agroecotourism as well as of its weak points and drawbacks, the following steps can be considered as possible priorities for further development of the sphere.

First, the network of estates must be developed first of all in those regions that are the most attractive and provide the largest number of objects of interest to tourists and the most travel opportunities. At the moment, the number of estates on such territories is small, and they are not able to meet the demand of a potentially possible number of tourists. The absence of competition affects the quality of services and their prices. Comparing the prices with the neighbouring Ukraine and Poland, some foreign tourists have noted that sometimes for the same money in these countries, you can get better and more diverse services.

Second, it is necessary to continue the production of promotional products, booklets, brochures, and catalogues.

Third, since in the recent years the number of estates in the country has tripled, a large group of owners has emerged who have not received any training and do not have sufficient practical work experience. In this regard, it is necessary to conduct regular trainings, seminars, and internships in order to learn the best practices in this field of activity in Belarus and abroad. This educational sphere is developing quite successfully, and the practice of episodic seminars has already turned into a coherent system of instruction.

Fourth, it is necessary to continue developing, marking and arranging pedestrian, bicycle and water routes, to research target groups and their requirements, to encourage their growth and to improve the quality of the service.

Fifth, it is necessary to do competitions among the owners of estates, as well as organize festivals of rural tourism.

Sixth, work in the agroecotourism sector must be built on the basis of an analysis of positive and negative experiences.

As the experience of arranging "green" routes (water, bicycle) has shown, their participants are not only domestic tourists, but also visitors from other countries. Summarizing the useful experience of implementing the "green" routes on the basis of the opinions of their participants from different countries, the following conclusions can be drawn: 1) the practice of organizing tours for foreign and Belarusian tourists has good prospects and should be continued in the future; 2) there are a number of positive factors that attract foreign tourists to Belarus. These are preserved nature, hospitality of people, the ability of the owners of estates to cook delicious healthy food, as well as the authentic Belarusian villages that cannot be found in Western Europe.

Negative factors restraining the development of tourism in this area include poorly developed infrastructure of tourist services (insufficient number of rural estates, hotels, catering facilities, etc.). In addition the rural estates themselves are often unable to provide quality service to their clients, having insufficient sanitary and hygienic conditions for this. The process lacks the required number of road signs and bicycle trails. There is no possibility to purchase detailed maps that would allow you to travel around in unfamiliar terrain without any problems.

The progressive trend in the growth of inbound tourism is also hampered by the need to open visas for the Republic of Belarus, the complicated procedure for registering foreign citizens in the bodies of the Ministry of Internal Affairs, i.e. bureaucratic procedures that our competitors in Ukraine and Poland do not have. At most border crossings, it is prohibited to cross the border on foot or by bicycle. An exception is the customs in Belovezhskaya Pushcha and the Augustow Canal.

For all these reasons, inbound tourism in the region, as well as in the country as a whole, is at the starting point of its development. Therefore, promoting the growth of the flow of foreign customers to Belarus is one of the priority tasks of rural tourism in Belarus.

References

Demyanchik, V.T. (2015). *Agroekoturizm v Pripyatskom Polesie* [*Agroecotourism in the Pripyat Polesie*]. Brest, Belarus: Alternativa.

Hursik, V. (2015). *Razvitie agroturizma v prigranichnyh regionah na primere Brestskoj i Grodnenskoj oblastej* [*Development of agroecotourism in border regions on the case of Brest and Grodno regions*]. Minsk: Smeltok.

Klitsunova, V.A. (2016). *Sozdanije regionalnyh kreativnyh turproduktov na osnove inter- pretatsii kulturnogo i prirodnogo nasledija* [*Development of regional creative tourism products based on the interpretation of cultural and natural heritage*]. Minsk: Otduh v derevne.

Kochurko, V.I. (Ed.). (2013). *Eko- i agroturizm: Perspektivy razvitija na mestnyh territo- rijah* [*Eco- and agrotourism: Development prospects in local areas*]. Minsk: Chetyre chetverti.

The National Statistics Committee of the Republic of Belarus. (2016). *Tourism and tourism resources in the republic of Belarus.* ISBN Publication No. 978-985-7115-41-9. Retrieved from www.belstat.gov.by

Poljakov, J., & Kalitenja, L. (2007). *Razvitie ustoichivogo selskogo turizma* [*Development of sustainable rural tourism*]. Minsk: Junipak.

Shadrakova, A.V., & Sharuho, I.N. (Eds.). (2015). *Regionalnyje tendentsii i faktory raz- vitija agroekoturizma Brestskoj i Grodnenskoj oblastej* [*Regional trends and factors of the development of agroecotourism in Brest and Grodno Regions*]. Minsk: Smeltok.

Tarasjonok, A.I. (Ed.). (2014). *Biznes v agro- i ekoturizme* [*Business in agro- and ecotourism*]. Minsk: Chetyre chetverti.

15 The market of the tour operators in Germany within a disruptive environment

Implications for the management and the resilient orientation of destinations

Martin Fontanari & Timm Ewald

1. The importance of resilient destinations for tourism and society

1.1 Introduction

All forms of holiday and leisure activities are always associated with safety and variety for travelers during their stay in the desired destination.

Over the past three decades, the phenomenon of international terrorism has increasingly shifted the focus of travel decisions to the security needs of guests (Hoffmann, 2008, p. 138; Glaeßer, 2005, p. 66f.; Kuschel & Schröder, 2002, p. 28), but also the perceived increase in environmental disasters, climate change, political unrest, epidemics and uncontrolled migration as well as selective media coverage have had a massive impact on the decision-making process of finding a destination for the holiday trip. In this context, the two main players in the tourism value chain – tour operators and destinations – must increasingly make strategic considerations on how to meet the challenges of the factors influencing the overall tourism experience in the long term, but still with the necessary flexibility. The aim is to sustainably maintain and consolidate the respective position in the tourism market.

The basic aim is to define the use of the concept of resilience for the tourism environment and to demonstrate its different meanings, applications and integrative function in an understanding of the various meanings; a different concept of resilience will emerge for a destination than for a tourism company, such as the tour operator.

Subsequently, it will be interesting to see to what extent the first ideal-typical concepts of a resilient destination can be roughly sketched out and what significance they could have for product portfolio planning from the point of view of the travel industry.

Empirically, the current understanding of the resilience of German tour operators is elaborated and compared with an assessment of the importance of resilient destinations.

1.2 Market relevance of resilience in the tourism context

If one assumes that the tourism scene is characterized by a safe, stable and consistent framework conditions for the provision and use of services, unforeseeable, permanent and temporary disturbances, depending on their severity, endanger not only the current destination or business model, but also the ability to act and react with an adequate and individual crisis management in the event of an incident, due to the associated change in demand.

In the natural and social sciences, but also in materials management, the term "resilience" has emerged in recent years, which describes the resilience of a system and the ability to return to its normal or equilibrium state after disturbances (Hartard, 2014, p. 201). By resilience, Sutcliff and Vogus understand that in the context of organizational psychology, resilience means maintaining an organization's reactive and proactive adaptability in the event of an incident, from crisis situations to systemic crises: "(resilience is the . . .) maintenance of positive adjustment under challenging conditions" (Sutcliff & Vogus, 2003, p. 95). In psychology and the social sciences, resilient persons are described as people with abilities that master critical situations well and emerge from them strengthened; they are able to make the best possible use of their abilities and skills from the resources and potentials available to them, at the moment or for the duration of the disorder, to master the crisis and to understand overcoming the danger situation as an opportunity for development (Welter-Enderlin & Hildenbrand, 2006, p. 16).

Derived from this the term, destination resilience refers to the ability and skill of a destination area to be optimally prepared for disasters and crises and to provide the minimum basic services in the tourism context (supply, infrastructure, transport services, security, health, guest care, etc.) or to guarantee them with the least possible delay; the preparation and orientation of a destination for a possible disruption should be carried out as early as possible in the planning stage.

In the ideal case, an efficient management of resilience leads to the fastest possible restoration of supply and functionality – both through internal and external resources, which are used in the course of resilience and crisis management.

Corporate resilience, on the other hand, describes the capacity of a company to accept external disturbances, shocks or distortions in the event of social, economic or political changes and to adapt to the new conditions as a bundle of individual resilience and organizational resilience (Di Bella, 2014, p. 168).

It must, however, be widened in such a way that sudden internal or endogenous distortions can also occur, which could have a massive impact on the service provider's production system or could bring it to a permanent standstill. As a working term for the resilience of touristic service providers, in particular tour operators, the term "corporate resilience" expresses a hybrid company organization which, with its own capabilities and skills, adapts itself to disruptions by means of scheduled operational changes and is able to restore its entrepreneurial performance in the best possible way.

1.3 The (touristic) importance and necessity of resilience in the context of globalization

The development of globalization has initially brought the industrialized world closer together, economically and politically; however, these developments also imply an ever-increasing degree of networking and dependence on industrial supply and sales processes in the hands of a few multinational companies and thus a concentration of economic power and control. However, the more complex, global and networked these new economic, technical and political structures become, the more intensively interwoven infrastructures are created, which require intensive technical maintenance and ongoing modernization, also driven by profit-oriented considerations (Fontanari & Kredinger, 2017, p. 2f.).

In times of temporary or latent crises which affect or influence a city, region or even several countries to the detriment of the functioning of its infrastructures or cause them to collapse partially or completely and in the context of the increasing dynamic change in tourism, it will therefore be important to deal with structures and approaches that address the safeguarding of the performance and competitiveness of companies and destinations.

This raises the question of the "counter-concept" for companies and regions, for example, which, with the increase in high-risk global developments and their dependencies, make it possible to separate them. The consequences of globalization and related worldwide crisis of financial, social and economic systems can lead to the collapse of a destination, region or country (systemic crisis) and cause the breakdown of economic and social networks in the system.

The trigger of a systemic crisis that leads to serious impairments of elementary partial and supply systems may be secondary to the systemic crisis (risk increase due to exponential high-risk developments such as those in the financial system, major natural disasters, armed conflicts and terrorism). The high degree of interdependence and cross-linking of the subsystems may lead to a domino effect in the event of system malfunctions. In the context of tourism destination development, resilient destinations are spaces that are largely detached from such dependencies, increasingly rely on inner strengths and authentic potentials and can thus contribute to added value and value creation on a global level. In this context, one can speak of *healthy destinations* that understand how to pick up and interpret trends at different levels, take socio-economic developments into account and react appropriately within the framework of the sustainability paradigm. Furthermore, these destinations gain more sovereignty, identity and a strengthening of the people's spirit of cooperation and interaction between all generations (Fontanari, 2016, p. 9). A corresponding resilience is given the more one dissolves from fragile supra-regional dependencies in supply and disposal and concentrates on self-sufficient regional or small-scale supply systems or closed-loop recycling management systems (Fontanari & Kredinger, 2017, p. 5).

2. Ideal model of a resilient destination

2.1 Dimensions of resilient destinations

As a destination or tourist destination, the terms "destination" or "destination area" are to be equated. Destination as such includes, among other things, the areas of economy, politics and the inhabitants' original habitat. The tourist offer consists of climatic, agricultural, historical-cultural, economic as well as other additional services and leads to attractive tourist offers and packages. The latter are therefore a complex network of individual success factors, which – combined to create an overall picture – form the basis for incoming business.

Crisis-resistant regions are regions that show weak or no negative effects on internal or external disturbances with regard to their development indicators. If negative effects occur, these regions quickly return to their system equilibrium and original performance after a short period of time, or even achieve better values. A resilient region thus has the ability to absorb internal and external disturbances through change processes, so that the functions, structures and relationships essential for the sustainable development of the region are maintained. These regions therefore have a low level of vulnerability and a high degree of resilience (Drath, 2016, p. 98f.).

Resilient destinations are also and above all characterized by autonomous systems or structures based on the aspects of regional economy. The term "regional economy" refers to value-added chains and exchange relationships between resources and actors that generate a regional closed-loop economy through their interaction.

An important success factor for the "marketable resilience" of a destination is the bundling of various elements into a product that is as unique as possible, so that there is little potential for substitution. Consequently, it can be concluded that a resilient destination has core competencies with which it generates competitive advantages, can prove to be a unique selling proposition in marketing and can differentiate itself from other target areas through a high degree of diversification.

Ideally, destinations will discover their market niche in the variety of resilient development opportunities and perspectives: They will link corresponding fields of development with the integration of locals and guests into product marketing and design. In order to ensure the continued existence of a sustainable and resilient goal, it is therefore essential that, in addition to the efficient cooperation of the service providers, the local population is also included in the planning process, as functioning infrastructures and self-sufficiency aspects are of the highest priority for both tourists and the local population.

The integration of the locals and tourists into such a resilient supply and activation system must also be communicated and marketed on the basis of knowledge and experience and must result in a win-win situation, i.e. a positive synergy effect, for both stakeholders and all tourism players. The evolution of resilience requires a dynamic adjustment and development process: thus, a destination in the strategic context can align its long-term development orientation according to the destination and market potentials with the family goal and thus go through a "double development".

Essentially, the basic resiliency goals of a destination are all development fields in the supply sector (agriculture, energy production, waste disposal and recycling) which result in a functioning autonomous regional closed-loop recycling system. Secondary goals of destination resilience are knowledge- and behavior-based goals, which aim at a change of attitude and mental strengthening of the locals and guests. Here, destination research faces the challenge of developing marketable tourism products and services that vertically expand tourism value creation in the sense of the closed-loop economy; on the other hand, cooperative, action- and project-oriented control systems must be developed for tourism regional management. It should be noted that such adjustments in the destination do not lead to exponential price increases for incoming tourism, as this can lead to shifts in the tourism flows.

The fact that the development of resilient structures in a destination context can also mean more sovereignty and identity, as well as a strengthening of the spirit of cooperation that has been invoked over and over again, as well as the interaction of all generations, is only indicated here with reference to the effects of "social agriculture", "effects of the second pillar of agricultural policy (regional agricultural accounting)" and "optimization of customer loyalty", etc.

2.2 Resilient destinations from the perspective of the travel industry

Destinations and tour operators form a mutually dependent coexistence in the tourism value creation, whose success depends on the resilience of the counterpart on the side of the destination (beneficiary, politics, population, environmental conditions). All service providers have their common vision for the destination in mind and work together to implement it. Cooperations that have a decisive influence on the long-term development of a destination are formulated, initiated and structured by means of strategic analyses.

Tour operators receive ideal-typical support from, for example, state tourist offices, whose regional knowhow, network and, not least, financial joint marketing measures enable them to collaboratively and sustainably develop the destination in a resilient direction.

A tour operator is also responsible for the long-term development of a destination and should be closely involved in the development process. This may also entail certain investment services that involve the development of self-sufficient supply systems or mechanisms, so it is a decision on strategic investments that are facing long-term amortization. This results in a different degree of commitment and cooperation between the destination actors and travel management.

Such a high or intensive degree of cooperation in turn presupposes a high degree of preliminary work and preliminary projects in the sense of confidence-building and intensive as well as professional information and communication structures that are to be maintained jointly: the associated higher transaction costs have to be taken into account in pricing again from a business point of view, but should flow into these in the long term in order not to act with exponential price increases on the market and thus reduce demand. In addition to the internal challenges of its organizational structure (resource allocation, adaptation of the operational and organizational structure to changing market conditions, etc.), tour operators have to rethink their product design approaches with a clear future in mind. In the course of the increasing share of information on target areas, product characteristics and in particular for comparison with competing offers, the organizers must realign themselves: the organiser must be able to adapt its product portfolio to the respective economic, social and (geo)political conditions at any time as quickly as possible.

This results in various aspects of the company's further strategic focus on resilient destinations.

2.2.1 Specialization level of a tour operator

Organizers with a high degree of specialization in a particular destination/region carry the risk of high economic dependence, as their portfolio and sales are strongly dependent on external influences and the mentioned possible disruptive factors and therefore cannot be influenced by the tour operator himself. As a result, the existing product portfolio is no longer in line with market requirements in the event of a long-term incident, and risk diversification is therefore impossible due to the lack of diversification. A tour operator with a balanced product portfolio, which includes resilient destinations, offers its customers the opportunity to switch to the same level of service in the event of a disturbance factor. In this way, the organizer, with a diversified and varied product portfolio, ensures that its customer base does not shift to competitors and that no economic damage occurs.

2.2.2 Guarantee risks and risk management

Many tour operators accept financial risks on the basis of guaranteed purchase, in some cases prepaid contingents. Even if the guarantees are sold out quickly in the event of short-term disruptive factors, this results in intensive economic damage to the vendor (price decline, cancellation costs, etc.). Accordingly, resilient organizers have comparatively low financial dependencies or additional insurance coverage from insurance companies (e.g. default guarantees). Resilient organizers therefore have an appropriate and well-functioning risk management system, which takes immediate effect in the event of a malfunction and minimizes potential damage ad hoc.

2.2.3 Product portfolio optimization compared to demand

For each type of tour operator, a diversified destination portfolio has to be served in such a way that the following aspects of marketing design can be realized for the customer in the context of a reliable offer design:

a. Consistency and continuity of supply (branding),
b. Sustainability impact,

c. Stable price/performance ratio and
d. Dealing with risks and goodwill regulations.

Consideration of these aspects is the basis for the formation of a relationship of trust, not only with regard to the demand side or with the actors of the destination, but also promotes an understanding of customer resilience. In this respect, the innovative tour operator is developing "resilience-sensitive customers", which in turn are increasing the demand for resilient destinations. Based on Rogers' innovation research and diffusion theory and his early-adaptor model, new strategic customer bases can be built up (Rogers, 1995). By building up a resilient thinking customer base and creating an appropriate range of resilient destinations, the tour operator is able to create its own upward spiral or generate a positive domino effect for itself.

Here too, it is important for the organizers to be on the market as early as possible with the corresponding products in order to turn potential customers into their own customers at an early stage.

3. Empirical evidence

3.1 Understanding resilience of German tour operators

3.1.1 Classification of the empirical investigation

From 17 May to 31 July 2017, an online survey of German tour operators took place within the ISM – International School of Management at Cologne. The empirical study on "Product design priorities and management approaches within the German tour operator market under special consideration of the factor resilience" was conducted within the lecture on "Practise and Research-Workshop".

More than 1000 tour operators based in Germany were contacted, leading to 141 valid interviews. Nearly 50 percent of the respondents stated that they held the position of managing director (48.9%), while a further 10.6 percent were members of the executive board, 9.9 percent respectively of division management, department management or middle management. In total, 89.2 percent of the respondents thus assigned themselves to the executive levels in their company, while 40.4 percent reported the total number of persons employed with up to 10 persons, 35.5 percent had between 11 and 99 persons in employment, 12.6 percent between 100 and 499 persons employed and 8.5 percent had more than 500 employees. The distribution of the executives surveyed also reflects the size distribution of the German tour operators' landscape, which in its structure is strongly influenced by small and medium-sized companies.

The survey covered a variety of topics, including the issues of general market and corporate development as well as the significance of sustainability and resilience. For this article, only data from the third survey part "Sustainability and Resilience Considerations of German Tour Operators on Destination Development" will be considered and analyzed.

3.1.2 Evaluation of the importance of sustainability in tourism

The year 2017, proclaimed by the UN as the "International Year of Sustainable Tourism for Development", led to a survey of the personal assessment of the importance of sustainability in tourism and subsequently to an assessment of the three pillars or dimensions of sustainability: Today, this is seen as a concept in which ecological, social and economic dimensions intertwine and all three dimensions need to be taken into account, even if this entails increased demands and corresponding complexity. In an initial assessment of sustainability, the managers surveyed rated sustainability as an important topic with 73 percent agreement.

In addition, those managers who consider sustainability to be significant in general were asked to assess the three dimensions of sustainability in a more differentiated manner. All three pillars showed a relatively similar evaluation pattern. In cumulative terms, environmental sustainability was rated as significant/very significant at 69.3 percent, economic sustainability was rated as significant/very significant at 58.5 percent and social sustainability was rated as significant/very significant at 61.4 percent. Surprisingly, the high proportion of those who did not want to make any further assessments is almost 25 percent. Reasons for this could be that the three-pillar model is not further known or that respondents have not yet dealt with the issue of sustainability in more detail.

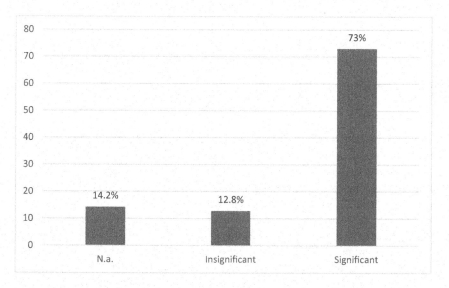

Figure 15.1 Meaning of the concept of sustainability in tourism
Source: Own illustration

Table 15.1 Question: "If you consider sustainability to be important, how would you evaluate it?"

	Ecological sustainability	Economic sustainability	Social sustainability
Very significant	21.4%	22.1%	20.7%
Significant	47.9%	36.4%	40.7%
Neutral	5.7%	15.0%	10.7%
Less significant	0%	2.1%	1.4%
Insignificant	1.4%	0.7%	0.7%
N.a.	23.6%	23.7%	25.8%
Total	100%	100%	100%

Source: Own illustration (n = 141)

Table 15.2 Question: "Which of these external factors have had the greatest positive or negative impact on your business development in the last three financial years? Select the three most relevant influencing factors."

	Positive factor	Ranking positive	Negativ factor	Ranking negative
Change in technology	53.9%	1	3.5%	7
Labour law regulations	5%	8	12.8%	5
Stability of political systems	18.4%	5	31.9%	2
Environmental changes/requirements	8.5%	6	12.8%	5
Increasing customer demands	27.7%	3	14.9%	3
Globalisation of the economy	28.4%	2	2.8%	8
Safety situation in destinations	20.6%	4	43.3%	1
Competition intensity/competitors	7.8%	7	13.5%	4

Source: Own illustration (n = 141)

During the final first part of the survey, managers had to identify the strongest three positive and negative factors among a selection of eight key factors influencing corporate development. Positive factors of influence were (1) technological change, (2) globalization of the economy and (3) increased customer demands. In contrast, (1) the security situation in destinations, (2) the stability of political systems and (3) the increased customer demands were cited as negative factors influencing the company's own development.

The high rating of the security situation in destinations (43.4%) – i.e. almost every second manager – and the stability of the political systems (31.9%), which classify just under a third of the managers as a strong factor influencing their own corporate development, make it indirectly visible how important the topic of security in product design and the choice of destination is in terms of stable corporate development. This result is of particular importance for the analysis of the resilience of destinations and tour operators. It is also striking that the increased customer demands are seen as both a positive and negative factor in the company's development. This can be justified by the fact that on the one hand, increasing customer demands result in tour operators adjusting or expanding their portfolio according to the new needs and thus new options in the product range, which open up new sales and profit potentials. On the other hand, increasing customer demands lead to an additional expense increase in the extension of the portfolio as well as to a higher time and transaction costs in the operative process of travel planning and execution. The reason for this is the growing demand for more individualized travel services.

In a further question section, it was essential to evaluate the critical design or influencing factors that will decisively impact the tour operators' product policy in the future. Prior to this, the most relevant design factors for product policy were selected in a preliminary study on an analysis of literature and studies, and the responses were submitted to multiple entries.

Submitting the first seven factors of a future-oriented product policy to the premises of sustainability, it can be concluded from this that the conceptual approach to product innovation is removed from the classical influencing factors (return on investment, offer design in depth and width, pricing policy,

Table 15.3 Question: "Future relevance of the design and drivers of product policy and innovation (multiple answers possible)"

	Ranking "very significant"	In percent
Travel safety	1	76.6%
Quality improvement	2	48.0%
Flexibility of the offer orientation	3	46.8%
Increased customer loyalty through customer enthusiasm	4	46.1%
Product innovation (based on competitive advantages)	5	39.0%
Stable service partners	6	38.8%
Quality standards	7	37.0%
Pricing policy for travel prices	8	34.8%
Profitability	9	27.0%
Goodwill in customer complaints	10	26.2%
Depth of product range/system solution	11	22.7%
Efficiency of service processes	12	21.3%
Brand management	13	20.6%
Wide product range/full range of products	14	15.6%

Source: Own illustration (n = 141)

goodwill, etc.) and developed in such a way that criteria such as security, quality, flexibility on the supply side, customer loyalty and stable service partners (hotels, destination management companies, etc.) are established in the future.

3.1.3 Resiliency awareness and macro-environment

For the introduction to the topic of resilience, the knowledge of the concept of resilience was examined, which was presented with the following description:

> *"Resistance, adaptability, ability to overcome disturbances in the tourist system caused by crises and conflicts of all kinds", but also "inner strength of employees and the company in dealing with crisis situations".*

Only 12.1 percent of the executives surveyed were unfamiliar with the term and rated it as unknown. In contrast, however, almost 30 percent stated that they were concretely concerned with the resilience ability. If one assumes that those 20.6 percent of the answers to this question who did not want to or were unable to provide any information on this question also make no reference to the term "resilience", then the cumulative figure of 32.7 percent of respondents is the same for managers who do not deal with the issue of resilience. At 37.6 percent, the relative majority of respondents pointed out that they had a rudimentary knowledge of the company's resilience, and that they dealt with it to a lesser extent:

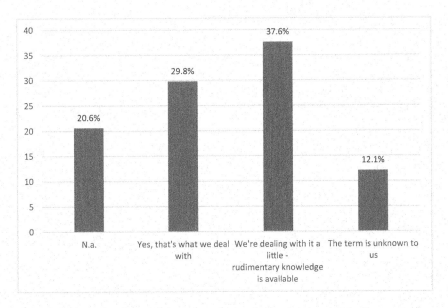

Figure 15.2 Knowledge of the concept of resilience in the company

Source: Own illustration (n = 141)

Directly with the knowledge of the concept of resilience for a company, the question arises which external determinants influence the stability and development of the company to what extent. The strongest negative influence is attributed to the following factors:

- "Political unrest" (56.4%),
- "Diseases and epidemics" (52.1%),
- "Clash of civilization" (45%),
- "Weather anomalies and climate change" (40.0%),
- "Cyber-attacks or corporate espionage" (36.4%),
- "New EU regulations and requirements" (31.4%) and
- "Global economic growth weakness" (32.1%)

In contrast, the majority of positive factors influencing the company's stability and development were:

- "Technological change and the digital society" (40.0%),
- "Globalization and networking" (39.3%) as well as
- "Demographic change and migration" (24.3%)

Here it becomes clear that the four most mentioned negative factors affecting the stability and development of German tour operators (political unrest, diseases and epidemics, clash of civilization, weather anomalies and climate change) affect the destination, whereas the three strongest positive external factors ("technological change and the digital society", "globalization and networking" and "demographic

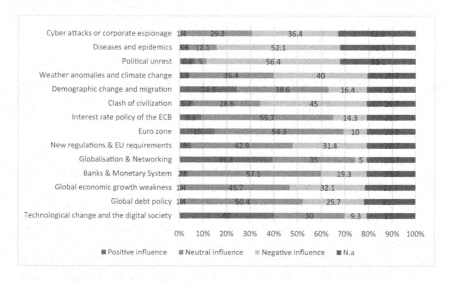

Figure 15.3 Negative and positive factors influencing corporate stability and development
Source: Own illustration (n = 141)

change and migration") have little or no connection to destinations and are seen as areas of opportunity/risk in the company's own corporate development.

From the tour operators' point of view, therefore, the greater risks and dangers of their own corporate development are the social, ecological and economic stability of the destination as well as the effects of the global framework conditions with regard to weather and climate change (which in turn have an impact on the destination).

In this context, a more important role is attached to the safe holiday stay and thus also to the ability of the destination to deal with crises, dangers and disturbances in the best possible way: In essence, this addresses the ability of the resilience of the destination.

Chapter 2 showed that it is possible to define the discussion and design of experimental destinations as a further development of the approach to environmentally compatible and sustainable destinations. In the further survey, the managers interviewed were asked to what extent they agreed with the thesis that "in future, environmental compatibility and sustainability should be assessed more strongly in terms of the degree of resilience of a destination". Exactly 50 percent of all respondents agree with this statement, whilst only 4.3 percent disagree with the question/thesis:

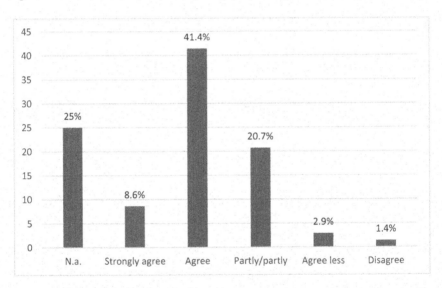

Figure 15.4 Thesis: "Resilience of a destination as a new "indicator" of environmental compatibility and sustainability"

Source: Own illustration (n = 141)

With regard to product development and marketing, a second question raised in the form of a thesis, namely whether "Destinations with a high resilience capacity will experience stronger demand in the future and thus assume a higher competitive significance". This statement records a further increase in agreement, with almost 53 percent of respondents agreeing to this correlation, whilst only 2.1 percent tend to deny it or reject it strictly. With 20 percent (partly/partly agreed) and 25 percent who did not want to provide any information, a large part of the respondents here still have uncertainty or the need for clarification.

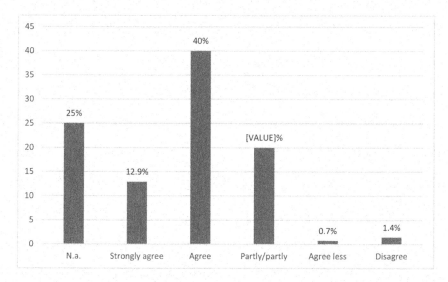

Figure 15.5 Thesis: "Increased resilience of destinations as a success factor in demand"
Source: Own illustration (n = 141)

According to German tour operators, destinations with a higher resilience capacity will tend to experience stronger demand and as a consequence, will have a stronger competitive importance in the context of external factors triggering the crisis. The importance of safety during travel and holidays is highlighted in numerous studies and publications. With this approach, destinations could thus make a central contribution to increasing competitiveness through product and communication design, while at the same time providing elementary infrastructures and product contributions via the scenarios of a closed-loop economy described in Chapter 2.

3.1.4 Approaches to a cooperative development of resilience between destinations and tour operators

In a concluding question on trends in market-oriented corporate development, theses were submitted that deal with the intensification of cooperation between destinations and tour operators in the context of greater/stronger destination resilience.

Specifically, it was asked for approval or rejection of the thesis that "top performers and stakeholders in tourism intensify their cooperation through a more intelligent use of resources and new business models". Specification of resources usage was not made here but was deliberately left open in order not to prejudge any limitation or diversion to possible resource potentials.

The statement of a more intensive cooperation in the area of resource use of a destination and a more intensive cooperation of tour operators for new business models is accepted by 41.5 percent of the managers, while only 8.6 percent of the respondents agree with this less – with no rejection of this thesis! Relatively speaking, this approval is even higher if the 25 percent of those respondents who were unable or unwilling to give any indication of this are deducted. Approximately one-quarter of the executives (23.6%) are neutral here (partial approval):

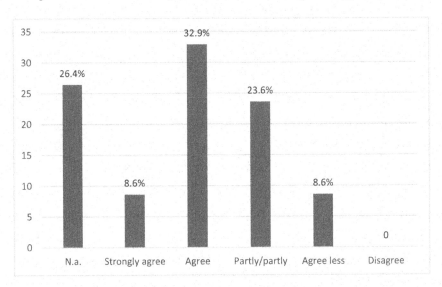

Figure 15.6 Thesis: "Service providers and stakeholders in tourism intensify their cooperation through a more intelligent use of resources and new business models"

Source: Own illustration (n = 141)

A further question dealt with the way of intensifying the cooperation between destination and tour operators; as a response, the vertical integration of tour operators from and with service providers in one destination was offered in order to work together more intensively in the long term under the guiding theme of increasing resilience and to enter into concentration processes. Here the agreement is in line with the previous question, and 44.3 percent of executives agree with a stronger vertical integration and the resulting concentration processes between the destination service providers and the tour operator; 5.7 percent agree with this strongly. Only one manager does not agree (0.7%), another 4.3 percent agree less, whilst another quarter of the respondents are neutral.

In order to increase resilience in destinations, but also to increase the entrepreneurial resilience of tour operators, various development strategies and packages of measures are available to illustrate the link between the "experimental coexistence" of destination and tour operator by means of an exemplary option. The managers were asked, for example, with which attribution of significance the providers of a destination would have to experience an increased sensitization and qualification for the greatest possible degree of self-sufficiency in the supply sector (energy, raw materials, foodstuffs, health). This was considered very significant by 34.3 percent of managers, while only 6.4 percent considered it insignificant. However, the majority are indifferent to this sensitization and qualification (38.6%), while one-fifth of the interviewees (20.7%) gave no indication of this.

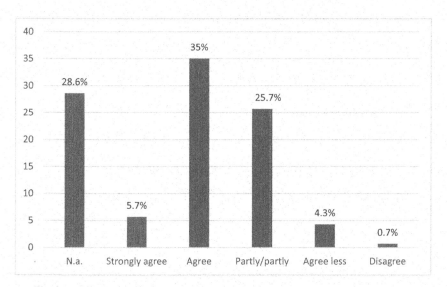

Figure 15.7 Thesis: "In the long term, the vertical integration of tour operators will experience increased concentration processes under the guiding principle of resilience"

Source: Own illustration (n = 141)

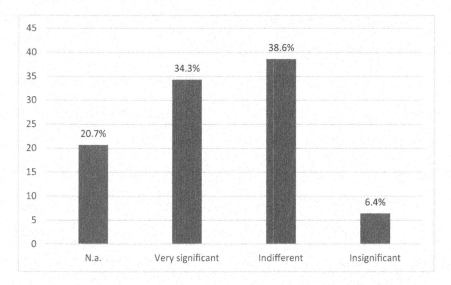

Figure 15.8 Question: "How do you assess the factor increased awareness and qualification of touristic service providers in the destination (e.g. through largely self-sufficient supply systems (energy, raw materials, food, health) which, from your point of view, means an increase in resilience for your company?"

Source: Own illustration (n = 141)

4. Derivations and recommendations

The empirical survey and analysis brings a surprising result: The managers of the German travel industry show a high sensitivity for the vulnerability of their business environment. There is a high awareness that the future business and product orientation, in an even closer development and cooperation context, must be seen and take place together with the service providers in a destination; the development of idle resources and potentials among service providers, which correspond to the idea of self-sufficiency and self-sufficiency, but also the development of new crisis response plans for overcoming disruptions and systemic crises, can only be realized in close cooperation between these two partners. With the reference to a "smarter use of resources", a more efficient and effective provision of services and thus, in the sense of sustainability, an optimal conservation of resources is also considered and thereby the basis for a reorientation of product and offer design.

In essence, tour operators are now being asked to set up a strategic working group with "their" destinations, together with the local service providers, in order to clarify at the outset the dimensions of desirable resilience ability and skills. Once the dimensions have been defined, it is essential to derive common target positions for the level of resilience on the destination side and to develop appropriate implementation strategies. With regard to the medium- and long-term implementation of "Resilience Realization Strategies", investment areas, project fields and design approaches will have to be derived and evaluated in detail, which require a cooperative investment within the framework of a public-private partnership (PPP). For tour operators, this would also mean a stronger sustainable commitment to the further development of destinations, which is in line with the sustainable coexistence approach.

Since, as a rule, different tour operators are involved in one destination both entrepreneurially and managerially as well the resilient destination development must now be understood as a joint development task, it is important to attract only committed tour operators for this project and to integrate them into a resilience network. Porter describes this state of competition-related cooperation as co-opetition (Porter, 2008).

This form of cooperation is common in highly industrialized sectors such as the automotive industry. In tourism, however, there may still be a lack of experience in this area. Nevertheless, a highly attractive network is emerging for the destination with its service providers and tour operators, in which synergies need to be realized that have never before been considered in this form: If the individual tour operators not only cooperate with each other (horizontal cooperation), but also with the local service providers of the upstream and/or downstream value-added stage (vertical integration), resident destinations can be integrated into the network. Within the strategic networks, the planning of resources can be more flexible. In addition, companies save time and resources in product development and the implementation of new products. The dependencies and barriers to entry within the networks may be considered very high at first, but in return the overall risk of financial and strategic risk is reduced. In addition, disruptions and systemic crises can now be mastered through self-help and a new culture of cooperation.

This raises the question of the organizational and developmental power of the design of junior structures and capabilities on an operational level in destinations and in the tour operator's company. This task can now be performed on a "small scale" – i.e. locally and regionally – in destinations and requires integration into a functioning strategic market system of providers and customers. Ideally, destinations discover their market niche in the diversity of development opportunities and perspectives: they combine corresponding fields of product design development with product marketing, involving local residents and guests.

The ultimate goal should be to design an innovative value-added process. Each part of the tourism value-added chain interacts with the participating service providers at a high level of cooperation and the associated reliability. A self-sufficient and resilient destination is created by the interaction of the individual players, subsistence businesses and the new, complementary range of services.

References

Di Bella, J. (2014). *Unternehmerische Resilienz. Protektive Faktoren für unternehmerischen Erfolg in risikoreichen Kontexten.* Dissertation, Universität Mannheim.

Drath, K. (2016). *Resilienz in der Unternehmensführung. Was Manager und ihre Teams stark macht* (2. Aufl.). Freiburg: Haufe Gruppe.

Fontanari, M. (2016). Zukunftsfaktor resiliente Gesellschaft. *JA! – Magazin für positive und gesunde Lebenswerte*, Nr. 10, Klagenfurt, S., 8–9.

Fontanari, M., & Kredinger, D. (2017). *Risiko- und Resilienzbewusstsein. Empirische Analysen und erste konzeptionelle Ansätze zur Steigerung der Resilienzfähigkeit von Regionen.* Working Paper, No. 9. Dortmund and Münster: Readbox Unipress.

Glaeßer, D. (2005). *Handbuch Krisenmanagement im Tourismus: Erfolgreiches Entscheiden in schwierigen Situationen.* Berlin: ESV – Erich Schmidt Verlag.

Hartard, S. (2014). Resilienz durch nachhaltige Ressourcenwirtschaft. In S. Hartard, A. Schaffer & E. Lang (Eds.), *Systeme in der Krise im Fokus von Resilienz und Nachhaltigkeit* (pp. 201–223). Marburg: Metropolis.

Hoffmann, B. (2008). *Terrorismus – Der unerklärte Krieg. Neue Gefahren politischer Gewalt.* Frankfurt am Main: Fischer Verlag.

Kuschel, R., & Schröder, A. (2002). *Tourismus und Terrorismus. Interaktionen, Auswirkungen und Handlungsstrategien.* Dresden: Schriftenreihe Tourismuswirtschaft.

Porter, M.E. (2008). The five competitive forces that shape strategy. *Harvard Business Review*, 78–93.

Rogers, E. (1995). *The diffusion of innovations* (5th ed.). New York: Free Press, Simon and Schuster.

Sutcliff, K.M., & Vogus, T.J. (2003). Organizing for resilience. In K. Cameron, J.E. Dutton & R.E. Quinn (Eds.), *Positive Organizational Scholarships* (pp. 94–110). San Francisco: Berrett-Koehler.

Welter-Enderlin, R., & Hildenbrand, B. (2006). *Resilienz – Gedeihen trotz widriger Umstände.* Heidelberg: Carl-Auer-Systeme.

Index

Note: Italicized page numbers indicate a figure on the corresponding page. Page numbers in bold indicate a table on the corresponding page.